e-COLORS

AUTHOR: Héctor Navarro Guere

© Carles Broto i Comerma
c/ Ausias Marc 20, 4º 2ª
08010 Barcelona, Spain
Tel.: +34 93 301 21 99
Fax: +34 93 302 67 97
info@linksbooks.net
www.linksbooks.net

ISBN: 84-89861-85-4
D.L: B-1444-2003
Printed in Barcelona

e-COLORS

INTRODUCTION

Ever since the advent of the computer screen as an important medium for communication, theorists, designers and website creators have been suggesting guidelines for designing more effective sites, especially those aimed at eliciting the active participation of users in interactive programs.

We cannot yet draw on a maturely developed paradigm for graphic interfaces; however, we can refer to a wide array of work that allows us to provide an outline of some stylistic, operative and functional principles.

Using a static mode of communication to explain the dynamic nature of online design is a paradoxical situation; however, it also implies that we should pause in order to examine the concept behind each of the constituent parts and to thereby evaluate their effectiveness.

Given the sheer amount of visual information to which we are subjected, it is a good idea to consider the scope of our subject and the new challenges which it brings. The field of user interfaces opens a series of complex issues, one of which is the use of color to convey information and to communicate. Thus can we speak of a semantics of color.

General knowledge of the cultural, psychological and contextual effects of color is oftentimes a determining factor in the success or failure of web design. Learned, or unconsciously acquired, criteria determine the effectiveness, suitability and usefulness of colors in planning strategies.

This volume is a collection of web projects, encompassing a wide range of different fields and representing a cross section of what sort of designs are currently to be found on the net. In compiling our collection, we have drawn on sites which have received outstanding awards and commendations from experts in the field, webmasters and graphic designers.

Each sample site is accompanied by a key which includes the site's original name, its field of activity, the technical resources used for creating and viewing it and the name of its designer or design studio. A point to which we have given special attention is what we call the 'rating' of originality, graphics and interactivity, to which we have assigned three icons: ☺,☺,☹. The criteria are as follows: Originality refers to the design's quality of freshness, its newness, to its capacity to surprise and make users take a second look. The category of graphics concerns the ideal creation and use of icons, images (whether fixed or in motion), pictograms, logos, sketches or whatever original element has been built into the design scheme. Finally, interactivity is judged on standards of hypertext navigation and its capacity to stimulate user participation.

We have also included a brief section on the principles and properties of color. Additionally, on the following pages is an overview of hexadecimal tones, which serves as a basic guideline for choosing colors and visualizing them on the screen. Without further words: the web designs.

Héctor Navarro Güere

COLOR AS GROUNDWORK

> In our highly visual culture, the concept of color is much more than the "impression which rays of light reflected off of an object produce on the retina of the eye" It can be conceptualized in any number of ways. On the one hand, there are human optical capabilities and, on the other, the semantics of the psychology of color, as well as the cultural implications of certain colors. Following are some reflections along these lines.

Generally, the color wheel includes 12 tones, of which three basic types are distinguished: primary, secondary and tertiary. Additionally this wheel shows other relationships between the colors. Theses are: Complementary colors, which are found opposite each other on the color wheel. The intermediate colors are those which are next to a primary color on the color wheel. Neighboring colors are those which are found side by side on the color wheel.

COLOR WHEEL

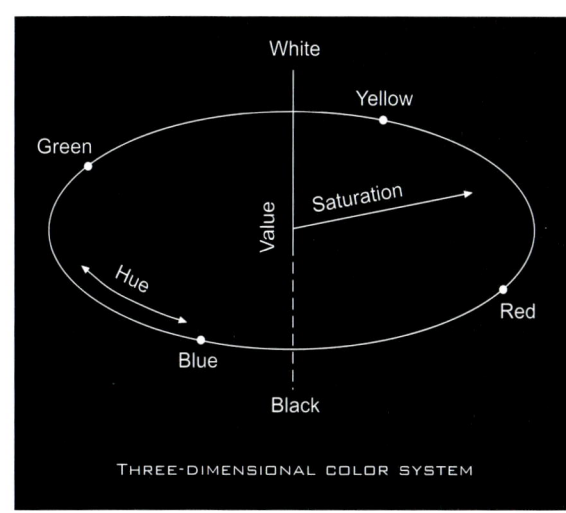

THREE-DIMENSIONAL COLOR SYSTEM

Light Colors: RGB

>These are the three primary colors of light composition. Also called RGB (red, green and blue). These colors are subtractive. When one of these colors is combined with another, the color is reduced or changed, which is why the sum of these three colors - red, green and blue - creates white (light).

When the human eye perceives a color, the colors which are really being activated are those which the perceived color needs in order to become light (white). Thus, for example, when we see the color red, in reality the colors which are at work are green and blue. This demonstrates that the effect produced by these colors is the opposite of what occurs in reality.

Computer monitors work with RGB and reproduce the color in 16.7 million tones. They use three channels, which contain 24 bits per pixel (8x3).

The CMYK colors - also called printing colors - are formed from combinations of the primary colors. These are: cyan, magenta and yellow. Additionally, the letter K, representing black, would be necessary for completing a complete range of tones.

The colors CMYK are used in printing and the separation of colors. They use 4 channels, which contain 32 bits per pixel (8x4).

PROPIERTIES

> ALL COLORS POSSESS A SERIES OF CHARAC-
TERISTICS WHICH CHANGE THEIR ASPECT AND
DEFINE THEIR FINAL APPEARANCE. AMONG
THESE PROPERTIES, SOME OF THE MOST USEFUL
TO KEEP IN MIND ARE:

HUE OR SHADE: THIS IS THE PURE STATE OF
THE COLOR, WITHOUT WHITE OR BLACK ADDED.
IT IS AN ATTRIBUTE ASSOCIATED WITH THE DOM-
INANT WAVELENGTH IN THE MIX OF LIGHT WAVES.
HUE IS DEFINED AS AN ATTRIBUTE OF COLOR
THAT ALLOWS US TO TELL RED FROM BLUE, AND
WHICH REFERS TO THE RANGE THAT A TONE DIS-
PLAYS FROM ONE SIDE OF THE COLOR WHEEL TO
THE OTHER. YELLOWISH-GREEN AND BLUISH-
GREEN, THEREFORE, ARE DIFFERENT HUES, OR
SHADES, OF GREEN.

SATURATION OR INTENSITY: THIS REFERS TO
THE VIBRANCY OR PALENESS OF A COLOR. IT IN-
DICATES THE PURITY OF COLOR AND IS RELATED
TO THE WIDTH OF THE STRIP OF LIGHT THAT WE
ARE SEEING. THE PURE COLORS OF THE SPEC-
TRUM ARE COMPLETELY SATURATED. AN INTENSE
COLOR IS VERY VIBRANT. AS WE RATE INTENSITY
IN OPPOSITION TO OTHER THINGS, THIS PROP-
ERTY IS ALWAYS COMPARATIVE. THE IMPORTANT
THING IS TO LEARN TO DISTINGUISH THE RELA-
TIONSHIPS OF INTENSITY, SINCE IT OFTEN
CHANGES WHEN A CERTAIN COLOR IS SET ON
THE BACKGROUND OF ANOTHER.

VALUE OR BRIGHTNESS: THIS IS HOW LIGHT OR
DARK THE COLOR IS, A PROPERTY WHICH REFERS
TO THE AMOUNT OF LIGHT PERCEIVED.
BRIGHTNESS CAN ALSO BE DEFINED AS THE
QUANTITY OF "DARKNESS" WHICH A COLOR HAS.
THAT IS, IT REPRESENTS HOW LIGHT OR DARK A
COLOR IS AS COMPARED TO ITS COLOR OF REF-
ERENCE. THIS IS AN IMPORTANT PROPERTY,
SINCE IT ALLOWS US TO CREATE SPATIAL SENSA-
TIONS THROUGH THE MEDIUM OF COLOR. THUS,
QUANTITIES OF THE SAME COLOR WITH STRONG
VALUE CONTRASTS HELP DEFINE SPACE AND
DEPTH, WHILE A GRADUAL CHANGE IN VALUE OF
A COLOR GIVES THE SENSATION OF CONTOUR, OF
THE CONTINUITY OF AN OBJECT IN SPACE.

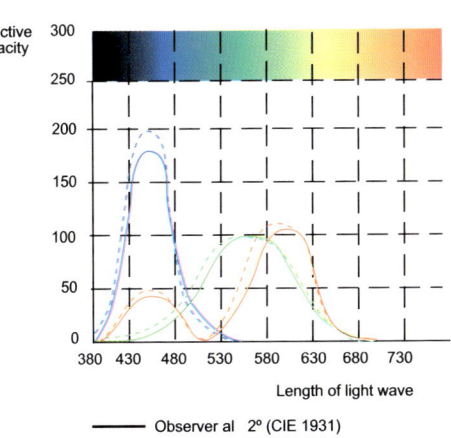

Observer al 2º (CIE 1931)
Observer al 10º (CIE 1964)

In 1931, the Commision Internationale de L'Eclairage
established a system of color order when specifying the
light source, the observer and the methodology for
identifying the values that describe color. It also proposed
the idea of a standard observer, based on the average
human population with normal color sight. Above, specific
numerical values for the responses of the average person
to different lengths of light waves.

Colors by Association

> The previous properties described serve to set color selection criteria by analogy and by contrast. By analogous colors, we understand the combination of colors that are contiguous on the color wheel. The contrasting colors are those tones which lie opposite each other on the color wheel; they are also the combination of two opposite colors. Here are some examples:

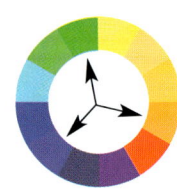

Complementary triad: Three colors which are equidistant from the center of the wheel and from each other; that is, with 120° between each.

Multiples: The scale of colors between any two colors, following a uniform gradation.

Complementary colors: colors which are symmetrically opposed on the color wheel. The shades vary by 180° between them.

Bright-tenuous mix: The selection of a pure bright color and a tenuous variation of its complementary color.

Close complementary colors: taking a given color from the color wheel as the basis and then another two that are equidistant from the first.

Black-white binomial: Exact contrast.

Double complementary colors: This refers to two pairs which are complementary to each other.

Other factors which play a part in the perception of colors are: shapes, the interplay of object and background, the time of exposure to a color and our memory of any given color. All of these variations are stabilized in the eye and effect the perception of our surroundings.

Psychological Color

> It is common knowledge that color has an impact on the emotions. Culture, traditions and fashion are factors that determine many associated emotional responses: to a particular color, to varying intensity of the same color, as well as to the different possible combinations of colors.

Each color is commonly related to emotions and associations of ideas. Thus, to cite only a few examples, we could establish the following:

Red: enthusiasm, passion, warning, excitement, strength, sex, danger, heat, fire, blood.

Yellow: enthusiasm, strength, spring, innocence, childhood, optimism.

Blue: truth, dignity, melancholy, sadness, trust, masculinity, sky, water, sensuality, comfort, elegance, freshness.

Orange: happiness, youth, warmth, summer.

Pink: calm, faintness, tranquility.

Green: nature, health, money, freshness, growth, abundance, fertility, plants.

Purple: abundance, sophistication, intelligence, spirituality, dignity, mystery, death.

Violet: fantasy, play, dreams, nightmares, madness.

Brown: age, antiquity, wood, brick.

Black: elegance, seduction, mystery, strength, evil.

White: purity, innocence, cleanliness, lightness, youth, softness.

Gold: prestige, money, elegance, religion.

Silver: prestige, coldness, science, space.

HEXADECIMAL TONES

>666699 >000099 >0000CC >009966 >999933 >CCCC00

>00CCFF >6699CC >0000FF >00FF99 >CCFFCC >66CCFF

>00FFFF >CCFFFF >CCCCFF >00FF66 >00FFCC >00CCCC

>CC00FF >9933CC >660099 >00CC00 >00CC99 >009999

>6600CC >993399 >993399 >660000 >006666 >666600

>CC3366 >CC0099 >CC3399 >CC9999 >990000 >996633

>FF0000 >CC33CC >FF00CC >FF9999 >FFCCCC >FFFFCC

>FF0099 >FF99FF >FF99CC >FF9900 >FFCC66 >FFFF00

SET AGAINST BLACK AND WHITE, THIS PALETTE OF LIGHT COLORS SUGGESTS EFFECTIVE
CONTRASTS AND HARMONY BETWEEN TONES.

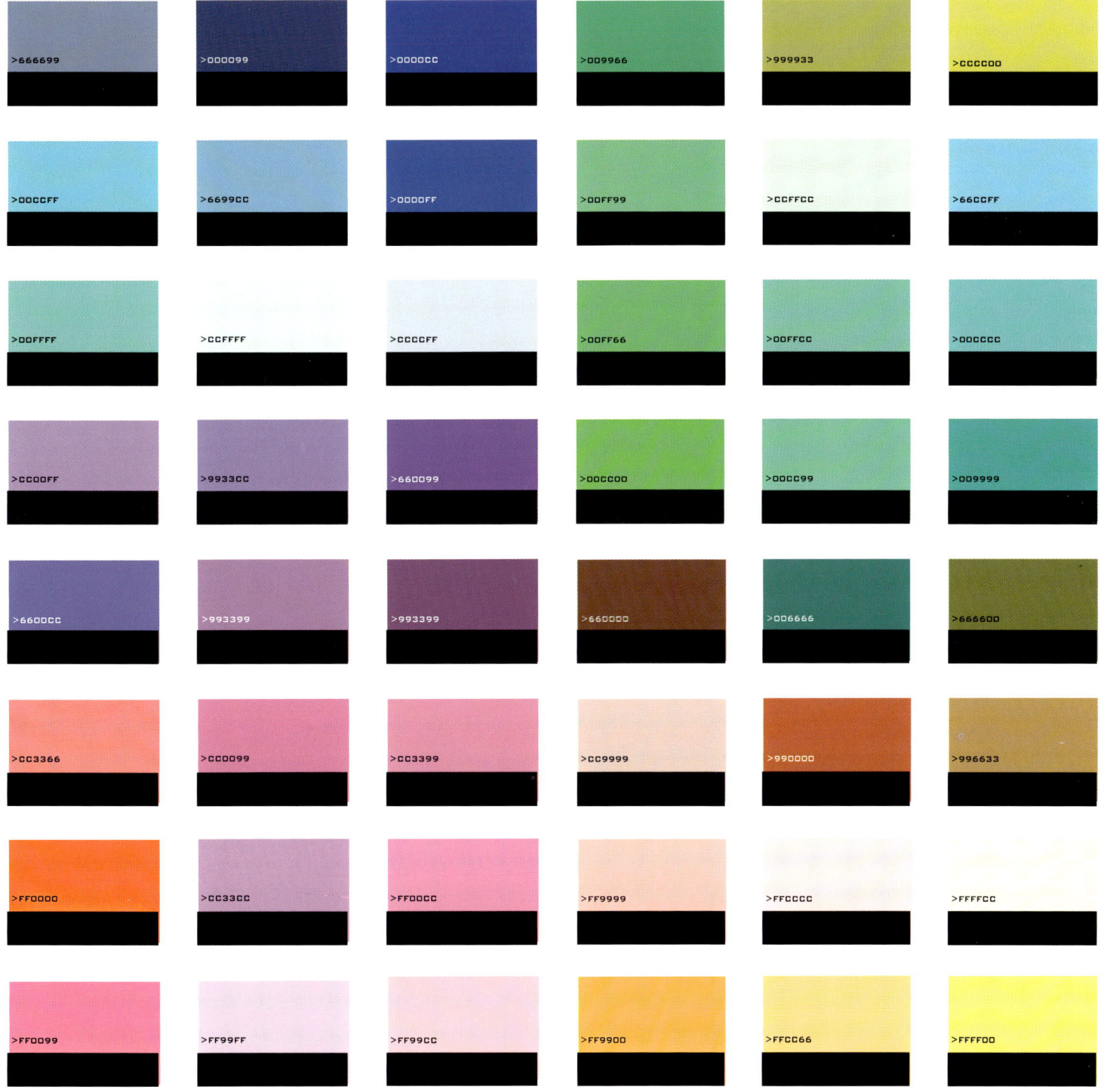

IN EACH OF THE PROPOSED COMBINATIONS, ITS EQUIVALENT IN THE HEXADECIMAL SYSTEM
IS SHOWN.

COLOR IS INFORMATION

WWW.ELIXIRSTUDIO.COM

> NAME: ELIXIR STUDIO > SECTOR: DE-
SIGN STUDIO > SPECIFICATIONS: FLASH,
HTML > RATING: ORIGINALITY ☺
GRAPHICS ☺ INTERACTIVITY ☺
> DESIGNED BY: ARNAUD MERCIER

THIS DESIGN PROPOSAL MAKES ITS
PRESENCE KNOWN WITH A RICH VARIETY
OF CREATED IMAGES, THE SUITABLE
CHOICE OF COLORS AND A PROPOR-
TIONAL PLACEMENT OF THE WINDOWS
OF THE SUB-SECTIONS.

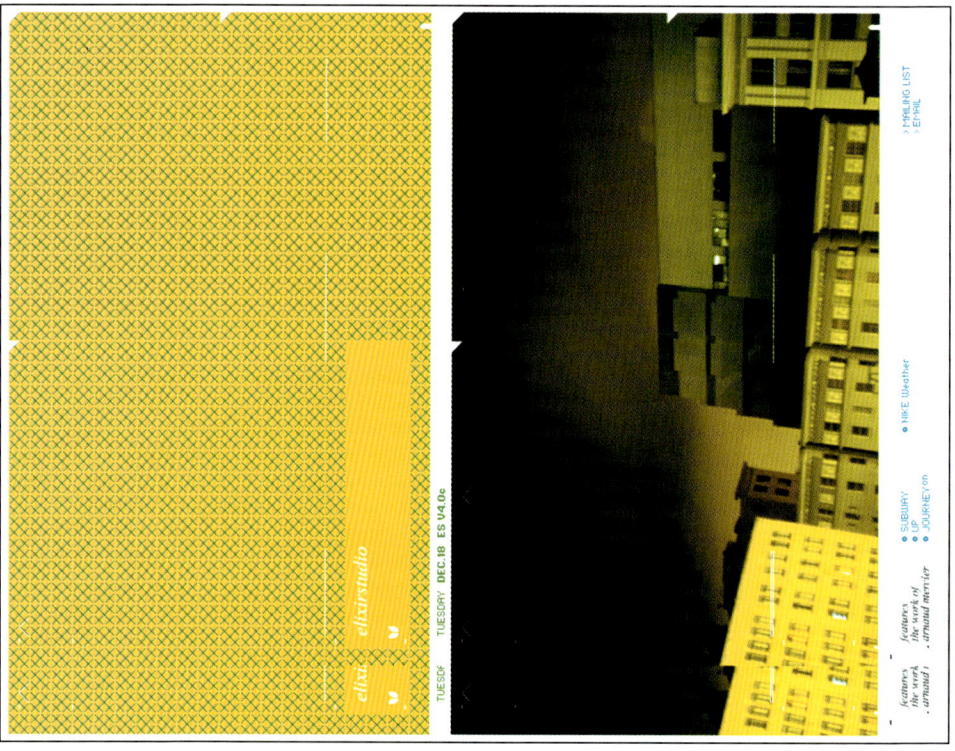

THE CREATIVITY OF THIS PROJECT IS
MADE MANIFEST IN THE CHOICE OF THE
SUBWAY METAPHOR AS A HIGHLY USEFUL
AND FAMILIAR REFERENCE FOR JOUR-
NEYS, COMINGS AND GOINGS, EN-
TRANCES AND EXITS. THUS, THIS MODE
OF COMMUNICATION BECOMES AN EFFEC-
TIVE PARADIGM FOR VIRTUAL NAVIGATING.

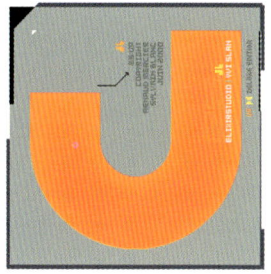
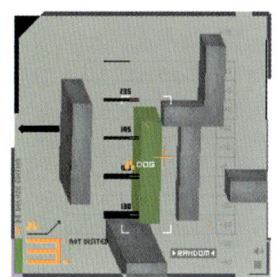

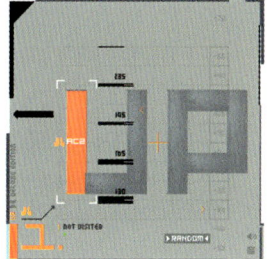
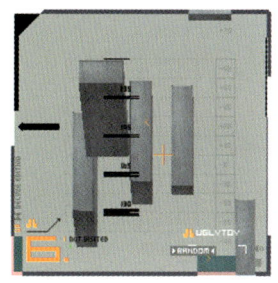
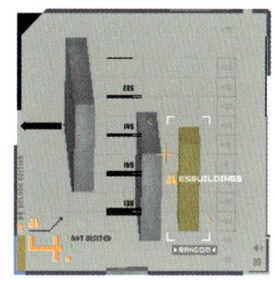

THE START-UP PAGE OFFERS THE OPTION OF ACCESSING THREE SUBSEQUENT SECTIONS, THEREBY THROWING THE TRADITIONAL IDEA OF A MENU OUT THE WINDOW. EACH SECTION, IN TURN, DISPLAYS AN INDIVIDUALIZED DESIGN WITH ITS OWN LIFE, DISCONNECTED FROM THE PRECEDING LINK.

AN AMALGAM OF SUPERIMPOSED, CLICKABLE GRAPHICS AND PHOTOGRAPHS IS THE COHESIVE ELEMENT IN AN OTHERWISE DISPARATE DESIGN SCHEME.

THE FIRST TWO PAGES PRESENTED REQUIRE USER PARTICIPATION, WHILE THE THIRD IS A LINEAR PRESENTATION.

```
>BB
 86
 82

>CC
 CC
 00

>FF
 CC
 66
```

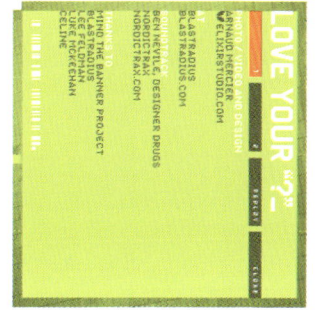
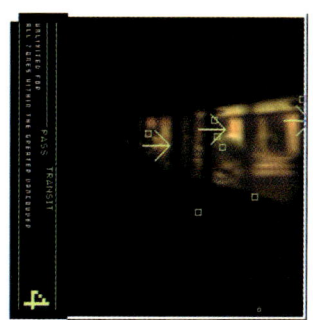

MENUS ARE THEREBY CREATED ON A
SINGLE PAGE. THE STRENGTH OF
THE DESIGN DOES NOT RELY ON THE
MENUS, BUT RATHER ON THE ENTER-
TAINING WAY THAT THE SECTIONS
ARE REVEALED.

WWW.CAOZ.COM

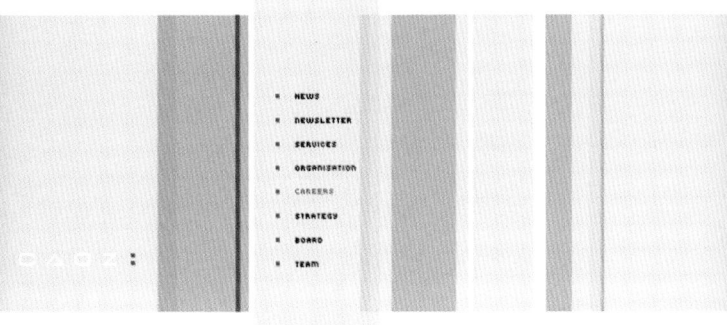

- NEWS
- NEWSLETTER
- SERVICES
- ORGANISATION
- CAREERS
- STRATEGY
- BOARD
- TEAM

CAOZ

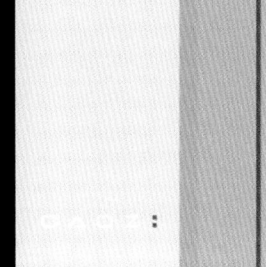

Careers

CAOZ is an energetic and creative team, always keen to embrace new talent.

The CAOZ team is a group of hard working and hard playing professionals. The employees are well informed, both about the organisation as well as their profession. We encourage and support our people to gain more knowledge, within and outside the company. By implementing appropriate processes, we ensure that our solutions are highly creative and professional, as well as delivered within time and budget. We facilitate our people with the latest tools and devices in a creative and fun atmosphere, to aid them in delivering world-class solutions.

- NEWS
- NEWSLETTER
- SERVICES
- ORGANISATION
- CAREERS
- STRATEGY
- BOARD
- TEAM

- CLOSE

> CC FF CC
> 00 CC 99
> 99 00 00

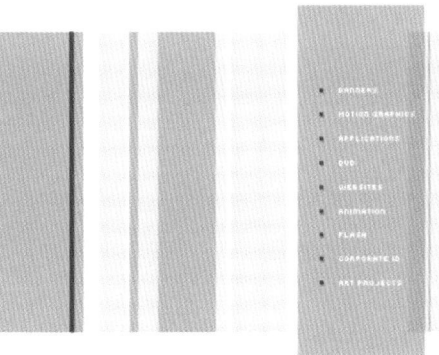

- BANNERS
- MOTION GRAPHICS
- APPLICATIONS
- DVD
- WEBSITES
- ANIMATION
- FLASH
- CORPORATE ID
- ART PROJECTS

CORPORATE IDENTITY: DESIGN AND CREATION OF IDENTITY PRODUCTS.

- VIRTUAL
- RELOCATION
- VIDEO PRESENTATION
- PRINT MATERIAL

- BANNERS
- MOTION GRAPHICS
- APPLICATIONS
- DVD
- WEBSITES
- ANIMATION
- FLASH
- CORPORATE ID
- ART PROJECTS

- CLOSE

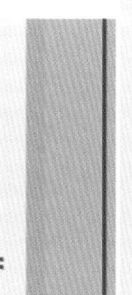

Organisation

CAOZ encourages employees to take reponsibility in their work. As much as possible the organisation is constructed of a flat hierarchy where the projects are the key drivers and the individual departments participate diagonally in each project.

- NEWS
- NEWSLETTER
- SERVICES
- ORGANISATION
- CAREERS
- STRATEGY
- BOARD
- TEAM

- CLOSE

CONSULTING

MOTION GRAPHICS

WWW.STYLEPARK.DE

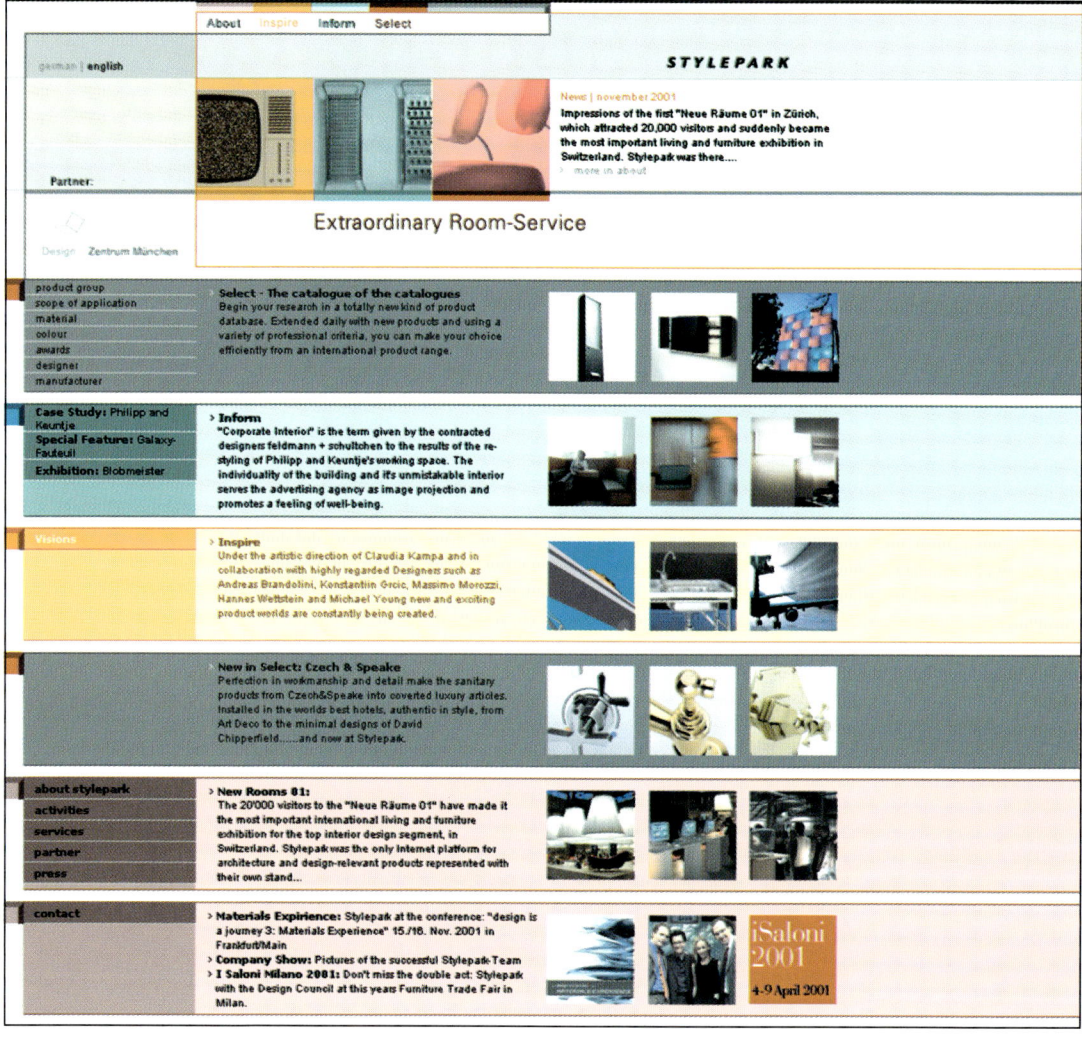

> NAME: STYLEPARK > SECTOR: INTER DESIGN > SPECIFICATIONS: FLASH, HTML > RATING: ORIGINALITY 🙂 GRAPHICS 😐 INTERACTIVITY 😐

THERE ARE VARIOUS WAYS OF PULLING UP PAGES ON THIS SITE. AN UPPER HORIZONTAL MENU AND ANOTHER VERTICAL BAR ON THE LEFT-HAND SIDE COHERENTLY AND CONCISELY MARK THE RHYTHM OF THE INFORMATION.

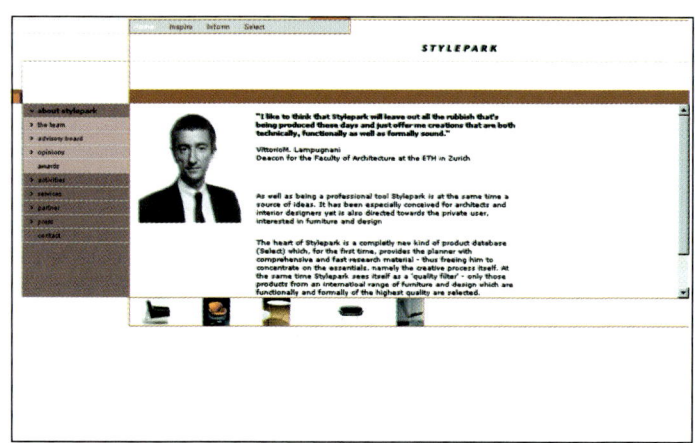

THIS SECOND SECTION GRANTS SU-
PREMACY TO THE PHOTOGRAPHS,
COMPUTER ANIMATION AND, IN GEN-
ERAL, TO COLOR.
IN ORDER TO PLACE MORE EMPHASIS
ON THE OBJECTS THEMSELVES, THE
GRAPHIC AND, TO A LESSER EXTENT,
TEXTUAL INFORMATION ONLY APPEARS
WHEN THE OBJECT IS SELECTED.

THE ANIMATION CREATES A SENSE OF
EXPECTATION IN EACH SECTION.

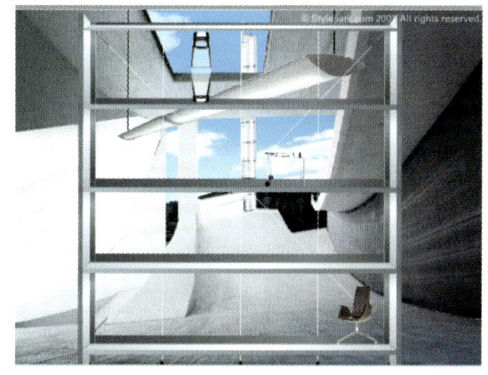

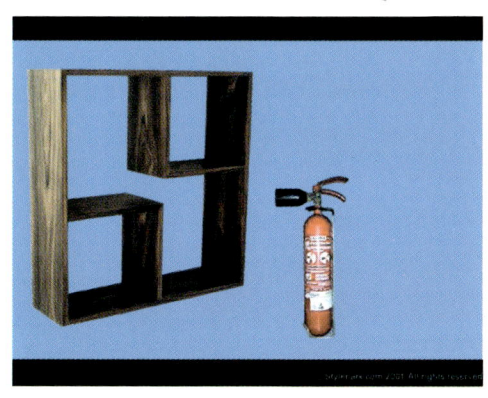

THE COLOR SCHEME, WITH THE AID OF A HORIZONTAL GRAPHIC DISTRIBUTION, FULFILLS THE FUNCTION OF SEPARATING AND CLASSIFYING THE CONTENTS, THEREBY MAKING FULL USE OF THE SCREEN'S OBLONG PROPORTIONING, ALTHOUGH THERE ARE ALSO VERTICAL ELEMENTS IN THE DESIGN.

IN THE TWO SECTIONS SHOWN ON THESE PAGES, BLUE AND GREEN OBEY THE PRINCIPLE OF HARMONIZING THEIR SUB-SECTIONS.

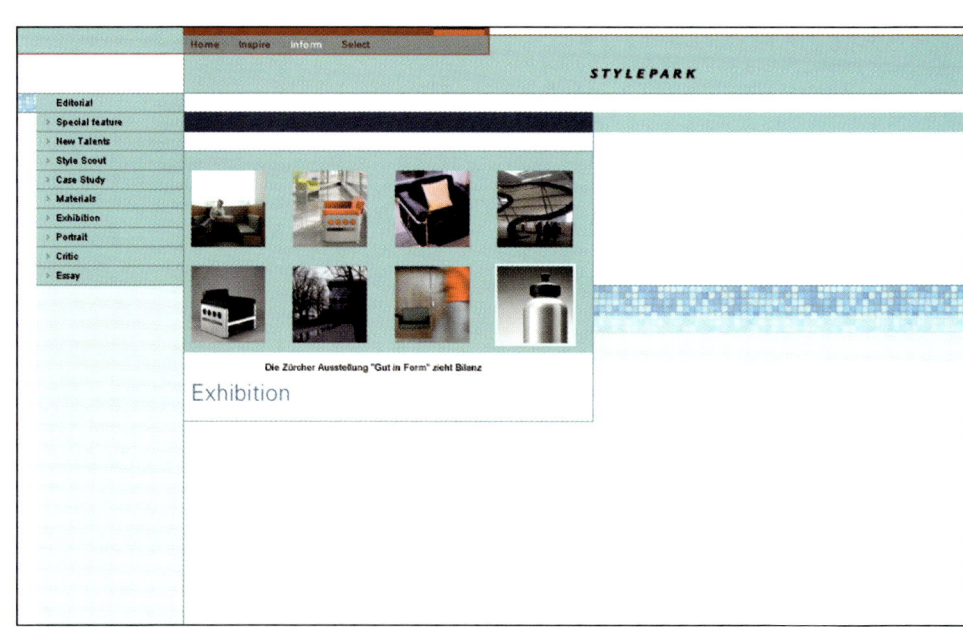

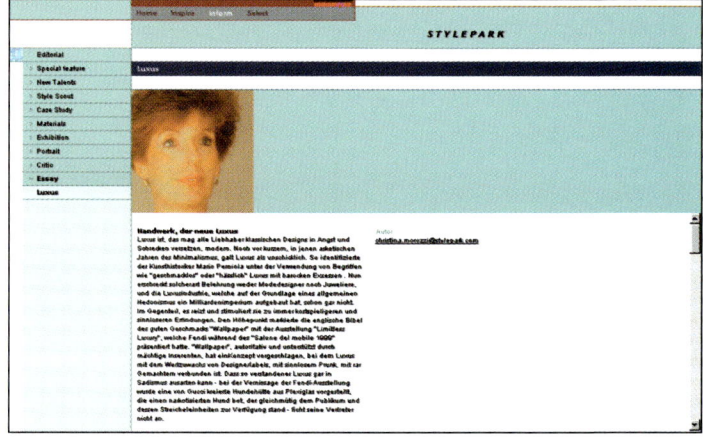

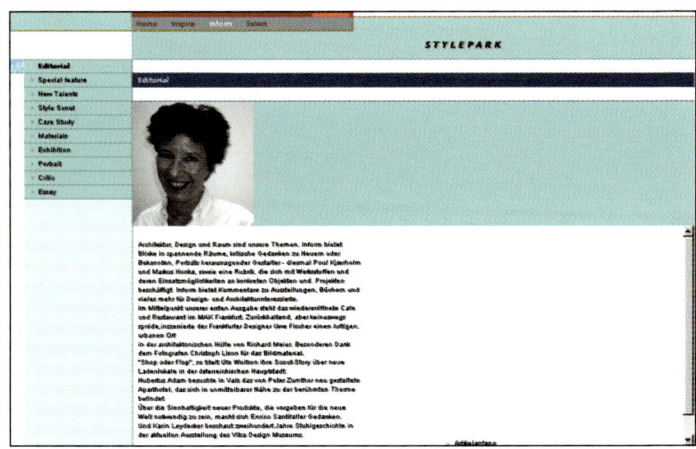

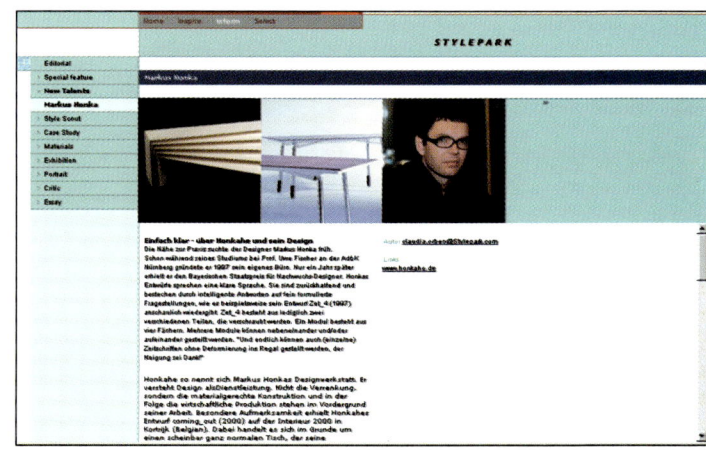

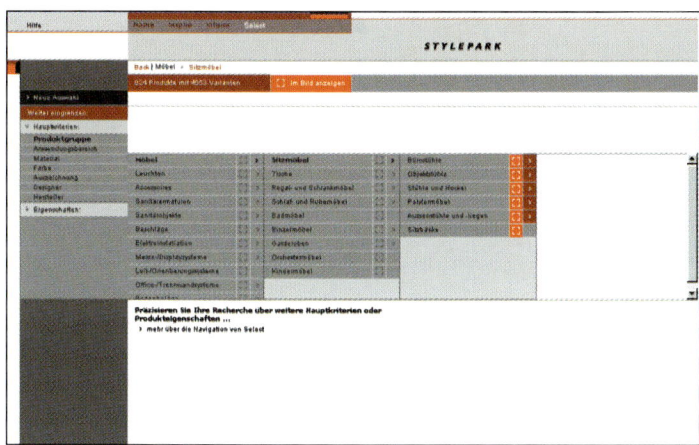

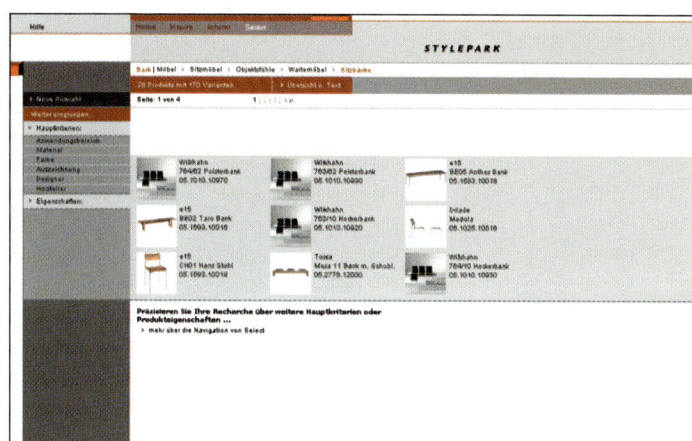

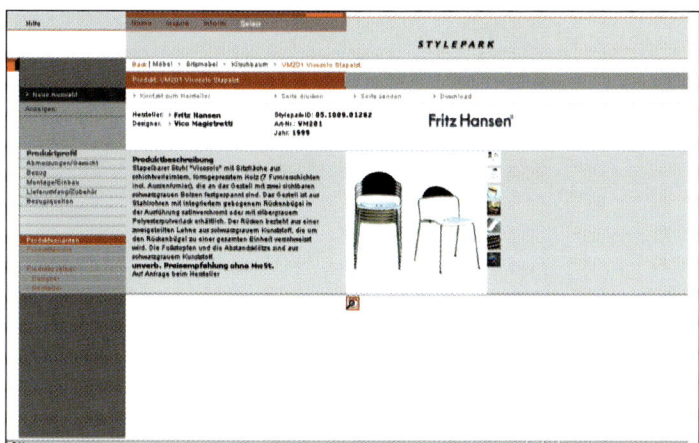

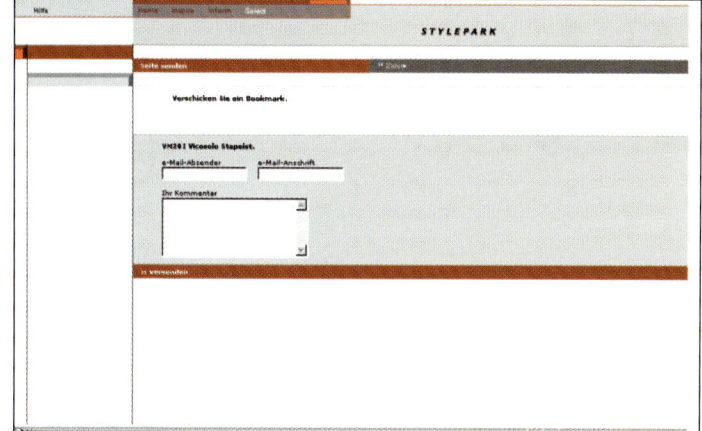

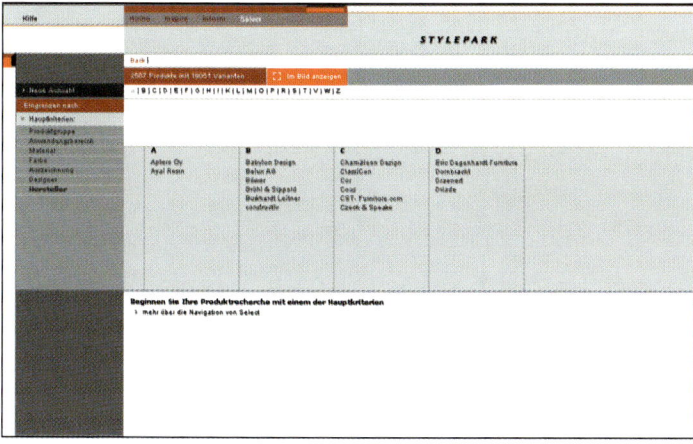

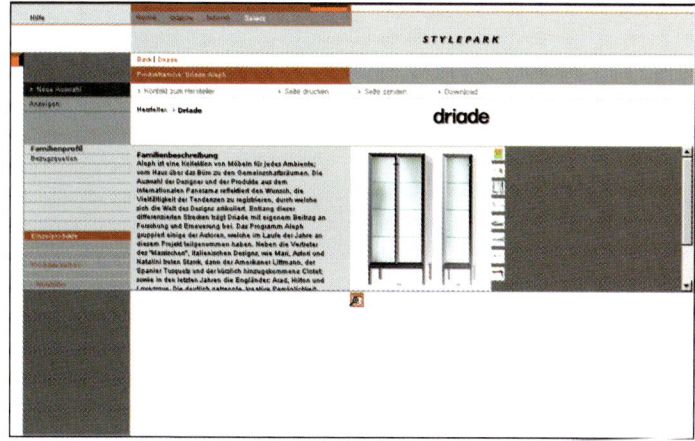

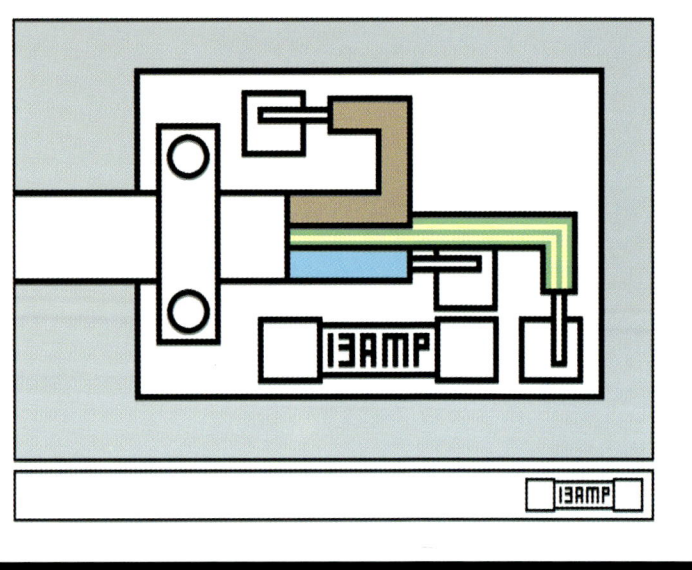

> NAME: 13 AMP > SECTOR: GAMES
> SPECS: FLASH, HTML > RATING:
ORIGINALITY ☺ GRAPHICS ☺
INTERACTIVITY ☺

CLARITY OF PURPOSE IS DENOTED BY A POLISHED COLOR SCHEME FOR FILLING IN THE BASIC SHAPES OF THE GRAPHICS. THE GOAL HERE IS TO PROVIDE ENTERTAINMENT: TOTAL ENJOYMENT OF INTERACTIVE, AUDIO-INCLUDED GAMES. THE GRAPHICS, COLORS AND CONTENTS ARE ALL UNAMBIGUOUS.

WWW.13AMP.TV

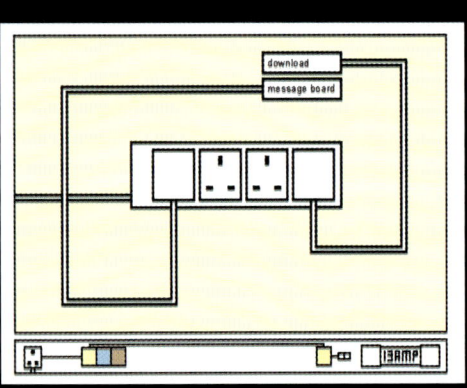

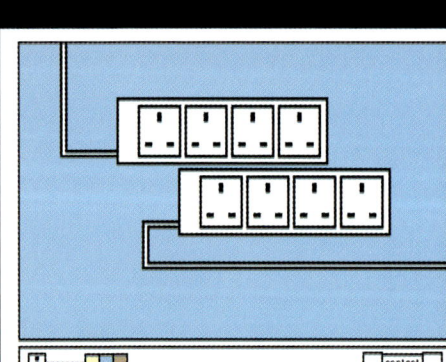

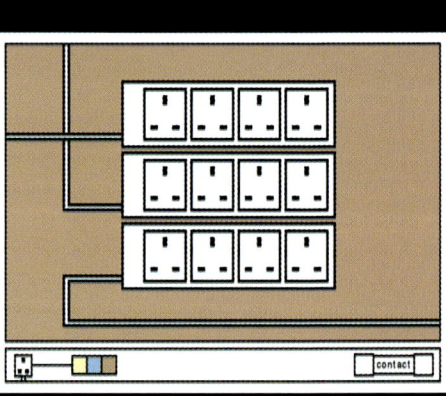

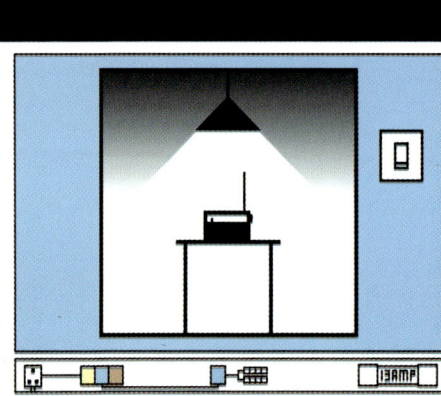

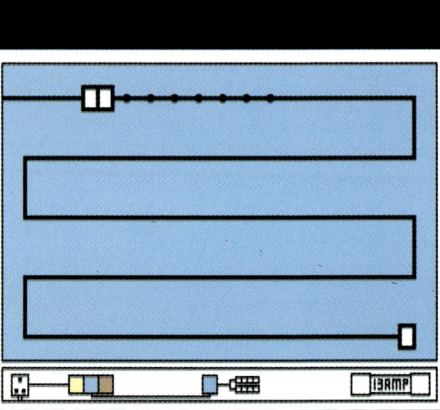

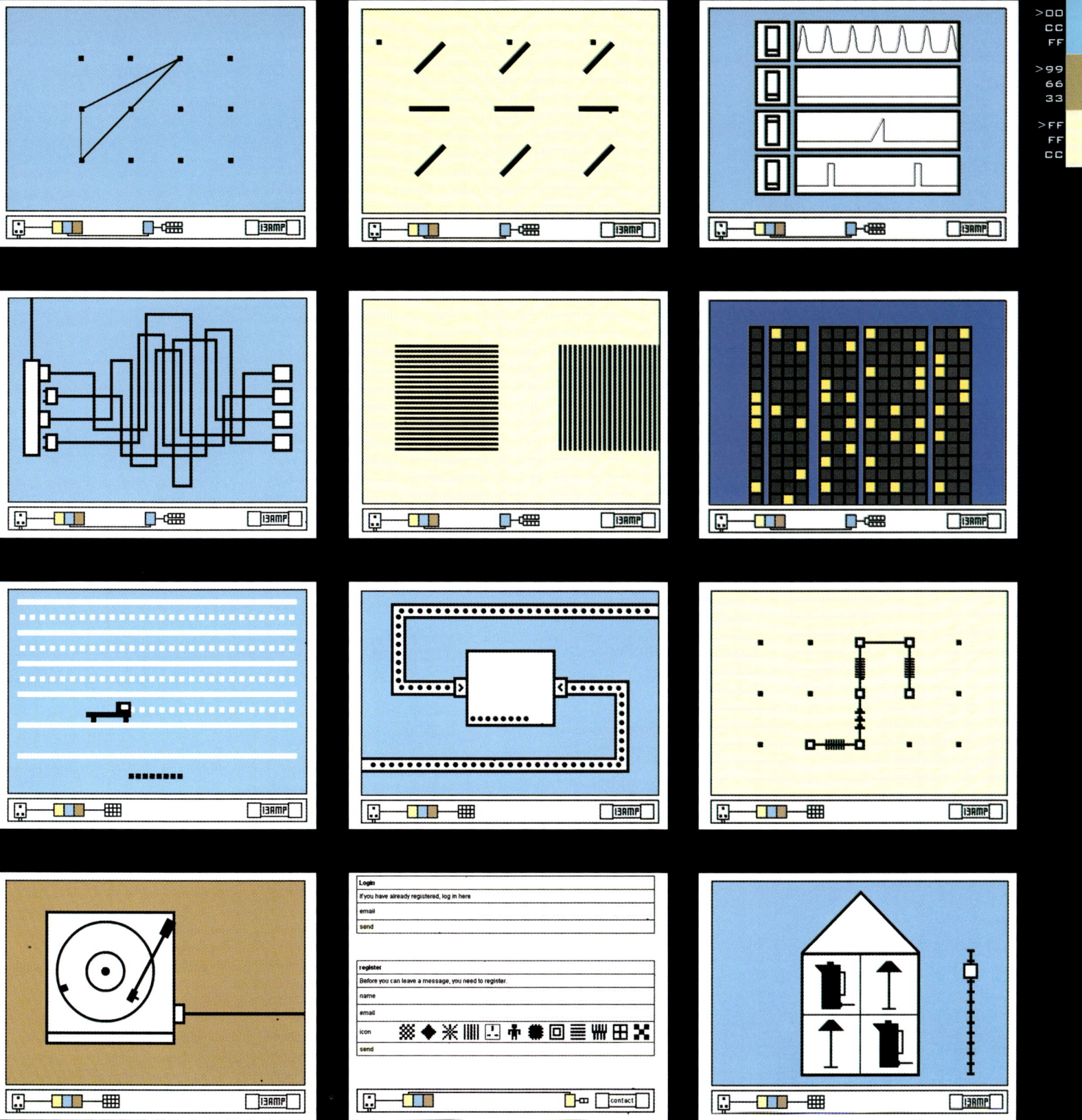

WEB.MADRITEL.ES/PERSONALES/

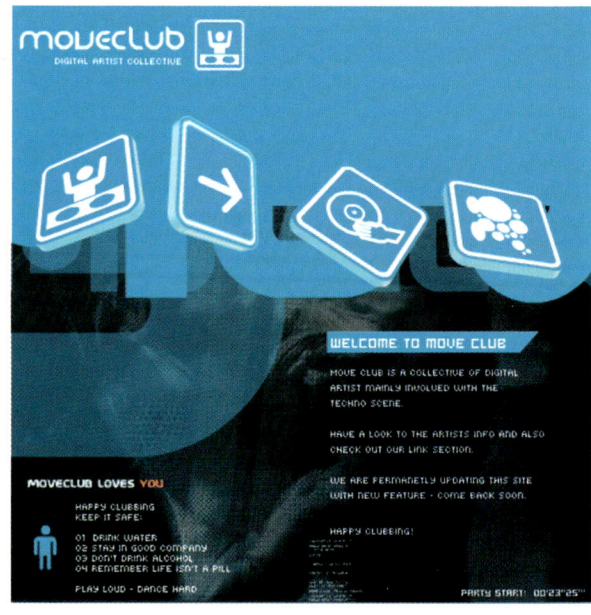

> NAME: MOVE CLUB > SECTOR: COLLECTIVE OF DIGITAL ARTISTS, DJS > SPECS: FLASH, HTML > RATING: ORIGINALITY ☺ GRAPHICS ☺ INTERACTIVITY ☺

THE DUALITY OF BLACK AND BLUE IS THE STRUCTURING PRINCIPLE THROUGHOUT THIS WEBSITE. CLICK ON ANY GIVEN SECTION AND THE BOTTOM OF THE BLACK SCREEN METAMORPHOSES INTO A NEW IDENTITY. THUS, A HOMOGENOUS GENERAL CONCEPT, WITH HETEROGENEOUS SUBSECTIONS, HAS BEEN CREATED.

THE MAIN MENU, WHICH COMES AND GOES, CONSISTS OF FOUR BASIC OPTIONS, IN THE FORM OF FREE-FLOATING, SQUARE-SHAPED ICONS.

STYLIZED GRAPHICS COMBINED WITH PHOTOGRAPHS FORM A COHESIVE WHOLE AND CREATE A FRESH, MOLD-BREAKING LOOK. THERE IS NOTHING SUPERFLUOUS; EACH ELEMENT SERVES ITS PURPOSE WELL.

CM10005574

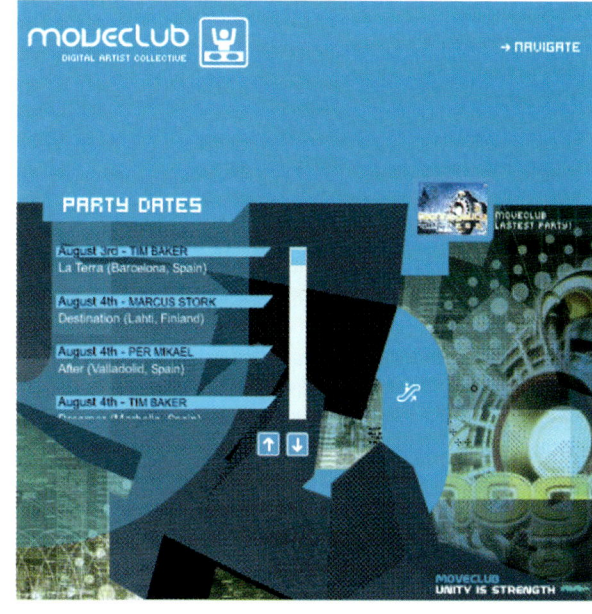

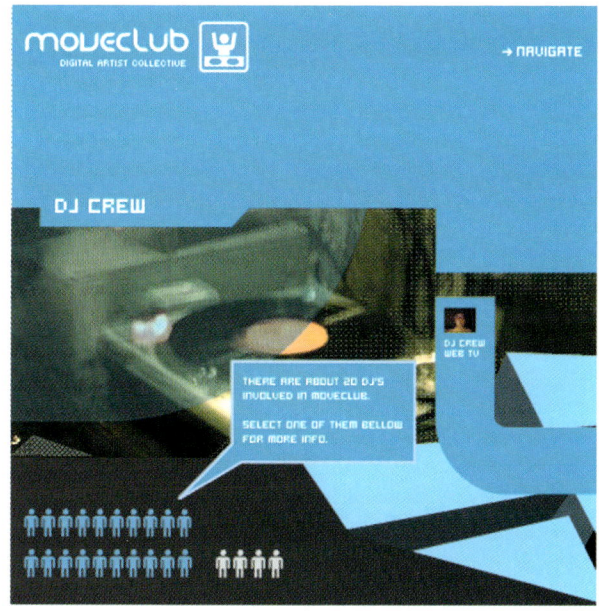

THE DELICATE CIRCLE IN A LAND-
SCAPE OF WHITE IS A STATEMENT IN
ITSELF. ITS INTRINSIC DYNAMISM
AND THE FEELING IT TRANSMITS OF
BEING IN CONSTANT MOTION MAKE
IT THE THREAD WHICH BINDS ALL OF
THE SECTIONS TOGETHER.

THE REST OF THE GRAPHICS, AS
WELL AS THE TEXTS AND ENHANCED
PHOTOGRAPHS, ARE SUBORDINATE
TO THIS SHAPE.
THUS, BASIC GEOMETRIC SHAPES ON
WHITE PROVIDE A STRUCTURAL BASIS
FOR CONTENTS IN PERPETUAL MO-
TION. VISUAL PROOF OF THE TRUTH
OF THE OLD ADAGE, "LESS IS MORE."

> NAME: PAPER(MEDIA) > SECTOR:
WEBSITE DESIGN > SPECIFICA-
TIONS: FLASH, HTML > RATING:
ORIGINALITY ☺ GRAPHICS ☺
INTERACTIVITY ☺ > DESIGNED
BY: PAPER(MEDIA)

WWW.PAPERMEDIA.COM

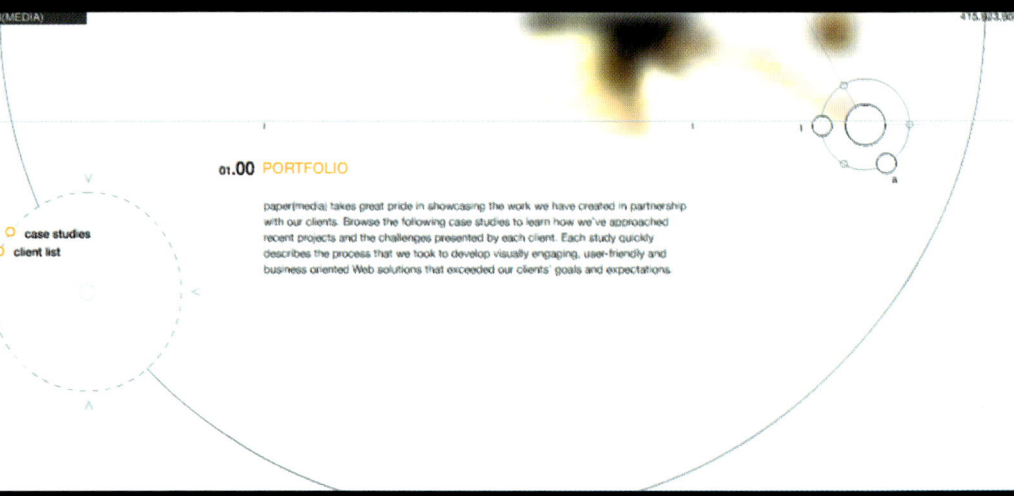

01.00 PORTFOLIO

case studies
client list

paper(media) takes great pride in showcasing the work we have created in partnership
with our clients. Browse the following case studies to learn how we've approached
recent projects and the challenges presented by each client. Each study quickly
describes the process that we took to develop visually engaging, user-friendly and
business oriented Web solutions that exceeded our clients' goals and expectations.

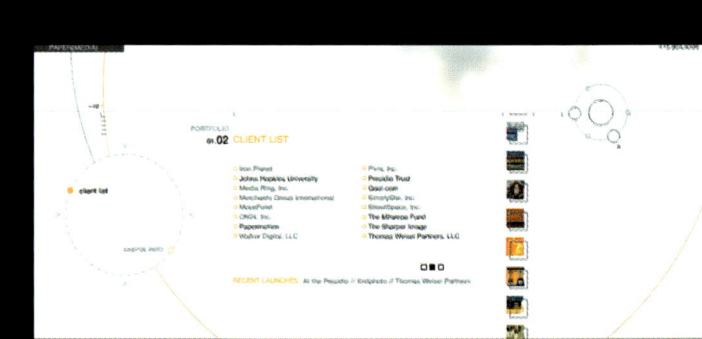

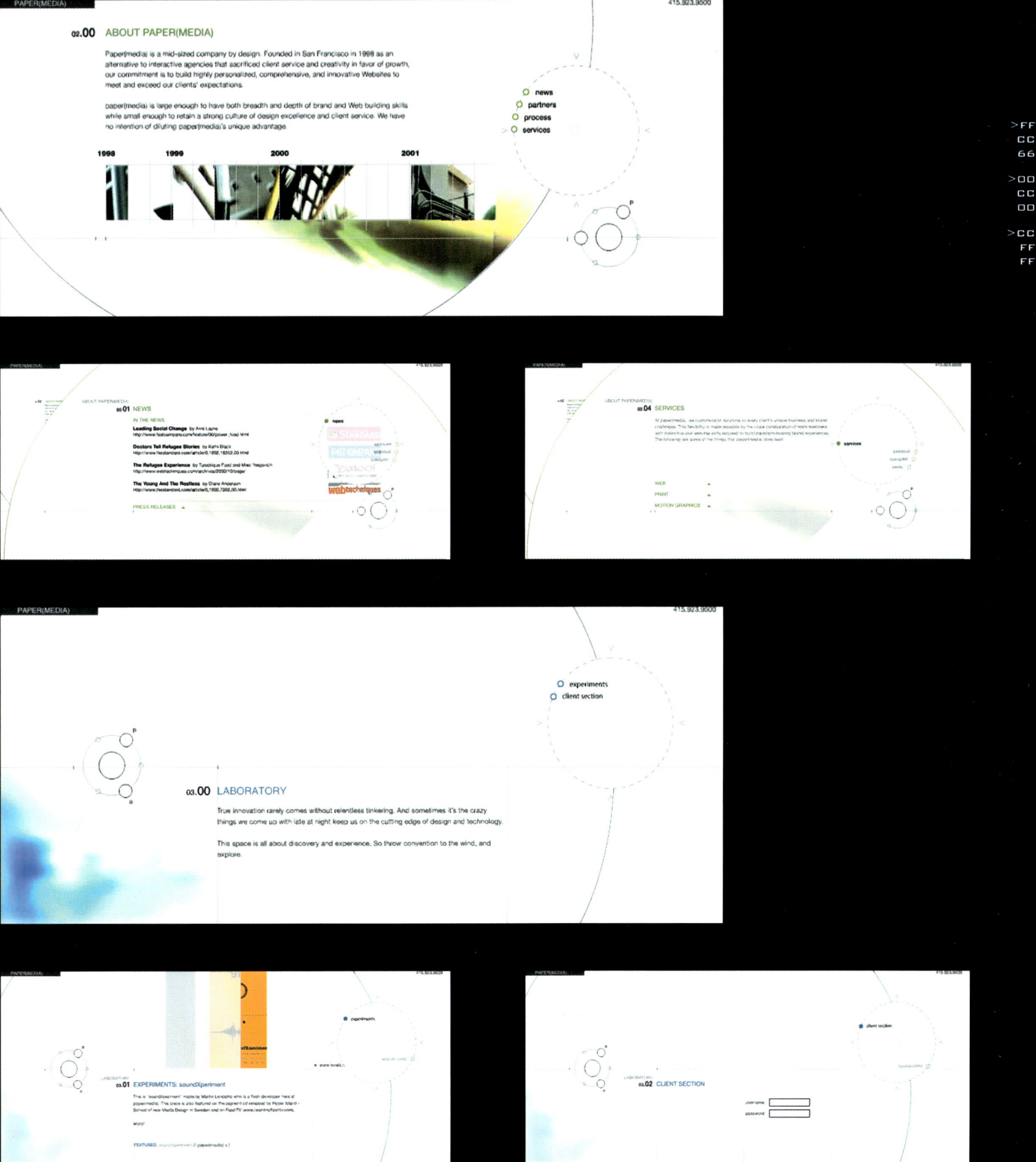

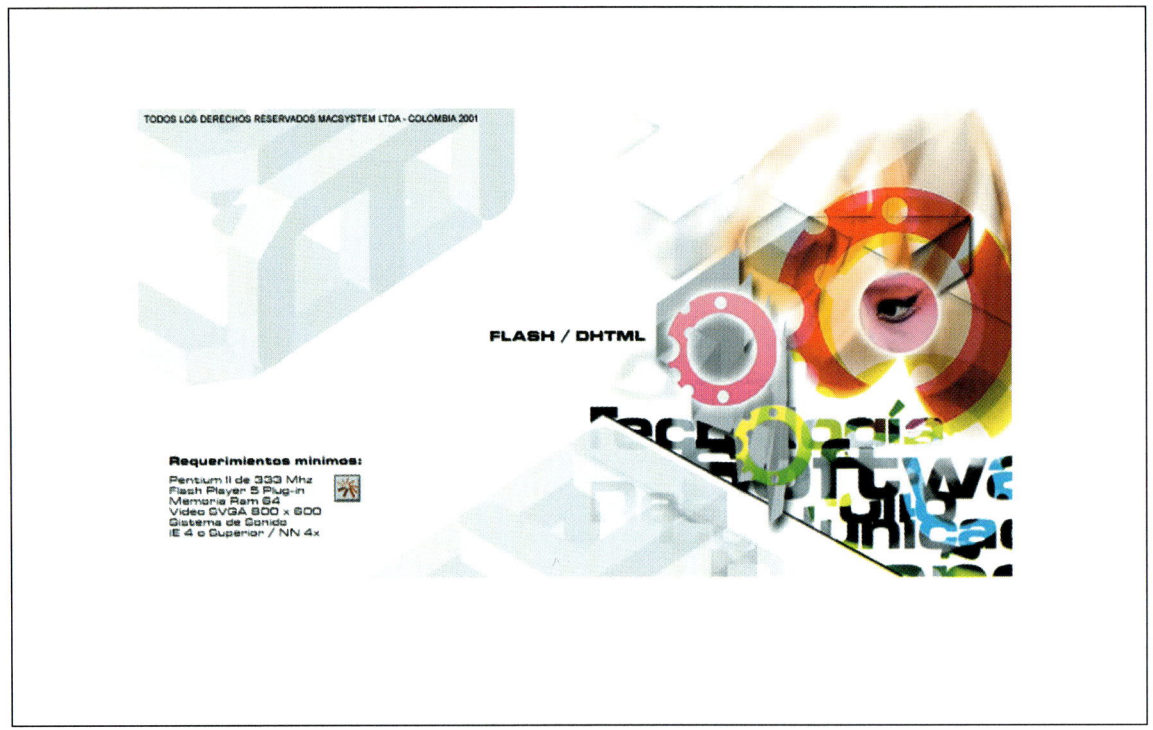

FLASH / DHTML

Requerimientos minimos:
Pentium II de 333 Mhz
Flash Player 5 Plug-in
Memoria Ram 64
Video GVGA 800 x 600
Sistema de Sonido
IE 4 o Superior / NN 4x

WWW.MACSYSTEM.COM.CO

> NAME: MACSYSTEM > SECTOR: MULTIMEDIA DESIGN AND SOLUTIONS > SPECS: FLASH, HTML > RATING: ORIGINALITY ☺ GRAPHICS ☺ INTER-ACTIVITY ☺ > CREDITS: INAVANSIS

AN IN-PERSPECTIVE REPRESENTATION CHARACTERIZES THE GRAPHIC COMPO-SITION OF THIS DESIGN. A DYNAMIC LOOK IS CREATED BY THE USE OF GEO-METRIC SHAPES THAT TAKE ON A THREE-DIMENSIONAL ASPECT ON THIS TWO-DIMENSIONAL PLANE.

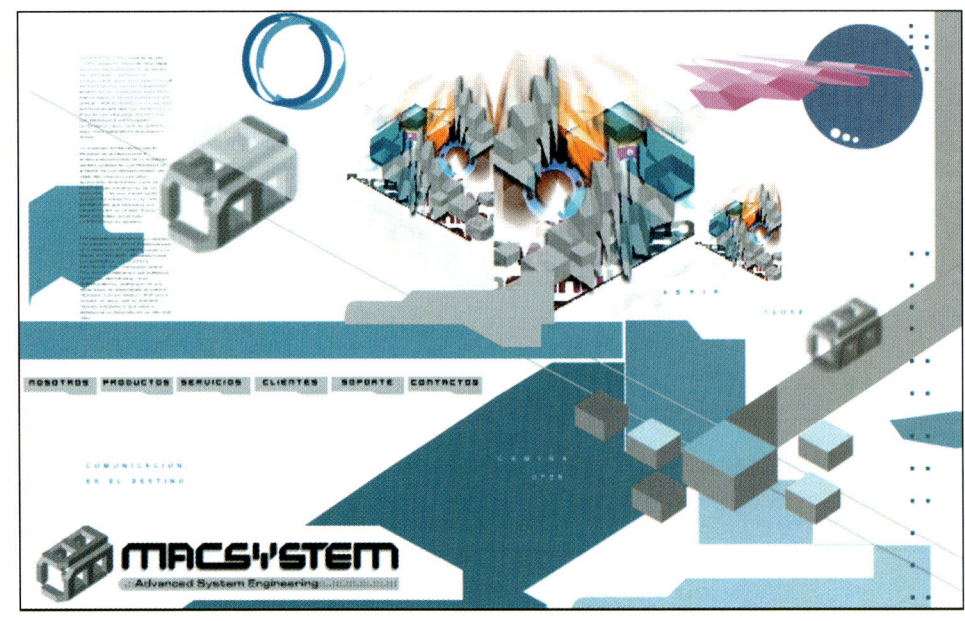

Each section enjoys an independent and coherent color scheme, with words and images conversing in equal circumstances.

Navigation through the six sections is done without complications. There is a clear, if limited, placement of the contents.

>00
99
99

>FF
CC
66

>FF
00
00

>CC
00
99

>00
99
66

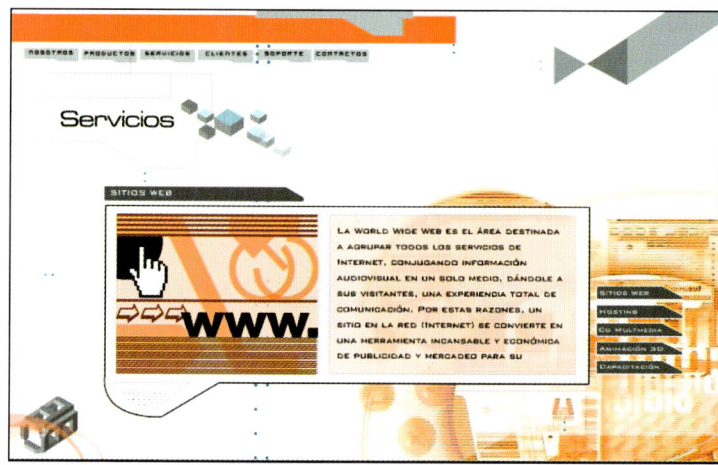

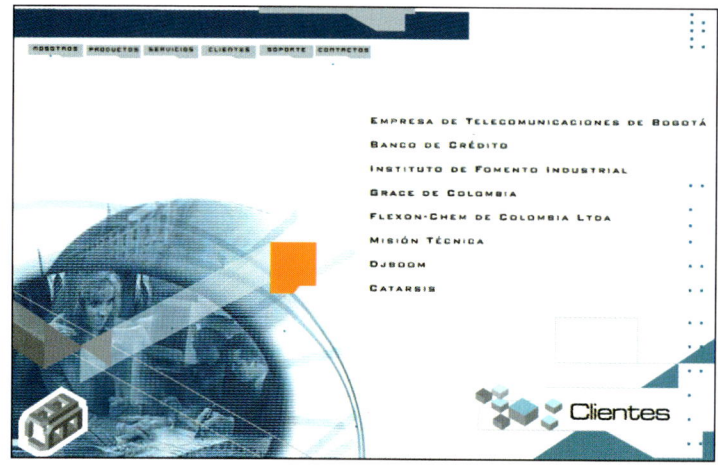

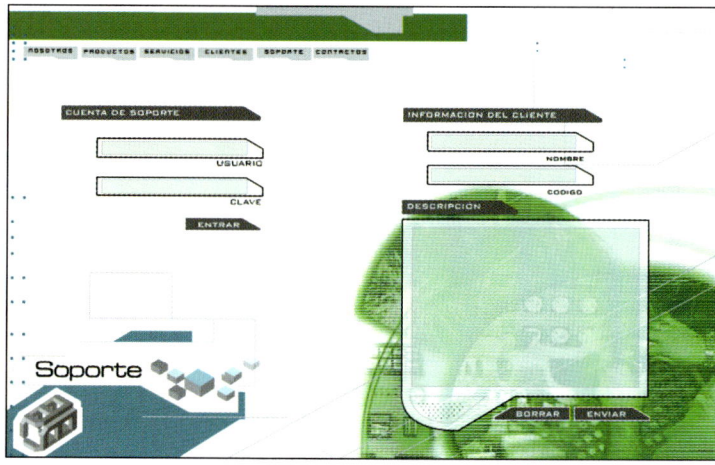

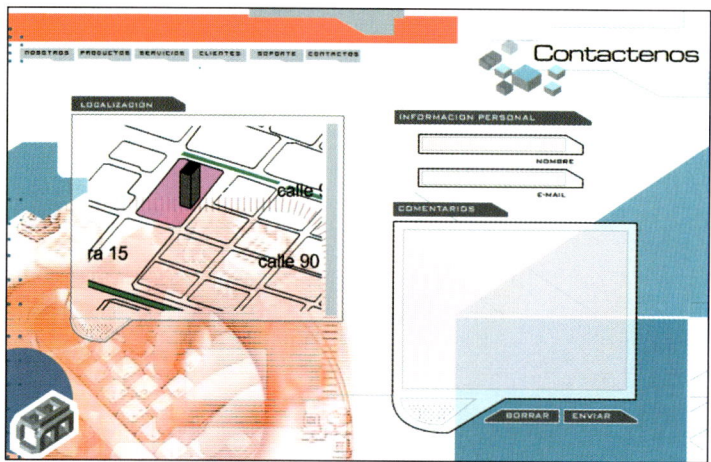

WWW.ALIVEIS.COM

> NAME: ALIVE > SECTOR: BEVERAGE ADVERTISEMENT > SPECIFICATIONS: FLASH, HTML > RATING: ORIGINALITY ☺ GRAPHICS ☺ INTERACTIVITY ☺ > CREDITS: PRELOADED

IF THERE IS ONE THING THAT STANDS OUT ABOUT THIS SITE, IT IS ITS EYE-CATCHING COLOR SCHEME. ORANGE IS THE UNCONTESTED STAR IN A SITE WHOSE TARGET AUDIENCE IS TEEN OR PRE-TEEN; THE WAY TO CAPTURE AT-TENTION IS THE USE OF VIBRANT TONES. BY THE SAME TOKEN, THE PLAYFUL INTERACTION OF THE ORANGE AND ELECTRIC GREEN IS A VISUALLY ARRESTING TECHNIQUE.

ANOTHER POINT OF VITAL IMPORTANCE WHEN DESIGNING A USER INTERFACE FOR KIDS IS THAT NAVIGATION SHOULD BE VERY EASY AND SHOULD NOT BE OPEN TO SECOND INTERPRETATIONS.

AS WITH THE COLOR SCHEME AND IN-TERACTIVITY, THE GRAPHICS ARE VERY CLEAR, EASILY UNDERSTOOD AND DIS-PLAY THE MESSAGE IN A STRAIGHTFOR-WARD MANNER, ALL OF WHICH IS ESPE-CIALLY IMPORTANT FOR THE ONLINE GAMES INCLUDED ON THIS SITE.

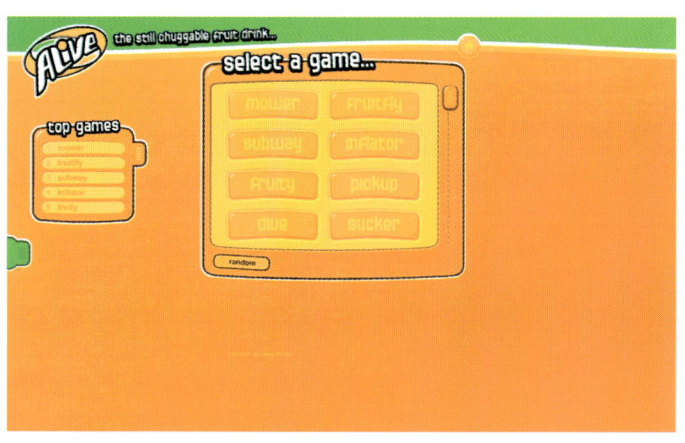

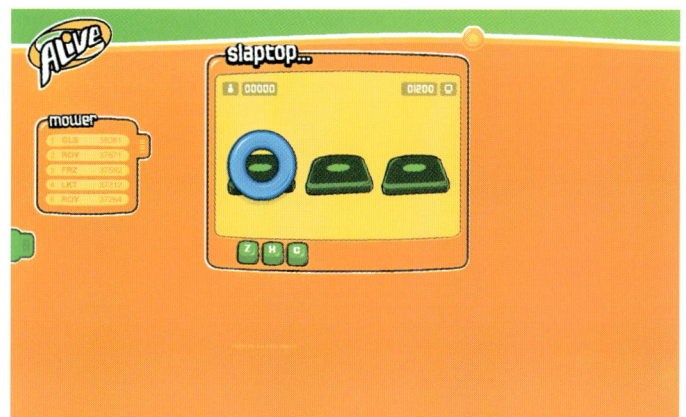

IT'S A STILL CHUGGABLE FRUIT DRINK...   MADE WITH FRUIT JUICE AND VITAMINS...   2 FAB FLAVOURS – ORANGE CASCADE AND TROPICAL TORRENT...   5% FRUIT JUICE

> CREDITS: MÚLTIPLO

THE USE OF RED WITH BLACK AND WHITE IS AN INEVITABLY EYE-CATCHING COMBINATION. THESE BASIC, CONTRASTING TONES ARE VISUAL RESOURCES WHICH NEVER GO WRONG.

THE MENU AND HEADING MAKE EFFICIENT USE OF THEM: A SUBTLE TOUCH OF RED CAPTURES THE ATTENTION, WHILE THE GRAY TONES IN THE PHOTOGRAPHS BRING US BACK TO THE SOBER MESSAGE OF THE SITE.

THIS KIND OF PORTAL NECESSARILY PLACES GREATER IMPORTANCE ON INFORMATION THAN ON GRAPHIC INGENUITY. HERE, THE WORDS ARE WHAT MATTER; THUS, THE SCREEN SCROLLS DOWN TO ALLOW MORE ROOM FOR LENGTHY TEXTS.

THE RECURRING MENU AT THE TOP PROVIDES THE OPTION OF BROWSING CONTENTS WITHOUT THE DANGER OF GETTING LOST OR HAVING TO WIND YOUR WAY BACK TO THE BEGINNING.

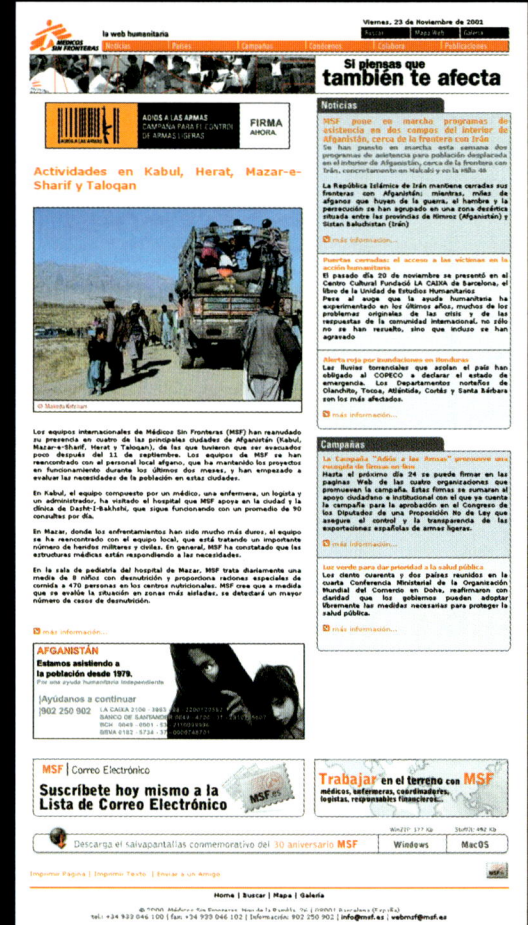

Viernes, 23 de Noviembre de 2001

Conócenos

Si quieres que las cosas cambien

Publicaciones

Si quieres que las cosas cambien

MSF**43** Memoria 2000

Publicaciones

Si crees que hay solución

Galería

Si quieres que las cosas cambien

Colabora

haz clic aquí

Formulario ON-LINE

Puedes hacerte socio
llamando al **902 250 902**

Mapa Web

haz clic aquí

WWW.ELEVENEYES.DE

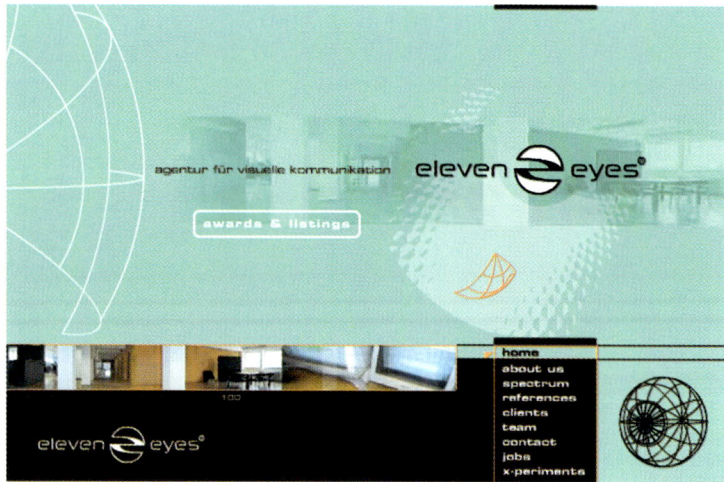

> NAME: ELEVEN EYES > SECTOR: VISUAL COMMUNICATIONS AGENCY > SPECS: FLASH > RATING: ORIGINALITY ☺ GRAPHICS ☺ INTERACTIVITY 😐

A SEARCH FOR DYNAMIC GRAPHICS HAS LED TO AN ASYMMETRIC COMPOSITION IN THIS DESIGN.

AN UNOBTRUSIVE COLOR SCHEME IS AN EXCELLENT RESOURCE FOR AVOIDING COMPETITION BETWEEN GRAPHICS AND TEXT. THUS, TEXT AND COLOR WORK TOGETHER IN HARMONY.

EACH SECTION CAN BE ACCESSED VIA MULTIPLE ROUTES. THUS, THE MENU IS CONFIGURED AS A USEFUL AND INDISPENSABLE TOOL FOR TAKING ON THE VARIOUS SECTIONS OF THIS SITE.

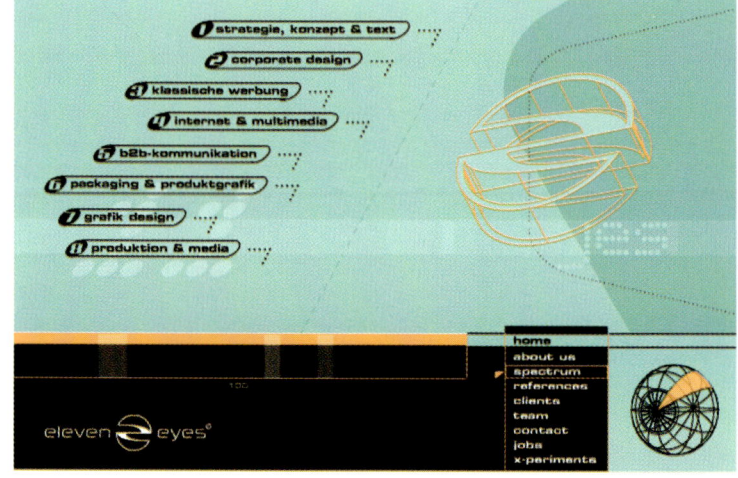

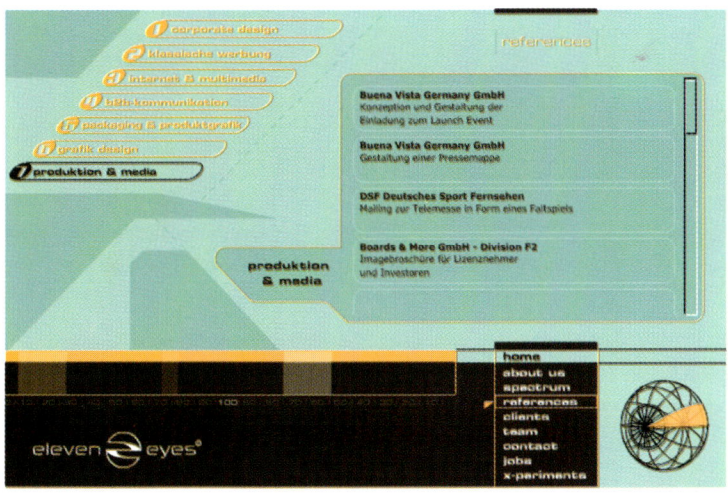

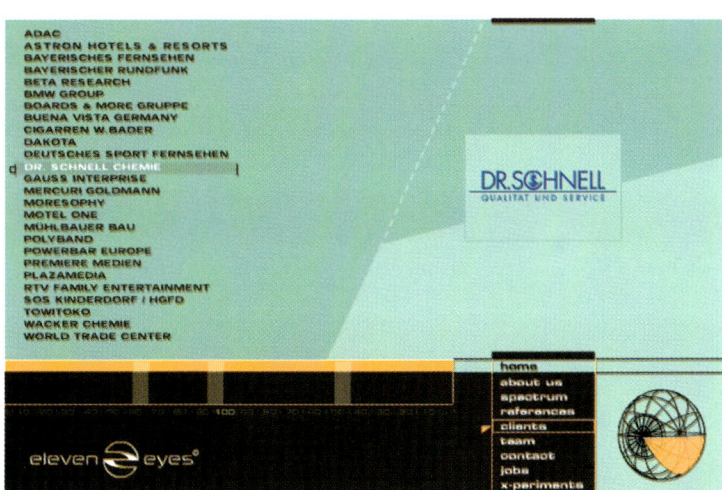
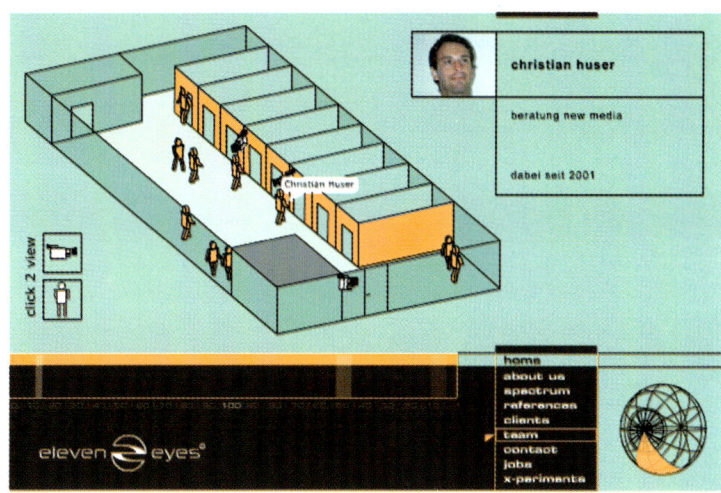
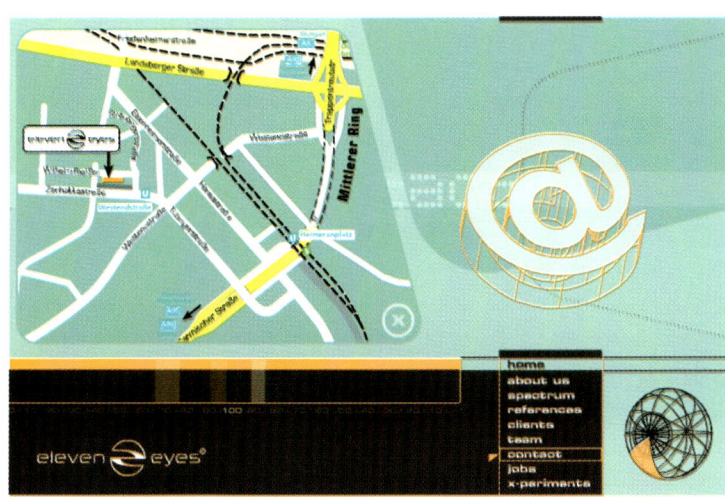
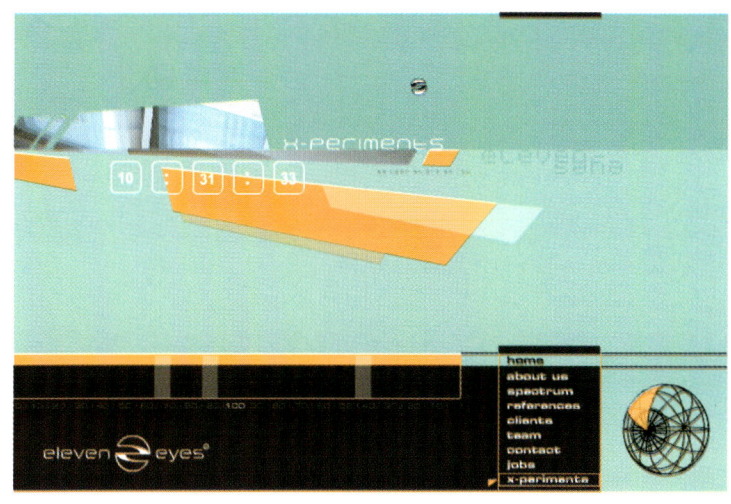

WWW.NEONSKY.COM

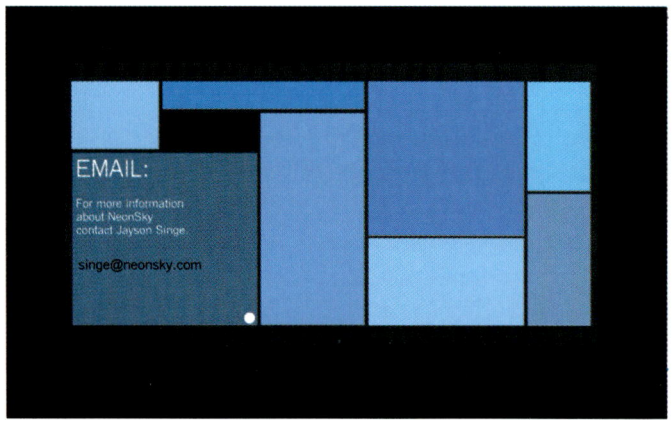

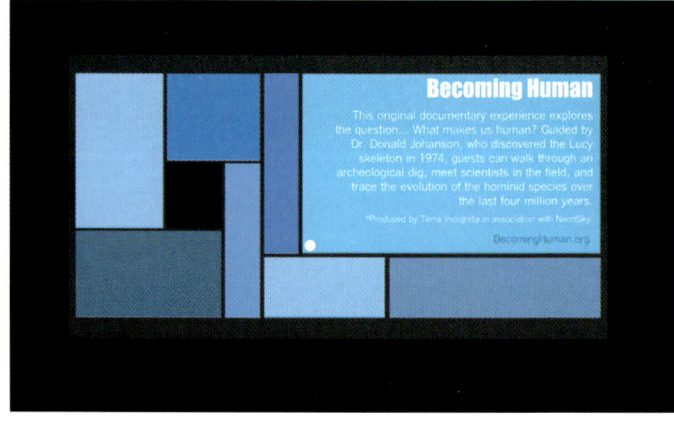

> NAME: NEONSKY > SECTOR: THEMED PORTAL, FLASH, ETC. > SPECS: FLASH > RATING: ORIGINALITY 🙂 GRAPHICS 🙂 INTERACTIVITY 🙂 > CRÉDITOS: NEONSKY CREATIVE MEDIA

As if part of a Constructivist composition by Mondrian, intercepted straight lines compose this interface, in which shades of blue play a central role. The use of a black background helps highlight contents, drawing attention toward the frames and the text.

The information is easy to access. By simply clicking on the white point located at one of the lower edges of each box, different contents are opened and closed.

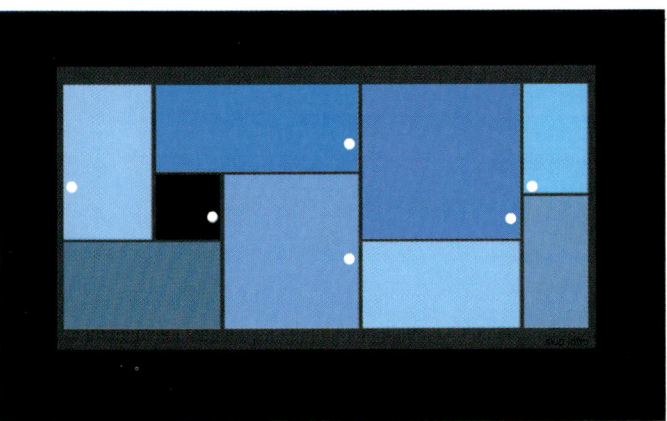

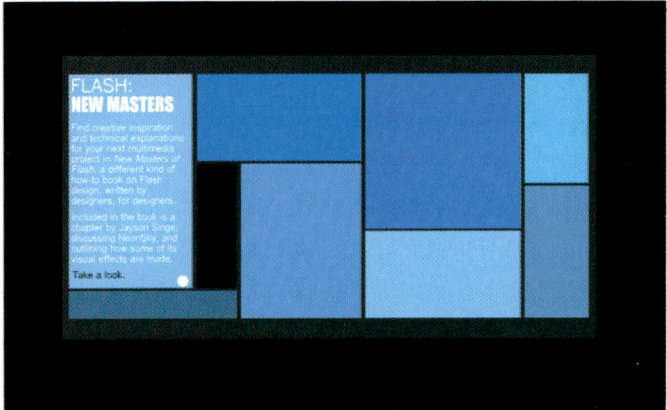

FLASH:
NEW MASTERS

Find creative inspiration and technical explanations for your next multimedia project in *New Masters of Flash*, a different kind of how-to book on Flash design, written by designers, for designers.

Included in the book is a chapter by Jayson Singe, discussing NeonSky, and outlining how some of its visual effects are made.

Take a look.

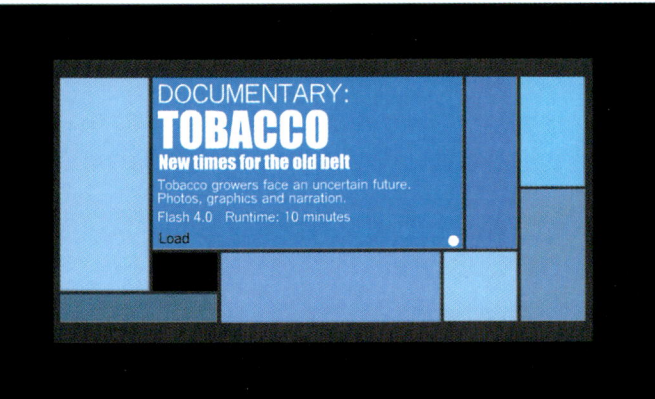

DOCUMENTARY:
TOBACCO
New times for the old belt

Tobacco growers face an uncertain future.
Photos, graphics and narration.

Flash 4.0   Runtime: 10 minutes

Load

DOCUMENTARY:
JOE THOMPSON
Old time fiddler

Joe Thompson is a living piece of history. One of only a handful of African-American old time fiddlers, he plays the music that his father played, music passed down through generations of slaves in the South.

Flash 4.0 and Quicktime 4.0
* video could take several minutes to load on slower connections

Load

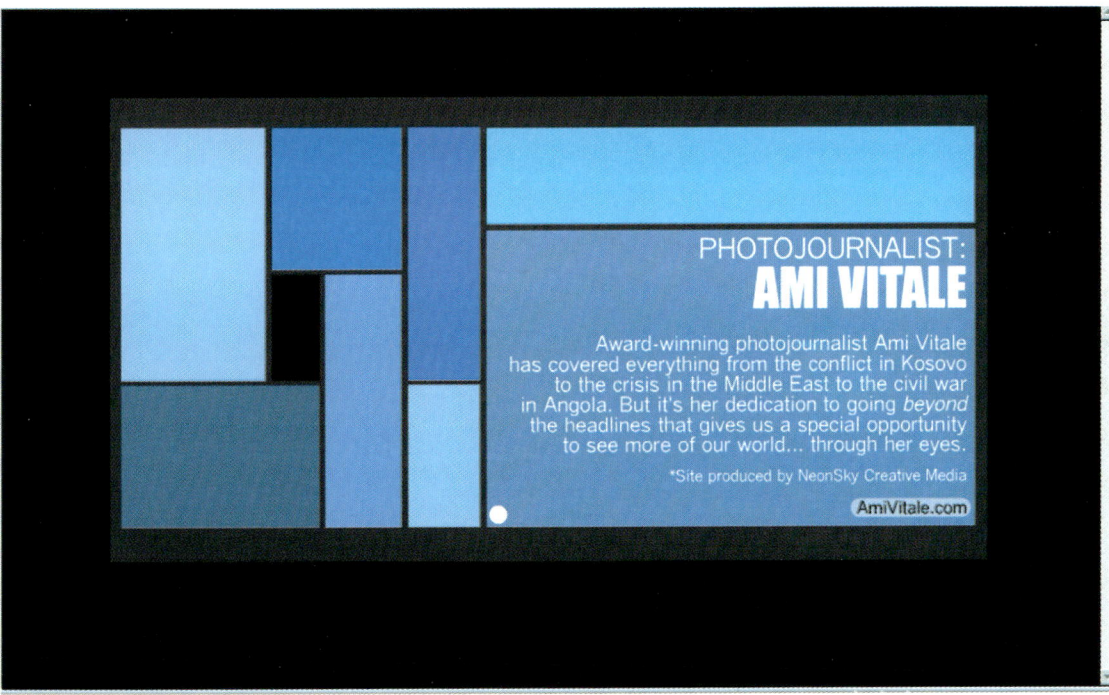

PHOTOJOURNALIST:
AMI VITALE

Award-winning photojournalist Ami Vitale has covered everything from the conflict in Kosovo to the crisis in the Middle East to the civil war in Angola. But it's her dedication to going *beyond* the headlines that gives us a special opportunity to see more of our world... through her eyes.

*Site produced by NeonSky Creative Media

AmiVitale.com

NAME: DIGITAL ROOTS > SECTOR: WEB DESIGN > SPECS: FLASH, HTML > RATING: ORIGINALITY ☺ GRAPHICS ☺ INTERACTIVITY ☹ > CREDITS: NET STRATEGIES

THE POINT OF DEPARTURE OF THIS INNOVATIVE DESIGN IS THE SIMPLIFIED GEOMETRY OF GRAPHICS WHICH USE CONTRASTING COLORS TO CREATE A DISJOINTED ATMOSPHERE. EACH SUBSECTION IS CONFIGURED WITH ITS OWN IDENTITY.

WITH A SINGLE CLICK, A MOVEABLE MENU LOCATES THE DESIRED CONTENT FOR SEAMLESS NAVIGATION.

LIKEWISE, THE INFORMATION IN EACH SECTION IS INDEPENDENT, WITH NO STANDARD CRITERIA.

TWO SAMPLES OF THIS PROJECT'S MOVING MENU, WHICH OPENS UP AND FOLLOWS THE CURSOR ACROSS THE PAGE. ITS NAME: DIGIPOD.

DIGITAL ROOTS
HUMAN FRIENDLY WEBDESIGN

ENTER
LOADED ||||||

AND IF IT ANNOYS YOU...

NOU DE LA RAMBLA 10. / 4.2 :: 08001 BARCELONA SPAIN   PHONE: +34.93.318.79.94 :: MAIL: INFO@DIGITALROOTS.ES

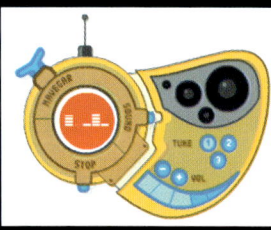

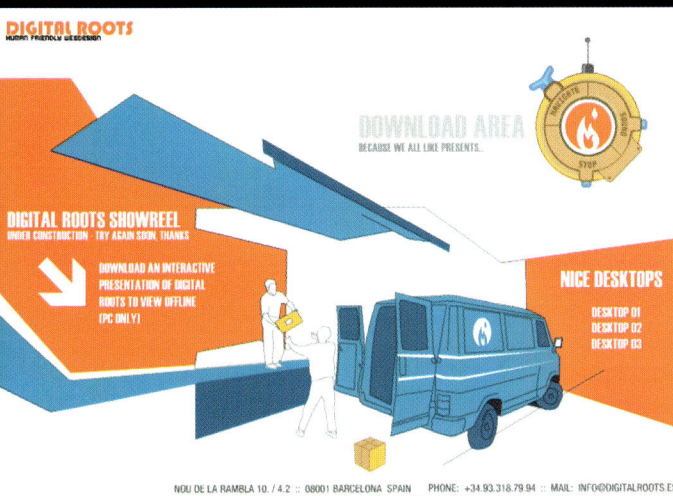
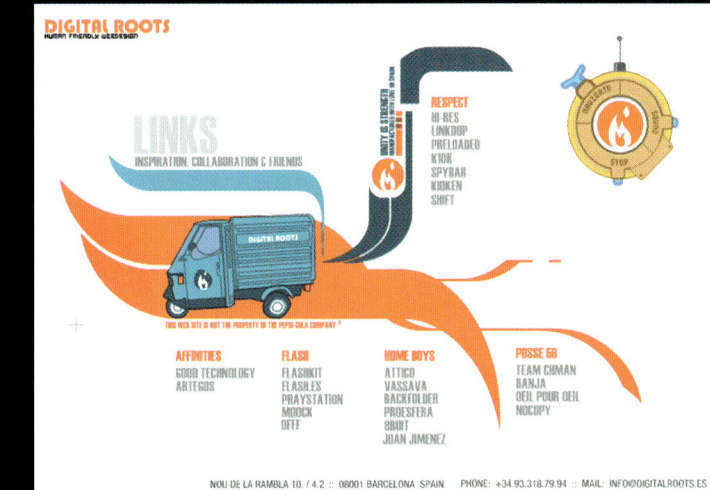
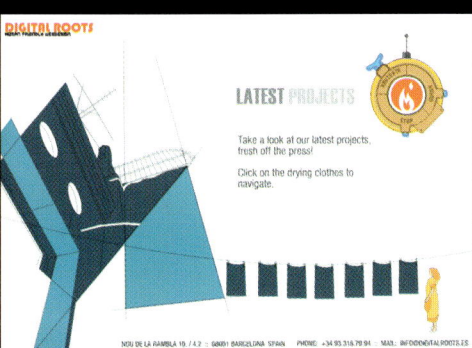
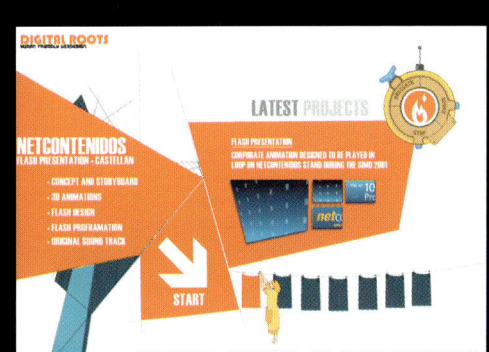

WWW.THETRUTH.COM

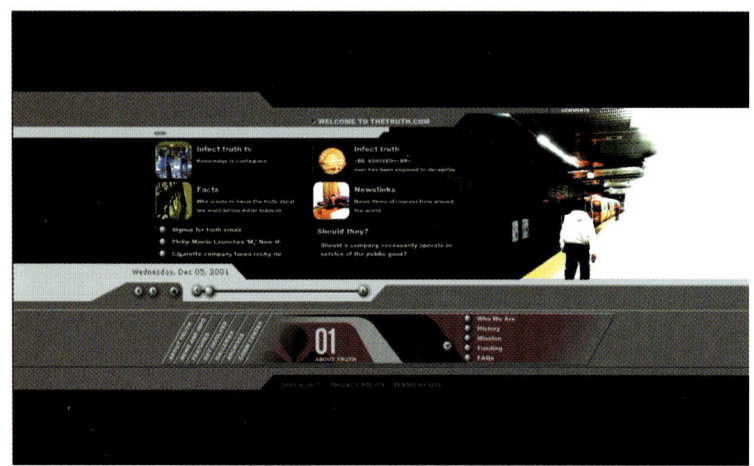

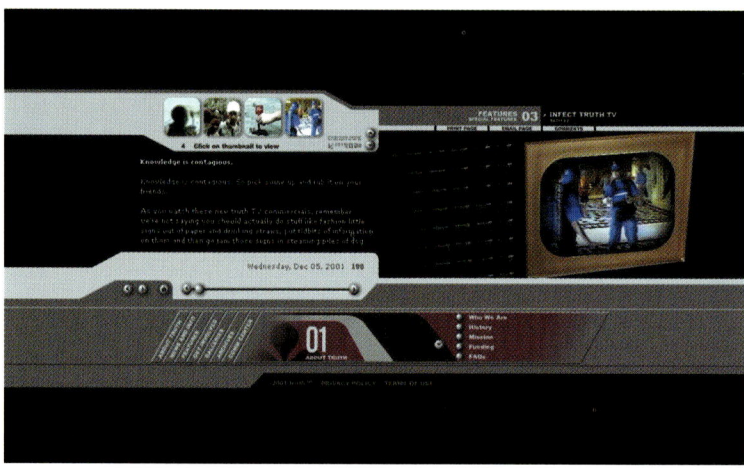

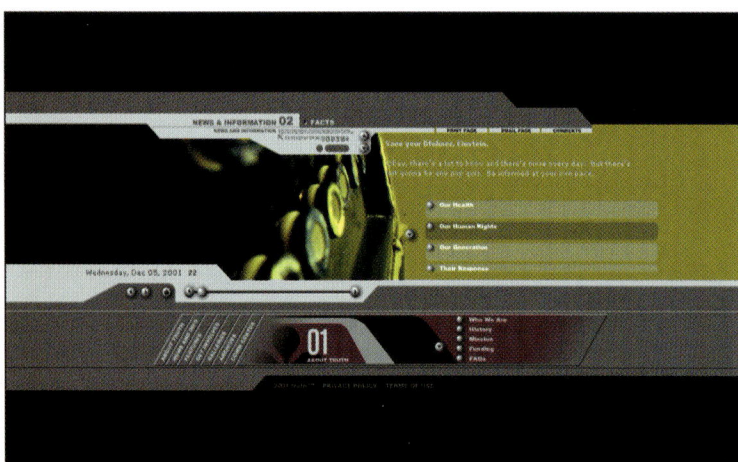

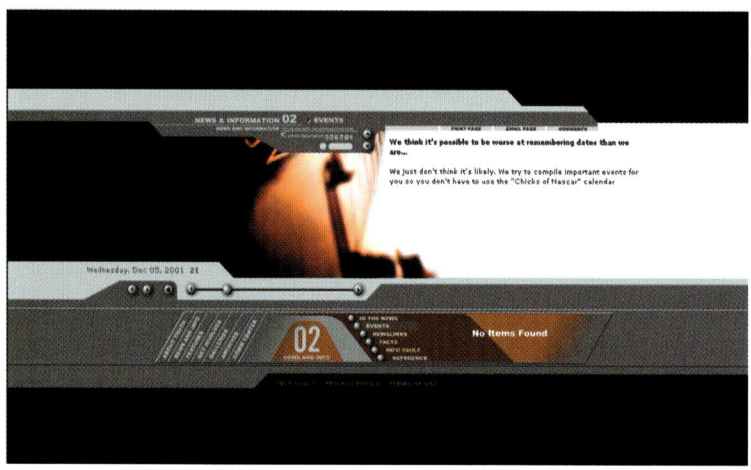

> NAME: THE TRUTH > SECTOR: ANTI TO-
BACCO INFORMATION > SPECS: FLASH,
HTML > RATING: ORIGINALITY ☺
GRAPHICS ☺ INTERACTIVITY ☺

THE SAME BASIC COMPOSITION
APPEARS THROUGHOUT THE
SITE. EACH OF THE SUBSEC-
TIONS USES A HORIZONTAL
GRAPHIC, WHICH IS HARDLY
MODIFIED FROM PAGE TO PAGE.
WITH THIS LAYOUT, THE USER
QUICKLY FINDS AND CONSULTS
THE RELEVANT INFORMATION,
WITHOUT THE NEED TO KEEP
PULLING UP ADDITIONAL PAGES.

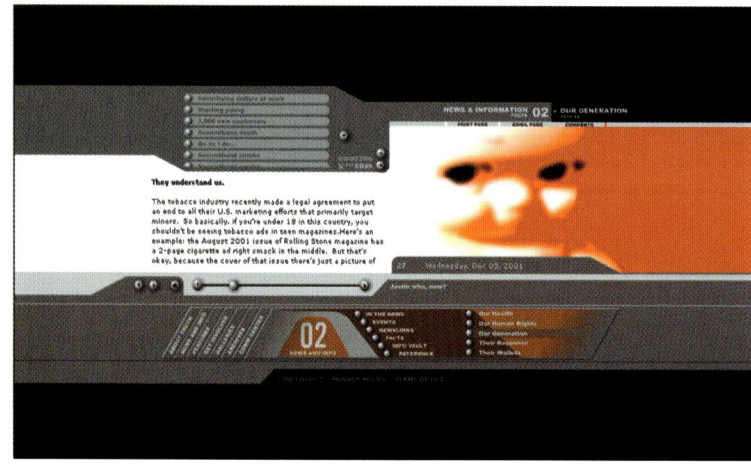

THE COLOR SCHEME CHOSEN FOR THE DESIGN IS DIRECTLY RELATED TO THE PHOTOGRAPHS, WITH INTRIGUING COMBINATIONS OF BLURRED AND DISPROPORTIONATE IMAGES.

THE CENTRAL GRAPHIC ELEMENT, WHICH IS SEEN THROUGHOUT THE SITE, IS A WINDOW CONTAINING ALL OF THE INFORMATION, INCLUDING THE MAIN MENU. IT IS NOT STATIC, BUT IS RATHER ADAPTED TO DIFFERING CONTENTS AND SECTIONS.

>FF
00
00

>99
00
00

>00
66
66

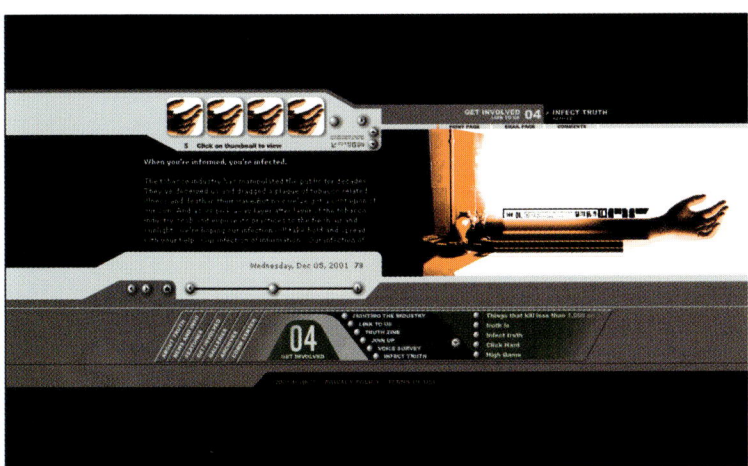

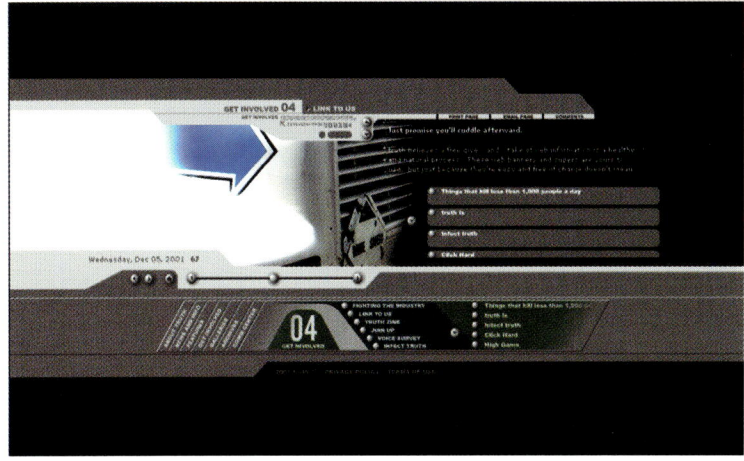

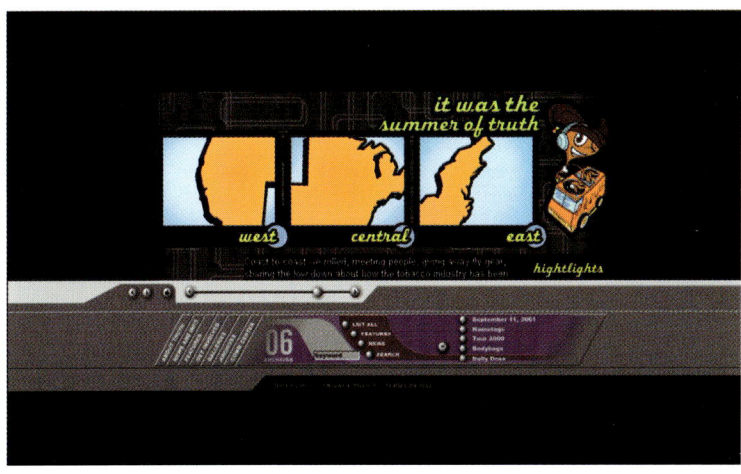

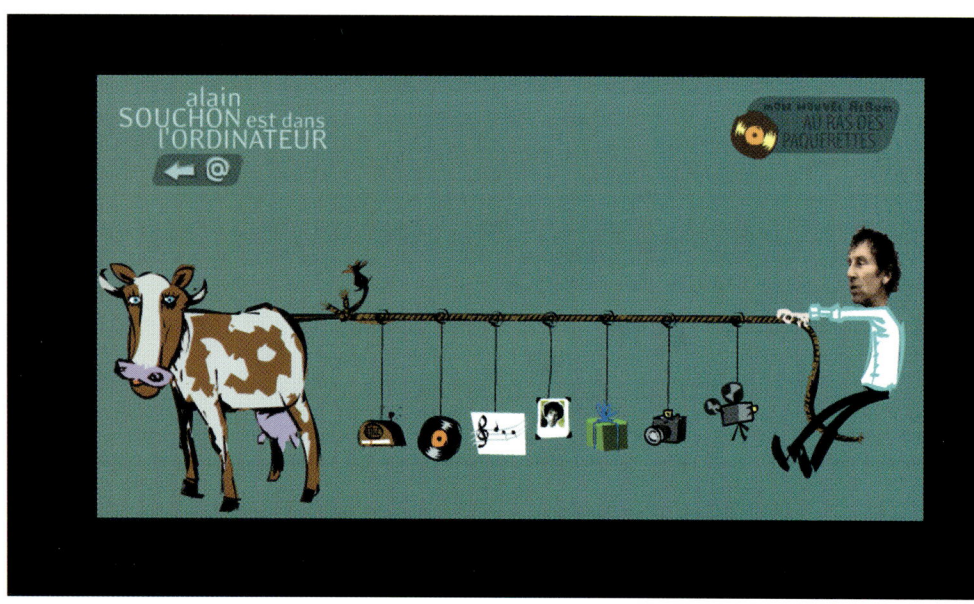

WWW.ALAINSOUCHON.NET

> NAME: ALAIN SOUCHON > SEC-
TOR: ADVERTISING > SPECS: FLASH,
HTML > RATING: ORIGINALITY ☺
GRAPHICS ☺ INTERACTIVITY ☺
> CREDITS: CEIL PORU CEIL > CON-
CEPCIÓN CHARLES SOUCHON

COLOR AND ANIMATION GIVE CHAR-
ACTER TO THIS ORIGINAL AND EX-
TENSIVE WEBSITE. COLOR EMPHA-
SIZES THE DRAWINGS; GREEN, IN ITS
VARIOUS HUES, IS AS UNOSTENTA-
TIOUS AS POSSIBLE, LEAVING THE
CLICKABLE ILLUSTRATIONS TO SPEAK
FOR THEMSELVES.

ON THE WHOLE, SUCH GRAPHIC
RICHNESS IS WHAT DETERMINES THE
PACE OF NAVIGATION, WITH THE TWO
MENUS FAMILIARIZING USERS WITH
THE VARIOUS SECTIONS.

A CLICK ON THE OPENING PAGES'
GRAPHICS LEADS TO ONE OF SEVEN
LINKS, EACH WITH AN INDEPENDENT
GRAPHIC TREATMENT.

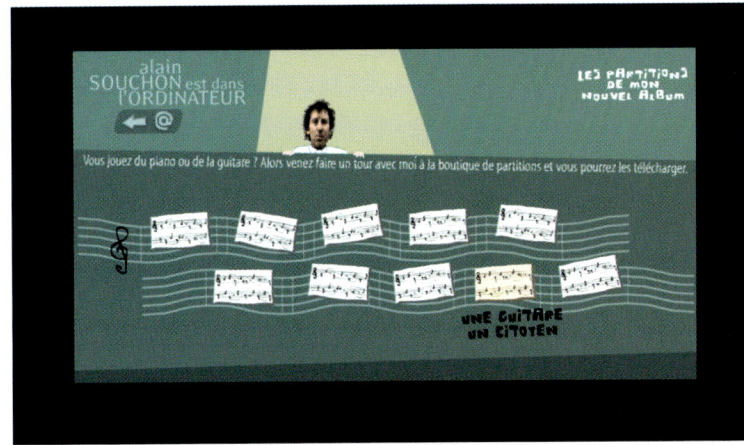

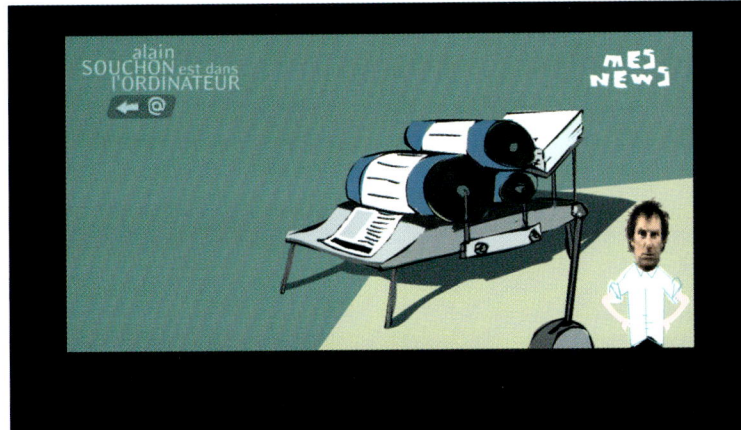

The second part of the website has a menu distribution closely resembling that of the original. Here, the treatment of color continues at the same rhythm, with varying graphics.

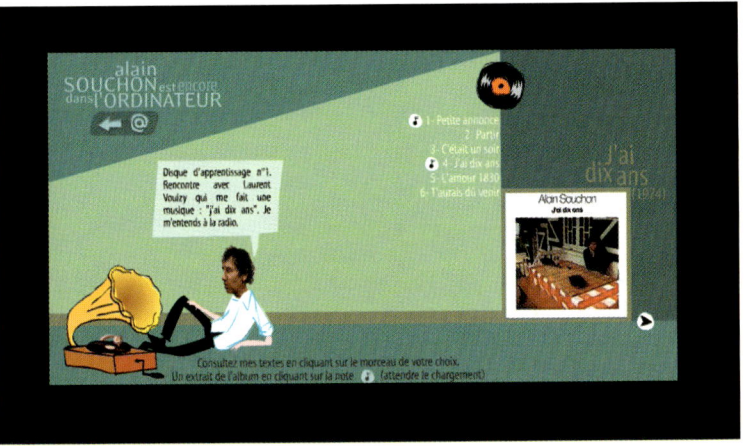

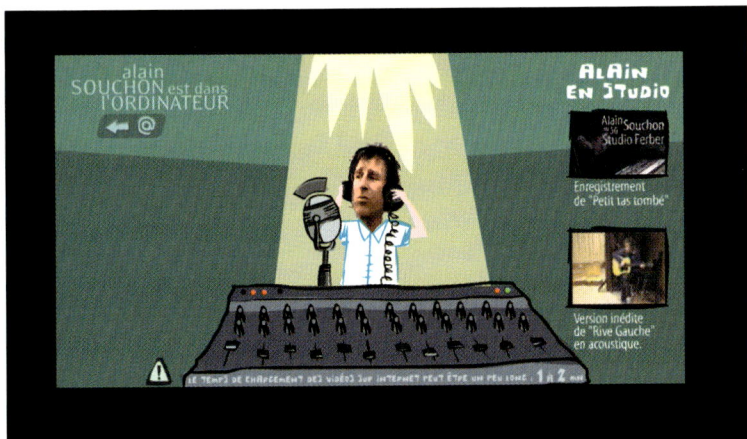

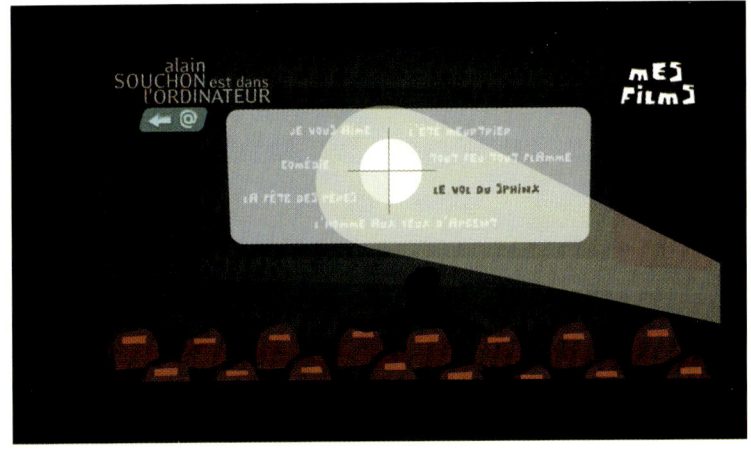

entrar .

REQUISITOS MINIMOS :
[Internet Explorer 4.+ / Netscape Navigator 4.+] + [Flash 5] + [Quicktime]

flúor
projectos
unit

HERE IS AN EXAMPLE OF THE MAXI-
MUM SYNTHESIS IN THE USE OF COL-
OR. A GENEROUS DOSE OF WHITE,
TEXT WRITTEN IN BLACK AND RE-
STRAINED TOUCHES OF COLOR ALL
CHARACTERIZE THIS EASY-ON-THE-
EYES DESIGN.
AN APPEALING ASPECT OF THIS SITE'S
LAYOUT IS ITS EASE OF NAVIGATION:
FINDING THE DESIRED INFORMATION
AND THE VARIOUS SUBSECTIONS IS A
STRAIGHTFORWARD PROCESS.

A VERTICAL MENU ON THE LEFT HAND SIDE OF THE SCREEN SERVES AS THE STRUCTURAL AXIS FROM WHICH THE THREE MAIN SECTIONS CAN BE ACCESSED. THESE, IN TURN, BRANCH OFF IN THEIR OWN DIRECTIONS. THIS SITE RELIES MORE ON THE TEXT AS A GRAPHIC ELEMENT THAN ON THE INHERENT ABSTRACTION OF ICONS.

>FF
FF
OO

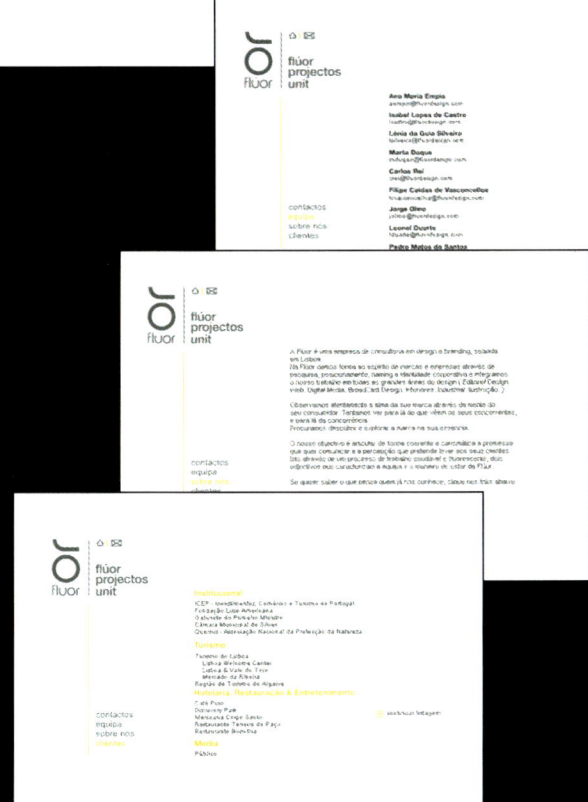

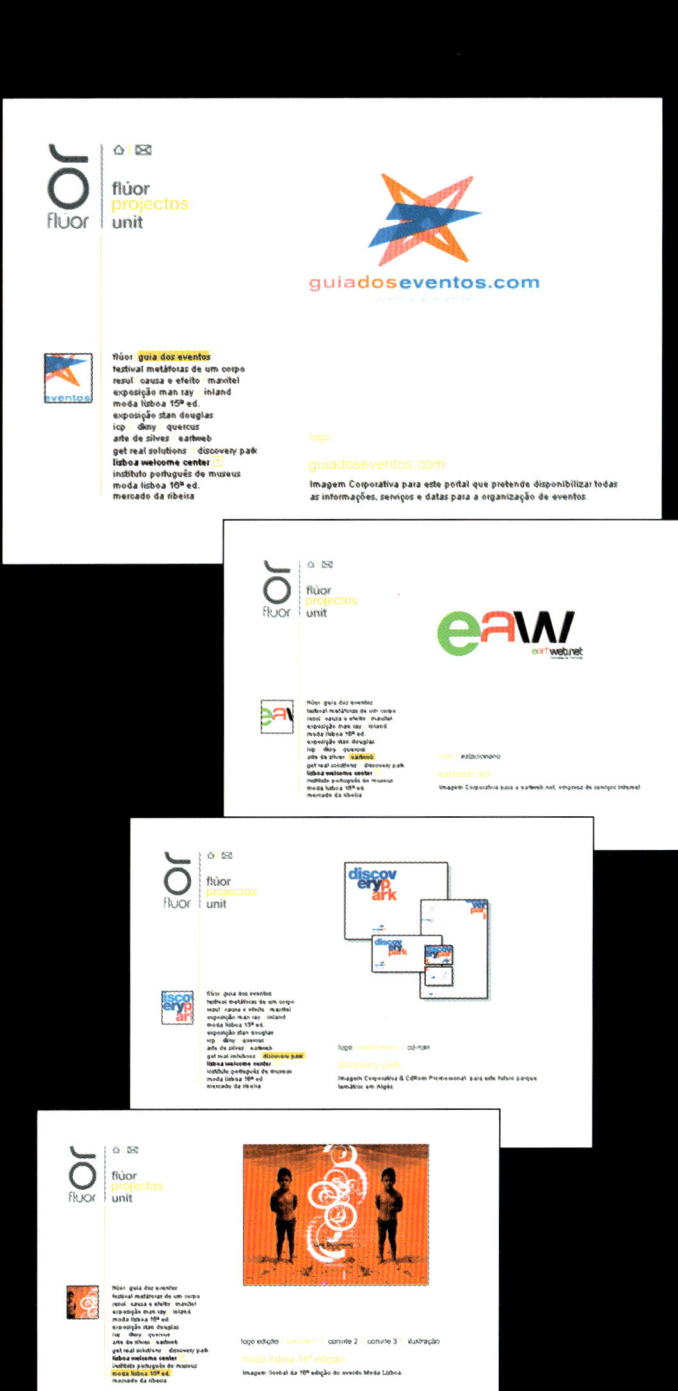

WWW.WMTEAM.DE

> NAME: WM TEAM WERBEAGENTUR

> SECTOR: ADVERTISING AGENCY

> SPECIFICATIONS: FLASH, HTML

> RATING: ORIGINALITY 😐

GRAPHICS 😊 INTERACTIVITY 😊

> DESIGNED BY: WM TEAM

USING PLAYFUL CARTOON IMAGES CAN BE AN EFFECTIVE AND FRIENDLY, ALBEIT UNSOPHISTICATED, WAY TO REACH A TARGET AUDIENCE.

THE SAME STRUCTURE IS SEEN THROUGHOT THE SITE, CHANGING ONLY SLIGHTLY WHEN ONE OF THE OPTIONS ON THE STATIONARY BAR TO THE RIGHT IS SELECTED. THE MESSAGES DISPLAYED ARE CLEAR, CONCISE AND UNAMBIGUOUS.

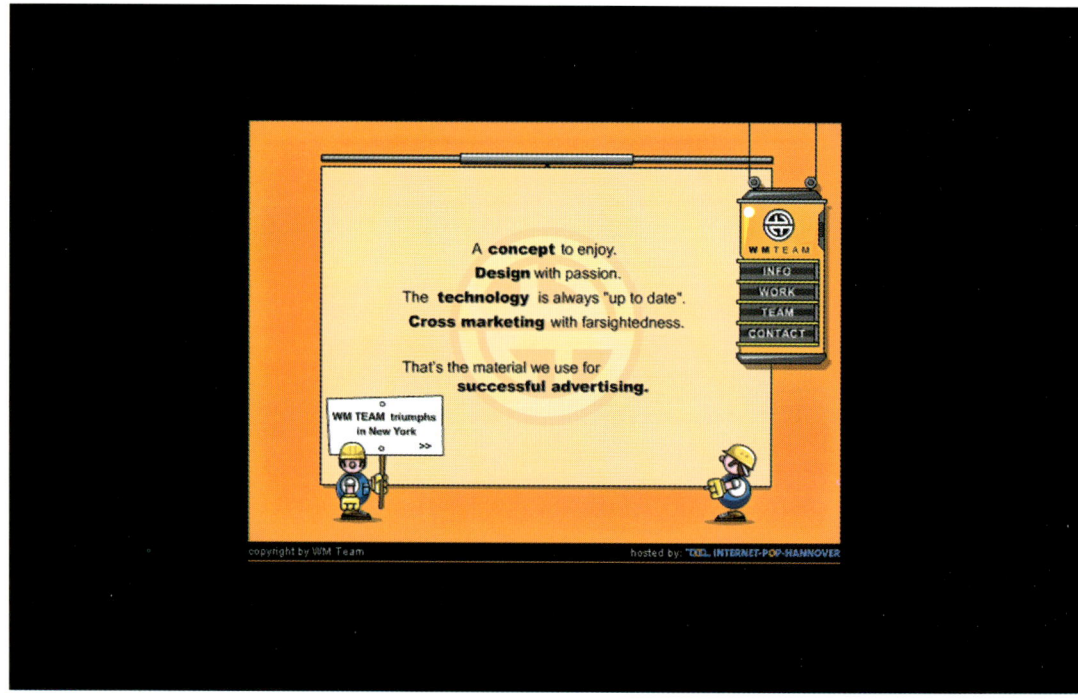

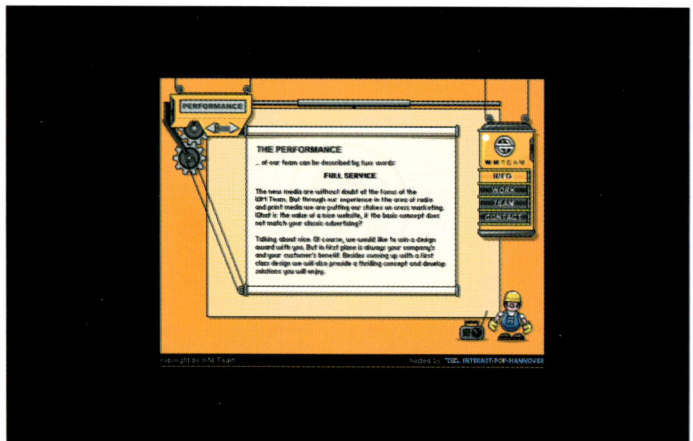

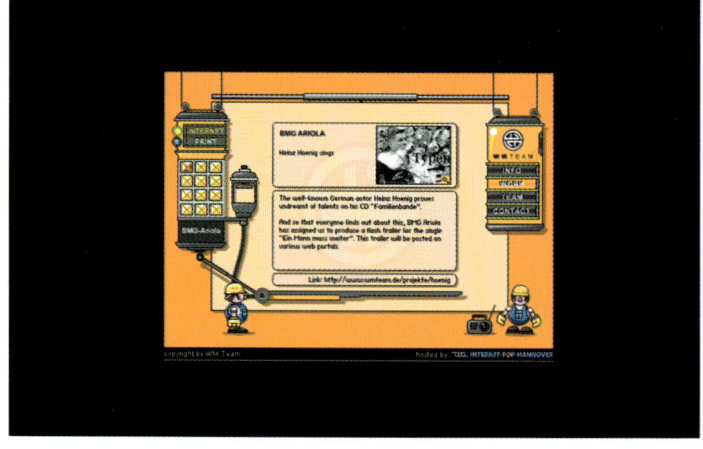

TEXTUAL INFORMATION IS INCORPO-
RATED INTO THE ILLUSTRATIONS IN
THIS DESIGN AND EACH SECTION
MAKES WELL-BALANCED USE OF TEXT
AND GRAPHICS.
THE NARRATIVE LINE CONTINUES
FROM ONE PAGE TO THE NEXT, OF-
FERING THE ADVANTAGE OF BEING
ABLE TO AVOID ERRONEOUS INTER-
PRETATIONS AND THE DISADVAN-
TAGE OF NOT BEING ABLE TO SKIP
WHAT YOU ARE NOT INTERESTED IN.

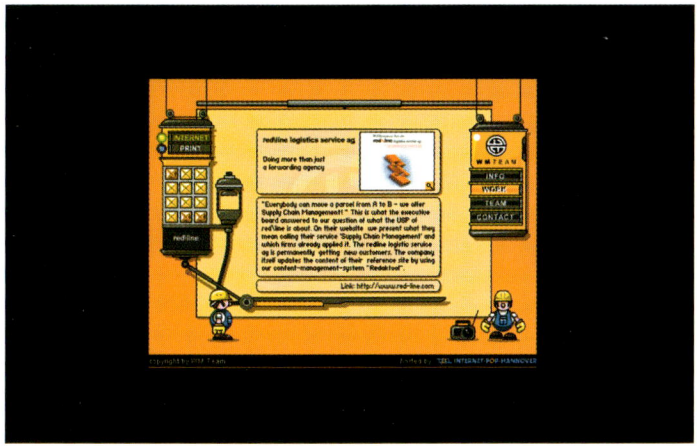

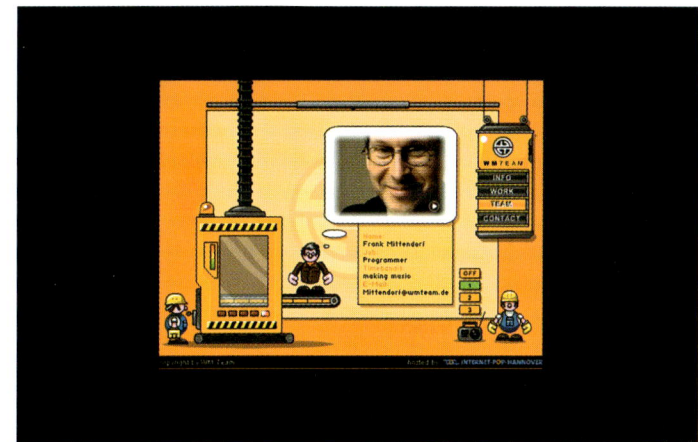

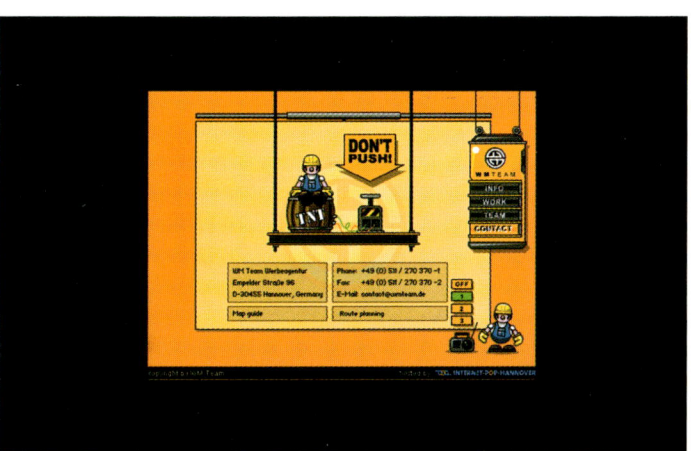

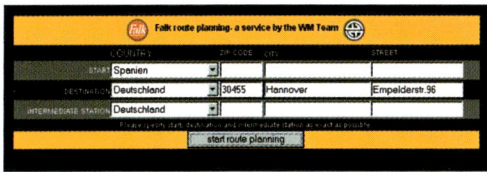

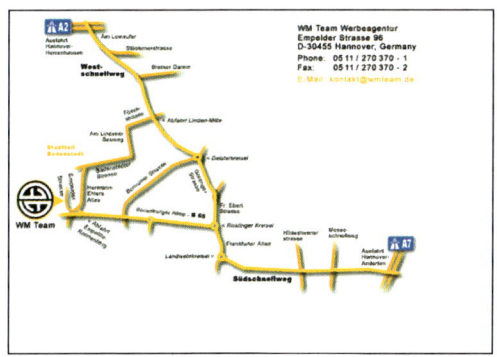

WWW.HELIOZILLA.COM

helios design
about helios
projects
clients
contact
Friday, November 30, 2001
Brand new ok47 website: go there
Stying, Profiling: New GEEK BOUTIQUE catalog
I'm OK, You're OK: New ok47 catalog
Broadcast Kings: New music video & commercials
Much Loved...

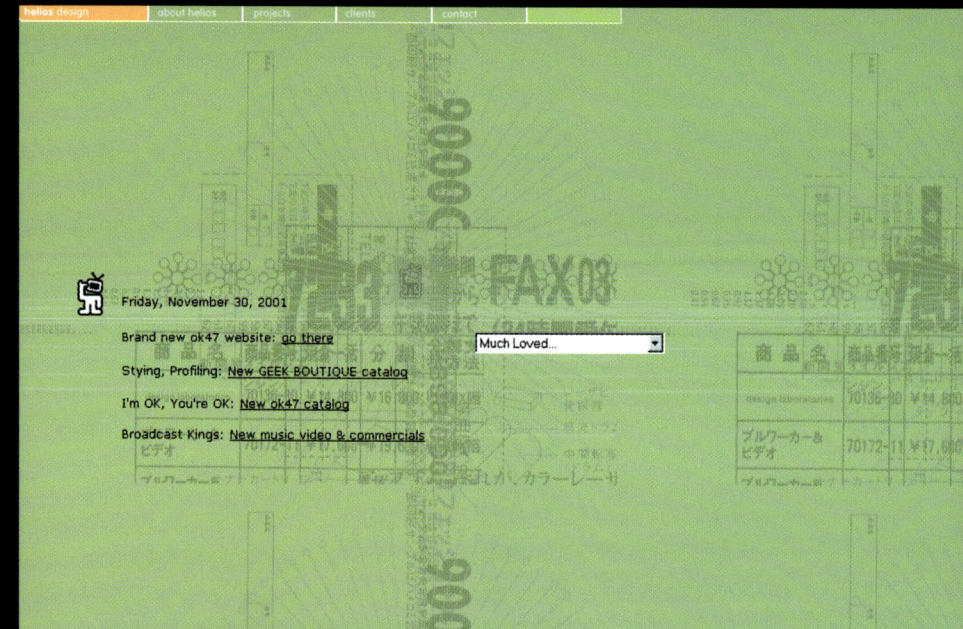

> NAME: HELIOS > SECTOR: DESIGN STUDIO > SPECS: FLASH, HTML > RATING: ORIGINALITY ☺ GRAPHICS ☺ INTERACTIVITY ☺

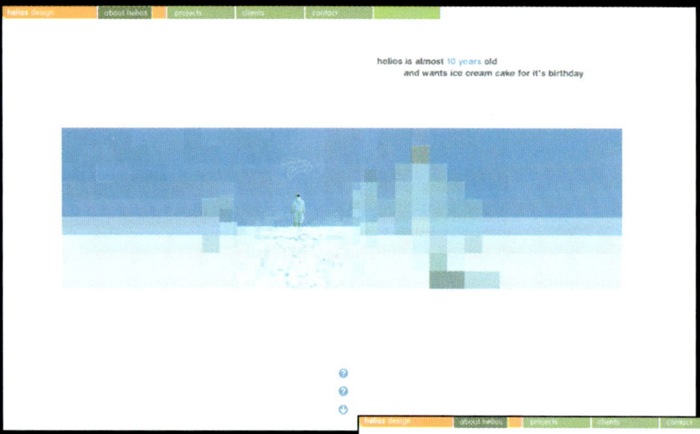

helios is almost 10 years old
and wants ice cream cake for it's birthday

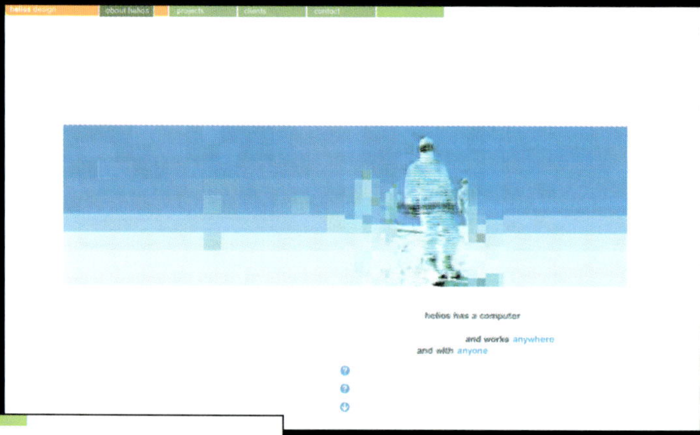

helios has a computer
and works anywhere
and with anyone

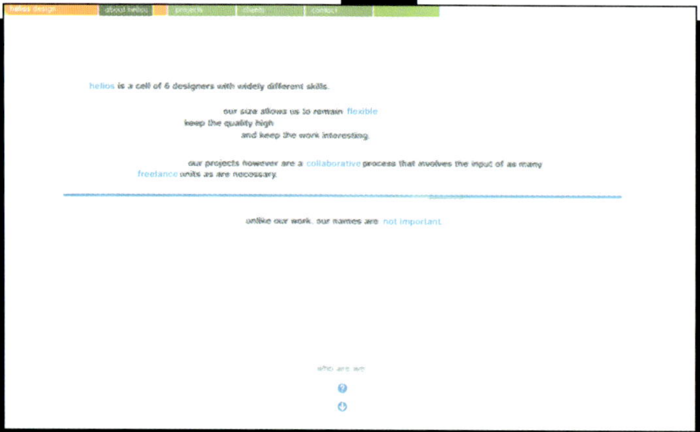

helios is a cell of 6 designers with widely different skills.
our size allows us to remain flexible
keep the quality high
and keep the work interesting.
our projects however are a collaborative process that involves the input of as many
freelance units as are necessary.
unlike our work, our names are not important.
who are we

GREEN, BLUE AND A TOUCH OF ORANGE ARE THE INGREDIENTS OF THIS EYE-CATCHING SITE, WHICH CREATES A SENSATION OF WHIMSY AND FUN AND WHERE USERS ARE ENCOURAGED TO DISCOVER THE VARIOUS INTERACTIVE NICHES FOR THEMSELVES.

THE GRAPHIC COMPOSITION SHOWS A TENDENCY TO RELY ON THE UPPER PORTION OF THE SCREEN; THE

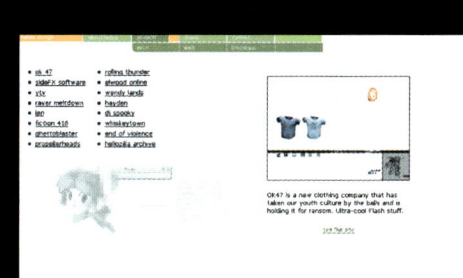

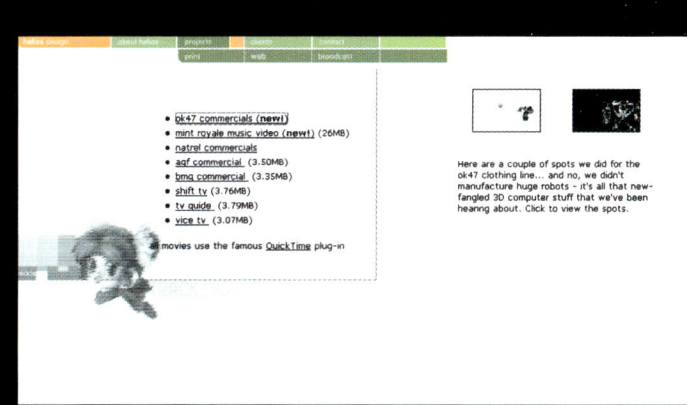

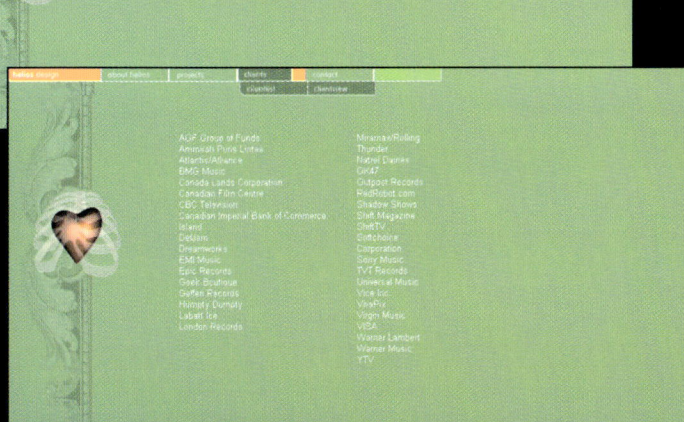

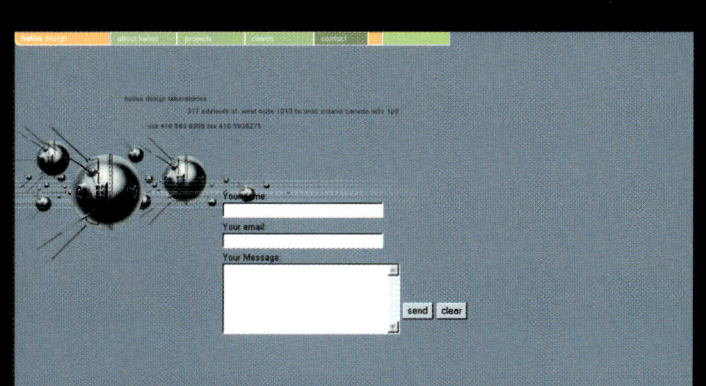

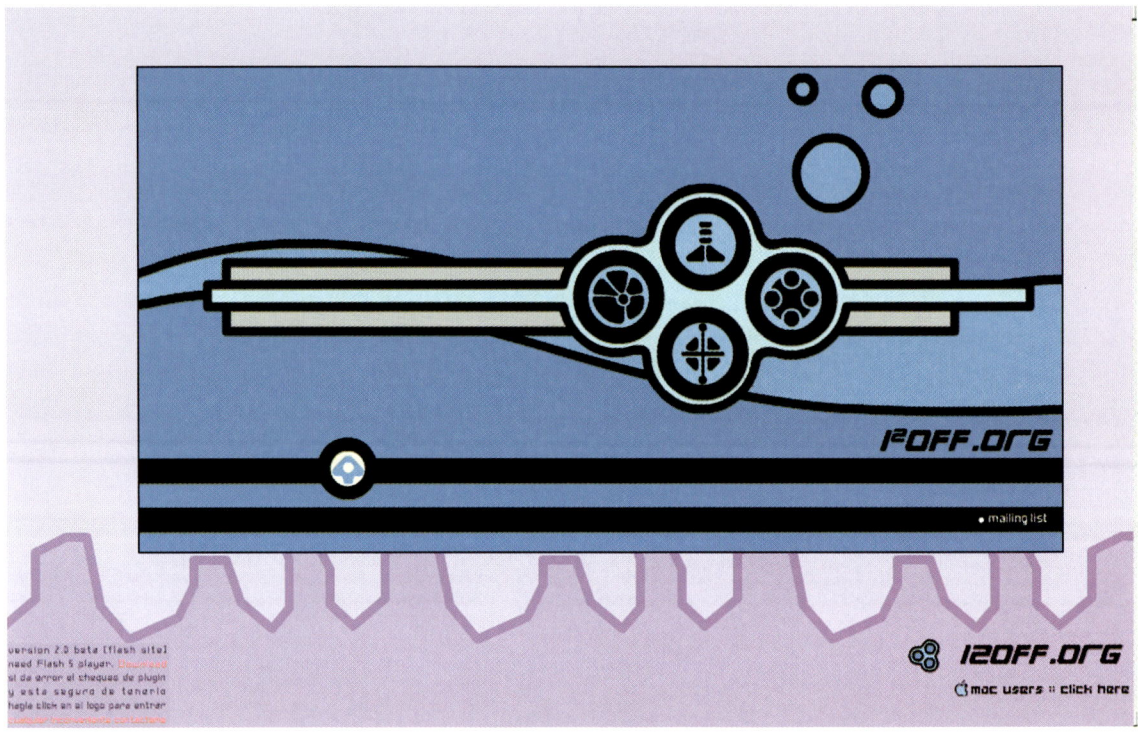

> NAME: 12OFF.ORG > SECTOR:
RESEARCH > SPECS: FLASH, HTML
> RATING: ORIGINALITY ☺ GRAPH-
ICS ☺ INTERACTIVITY ☺ > CRED-
ITS: IVAN IVANOFF

WWW.12OFF.ORG

THIS SITE HAS ESPECIALLY ORIGI-
NAL ICONS, EACH LEADING TO A
DIFFERENT SECTION. A SERIES OF
INFORMATIVE WINDOWS APPEAR AT
THE USER'S COMMAND.

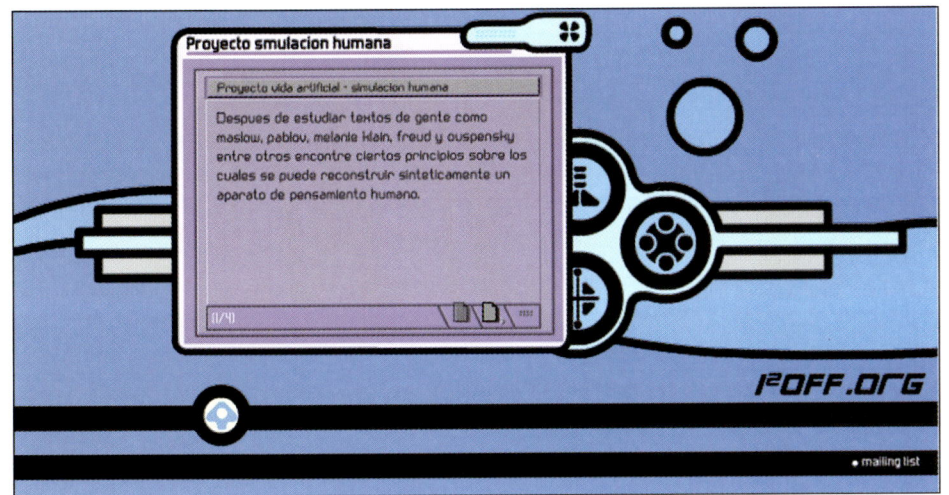

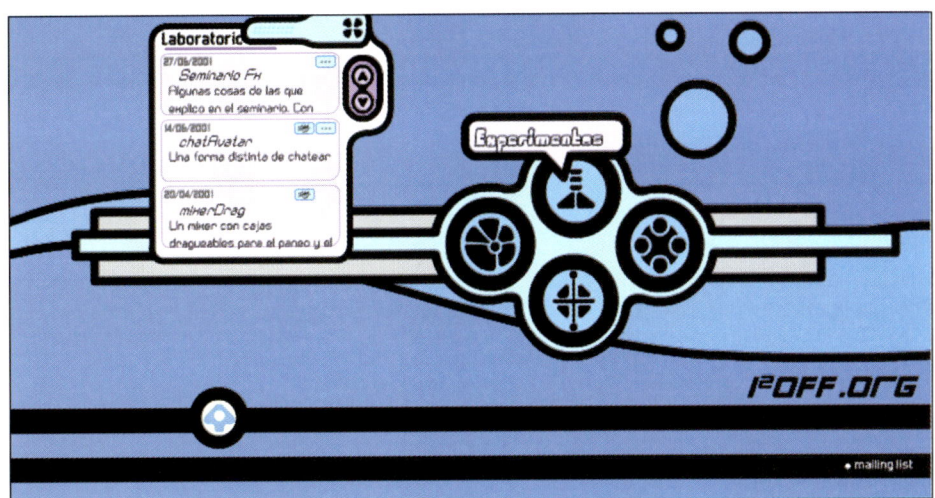

The graphic structure of this website remains constant throughout, changing only when contents are located.

Blue tones and their complementary colors support the graphics and compete with textual information in the visual hierarchy.

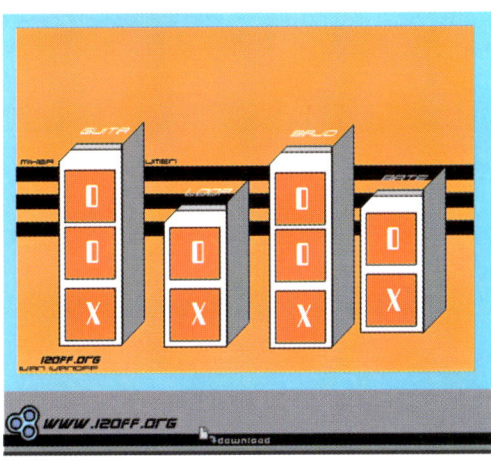

> NAME: ORBY INTERACTIVE

> SECTOR: CREATION AND DEVELOPMENT OF DIGITAL SERVICES

> SPECIFICATIONS: FLASH, HTML

> RATING: ORIGINALITY ☺ GRAPHICS ☺ INTERACTIVITY ☹

THE EXPRESSIVE STRENGTH OF OR-ANGE DEFINES THE CHARACTER OF THIS SITE. THE CONTENTS SEEM TO SPRING FROM AND BE DICTATED BY THIS SINGLE ELEMENT.

WWW.ORBY.COM.BR

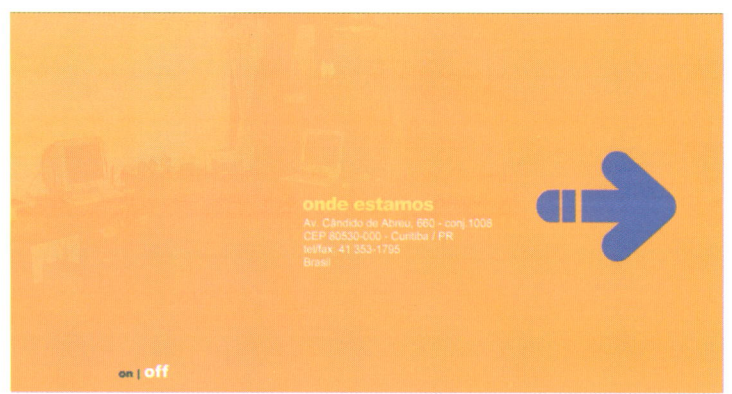

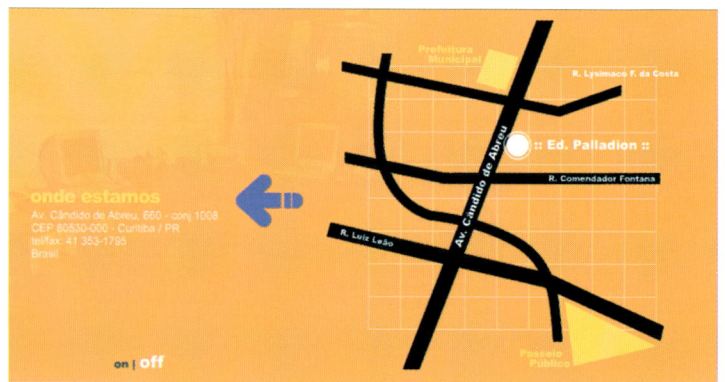

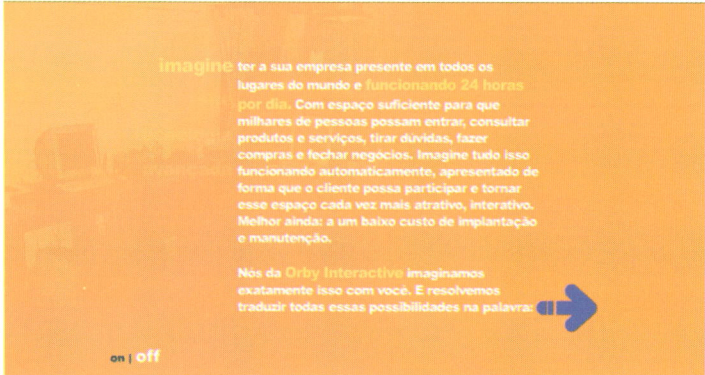

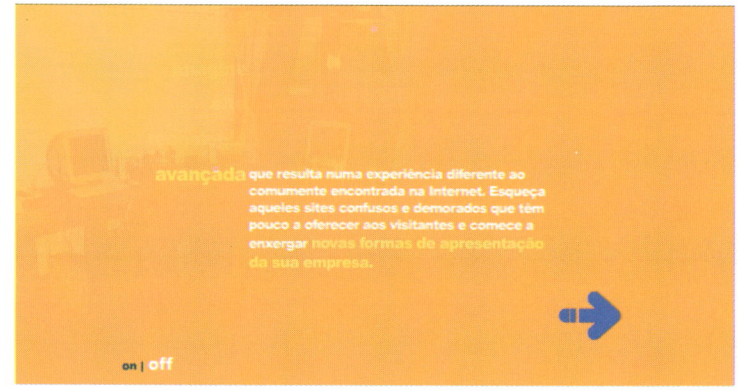

THE TEXTUAL CONTENTS ACQUIRE THE
STATUS OF GRAPHICS CAPABLE OF IL-
LUSTRATING AND GIVING LIFE TO EACH
SECTION, WHILE THE BACKGROUND
PHOTOS ARE ALSO IMPORTANT DEFIN-
ING ELEMENTS. THE UNIVERSALLY
USED AND UNDERSTOOD ARROW EF-
FECTIVELY SERVES ITS PURPOSE
HERE: ORIENTATION.

>FF
00
00

>00
CC
00

>00
00
99

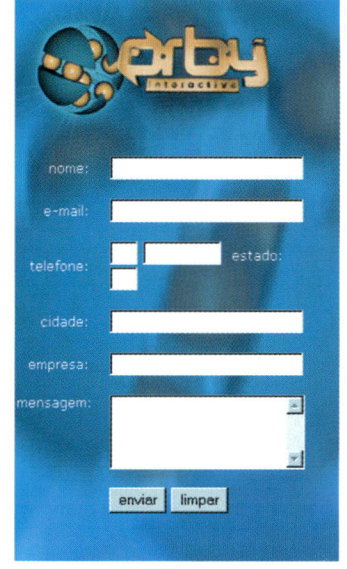

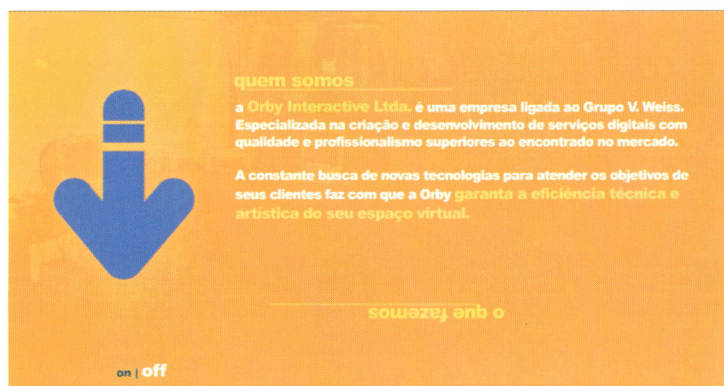

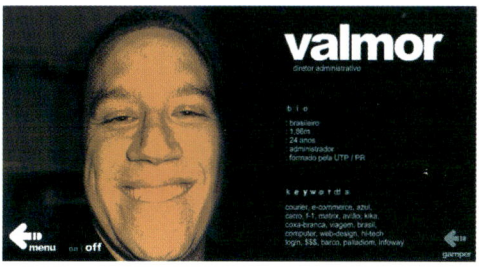

> NAME: MYLG019 (LG TELECOM FAMILY
SITE) > SECTOR: COMPANY PORTAL
> SPECS: HTML > RATING: ORIGINALITY ☺
GRAPHICS ☺ INTERACTIVITY ☺

WWW.MYLG019.CO.KR

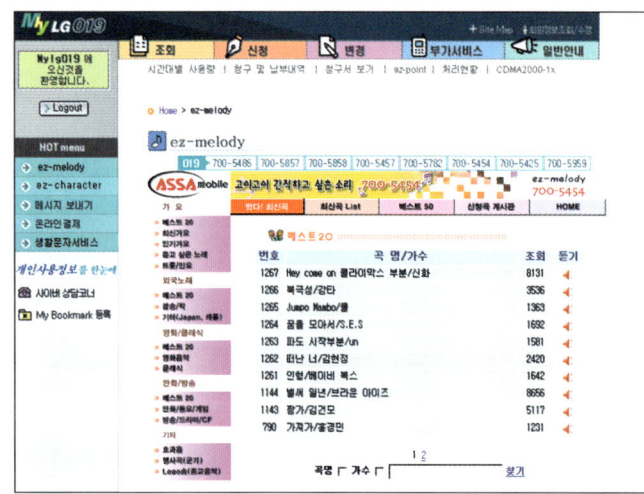

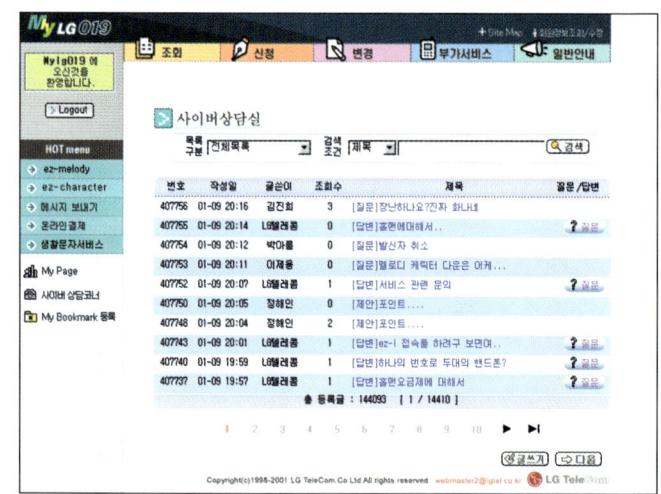

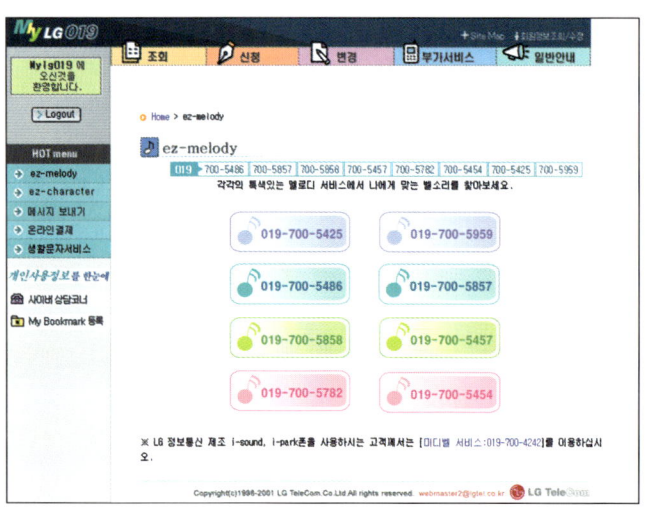

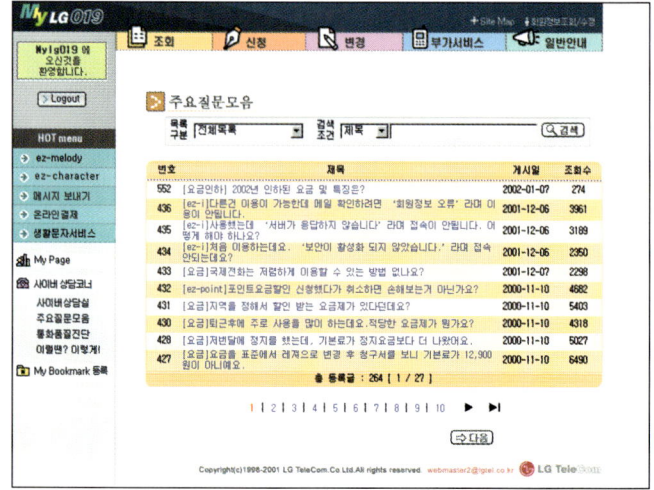

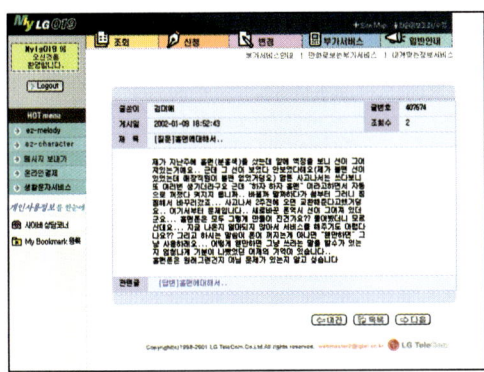

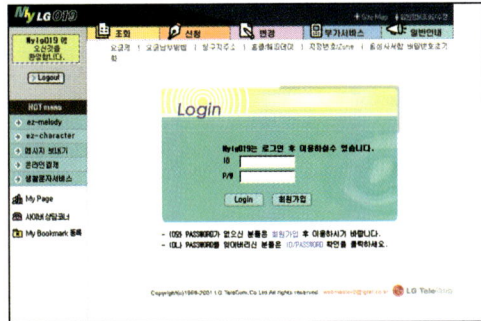

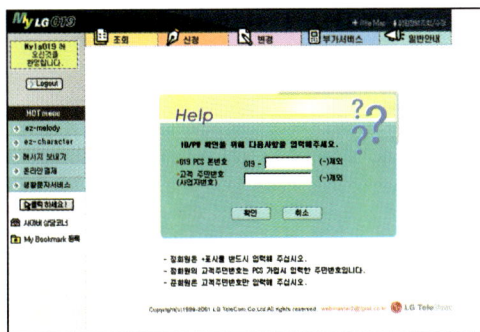

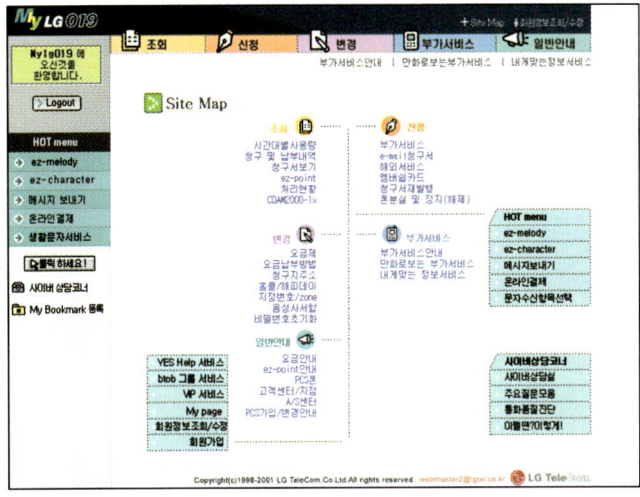

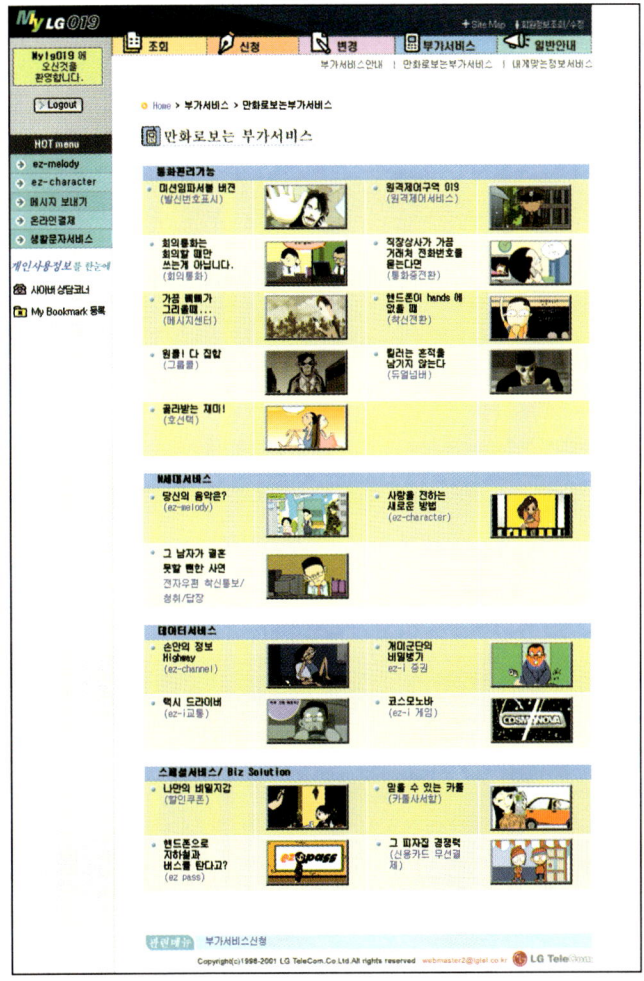

There's no more effective method for trying out the success of a design than creating a web in a language which one is not entirely familiar with. The suitability of the icons and graphics can thus be verified, with users recognizing the images as a familiar resource for choosing this or that path.

This portal has made an attempt at just that, using color as a powerful resource for classifying and discriminating.

WWW.SPORTLOCO.COM

> NAME: SPORT LOCO > SECTOR: SPORTS INFORMATION > SPECS: FLASH, HTML > RATING: ORIGINALITY ☺ > GRAPHICS ☺ > INTERACTIVITY ☺

THE NATURE OF A PORTAL OF THIS KIND IS HIGHLY COMPLEX. ON THE ONE HAND IS THE OPTION OF INCLUDING A WIDE VARIETY OF SECTIONS, WHILE TAKING GREAT CARE IN THE DESIGN OF EACH AND ENSURING SIMPLE NAVIGATION. ON THE OTHER IS THE WISH TO MAKE A HOMOGENOUS, UNAMBIGUOUS DESIGN.

THIS PARTICULAR SITE HAS COME TO A SATISFACTORY MIDPOINT BETWEEN THE TWO, WITH THE CREATION OF INDEPENDENT, INFORMATIVE UNITS WHICH, IN SOME CASES, VISUALLY COMPETE WITH EACH OTHER, WHILE ALWAYS ACHIEVING A SENSE OF HARMONY IN THE OVERALL LAYOUT.

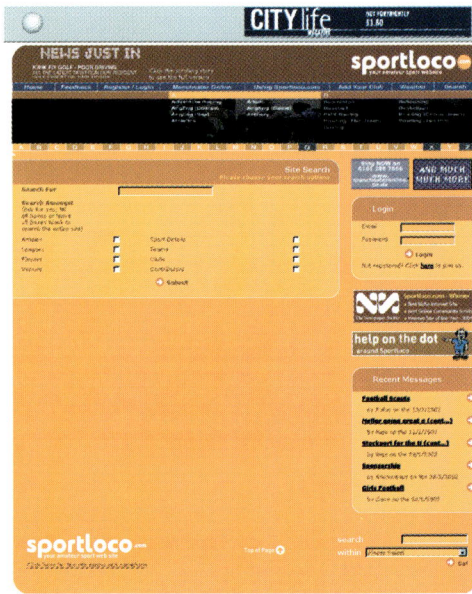

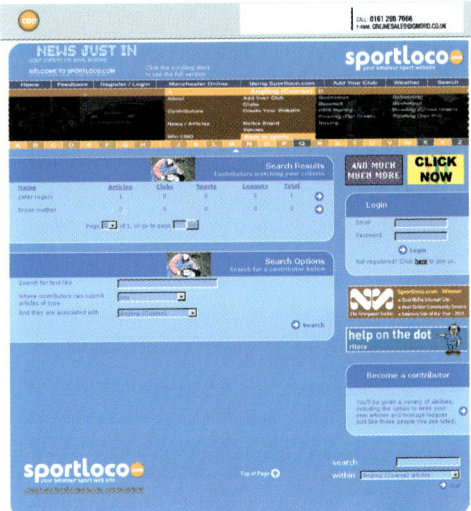

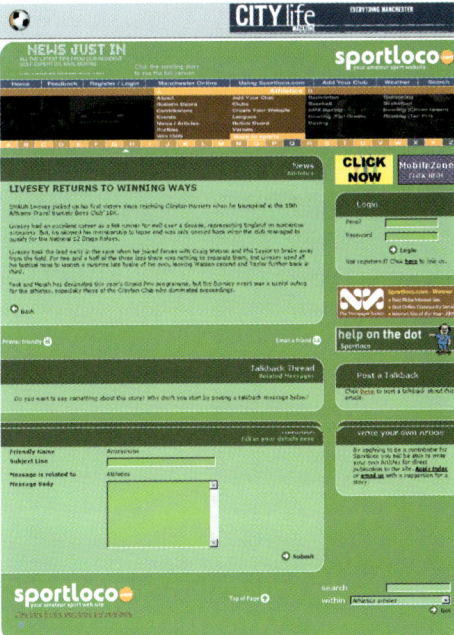

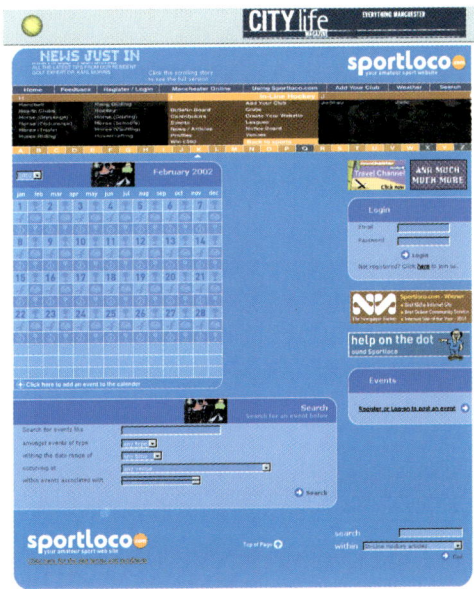

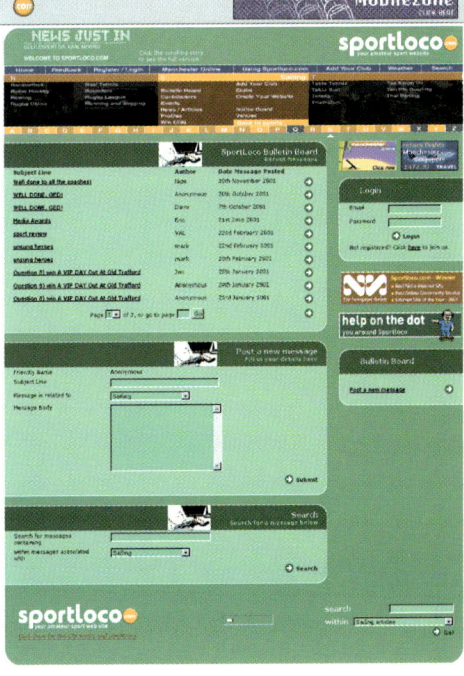

SECOND PLEASE
›THE WORLD OF MONSOON

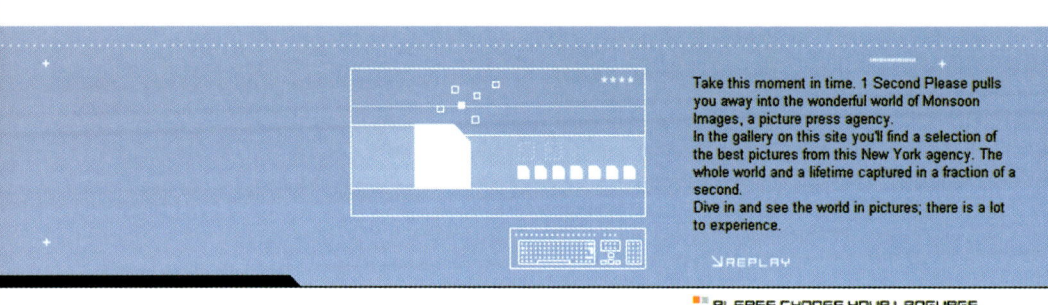

Take this moment in time. 1 Second Please pulls you away into the wonderful world of Monsoon Images, a picture press agency.
In the gallery on this site you'll find a selection of the best pictures from this New York agency. The whole world and a lifetime captured in a fraction of a second.
Dive in and see the world in pictures; there is a lot to experience.

›REPLAY

■■ PLEASE CHOOSE YOUR LANGUAGE
ENGLISH
DEUTSCH

PICTUREPRESS

SECOND PLEASE
›THE WORLD OF MONSOON

GALLERY ■■■■■■

GALLERY

Wander through the 1 Second Please gallery. The picture worlds from our extensive galleries take you on a journey around the globe. Experience the variety that 1 Second Please offers you. All images are available for download, free. To do so, please read our Terms.

■■ IMAGINE THE WORLD

QUICKNAVIGATION

> NAME: 1 SECOND PLEASE > SECTOR: PICTURE PRESS AGENCY > SPECS: FLASH, HTML > RATING: ORIGINALITY ☺ GRAPHICS ☺ INTERACTIVITY ☹ > CREDITS: ELEKTROMEDIEN

A HORIZONTALLY ORIENTED STRUCTURE IS SEEN FROM BEGINNING TO END. FAR FROM BEING STATIC, IT IS CONSTANTLY UPDATED AND ADJUSTED TO THE NEEDS OF EACH SECTION.

As is customary in hyper-text navigation, this design constantly reminds users where they are. Contents can be located both on the pop-up menu, located at the top of the page, and the linear menu at the bottom.

There is a marked tendency toward using a minimum amount of color, a logical choice in a site where the goal is to call attention to the product: in this case, pictures.

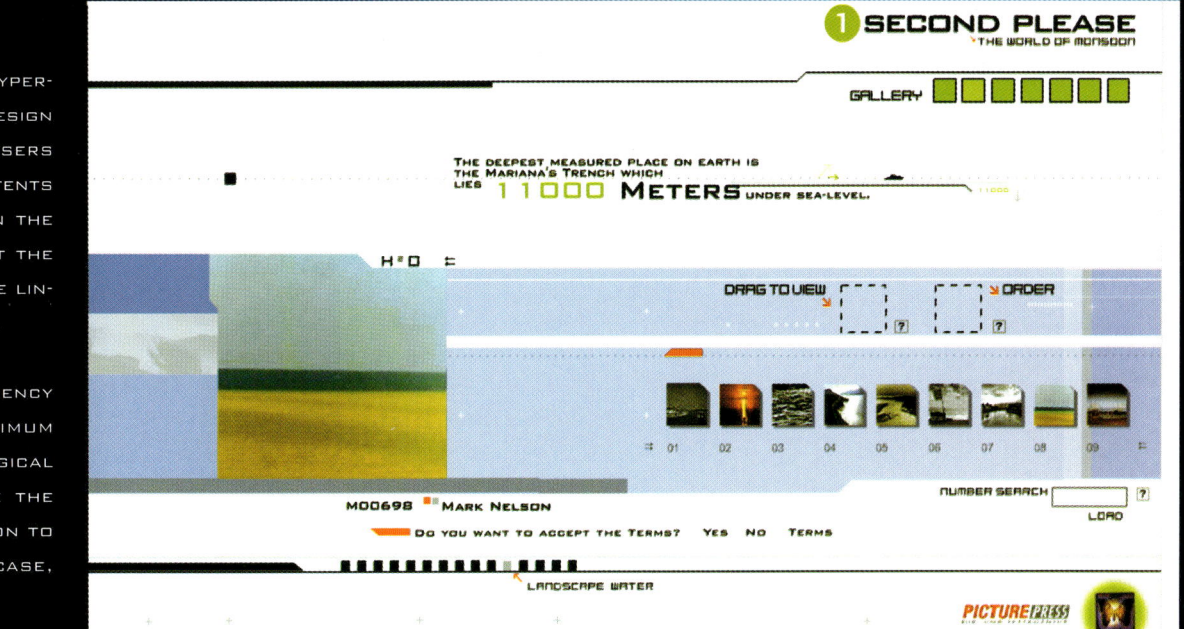

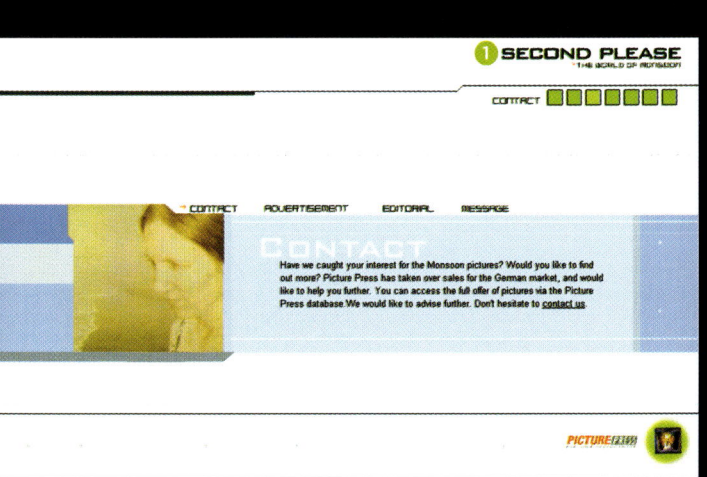

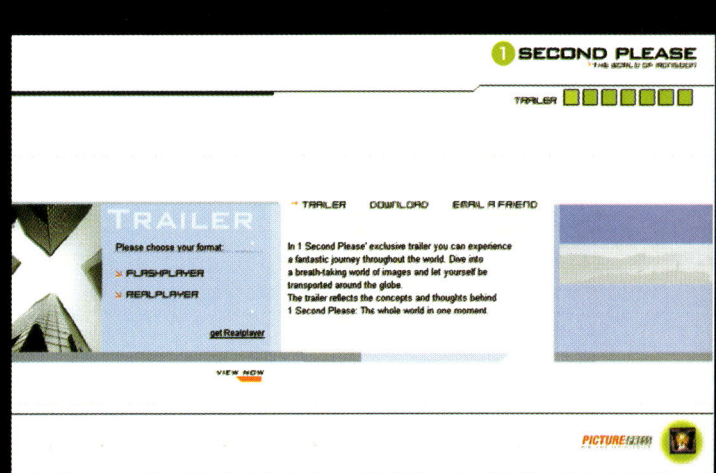

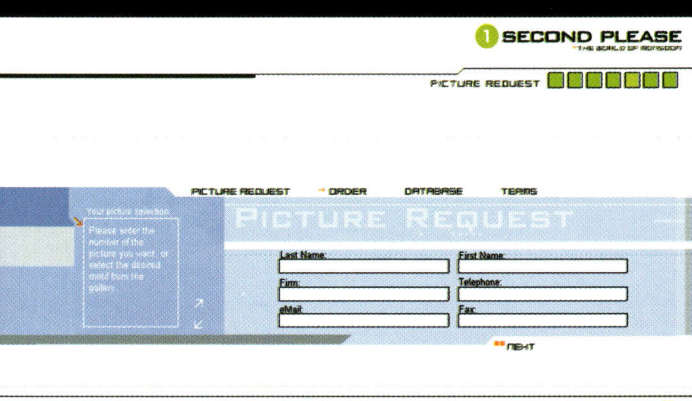

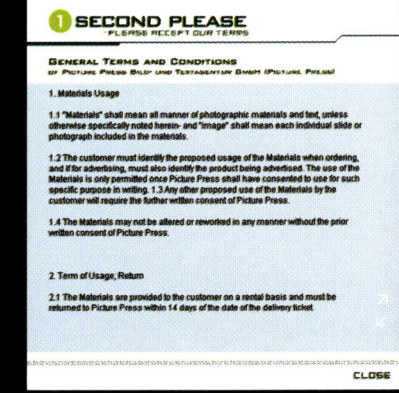

WWW.FREEFARM.CO.UK

> NAME: FREEFARM > SECTOR: PROMOTION OF ALTERNATIVE MUSIC > SPECS: FLASH > RATING: ORIGINALITY ☺ GRAPHICS ☺ INTERACTIVITY ☺ > CREDITS: THE DESIGNERS REPUBLIC

A GOOD EXAMPLE OF THE USE OF FEW GRAPHIC RESOURCES, A SINGLE TONE AND A LOT OF IMAGINATION.

GREEN WAS CHOSEN TO DEVELOP A WEBSITE THAT USES THE FLUID SHAPE OF A CIRCLE, DELIBERATELY EVOKING A RECORD OR CD. HERE, THE LAYOUT IS STRUCTURED ON THE BASIS OF AN APPARENT IMBALANCE, THEREBY GENERATING AN ARBITRARY SPACE WHERE THE PRIMARY FOCAL POINT IS CONSTANTLY IN A DIFFERENT PLACE, CREATING SCREENS THAT ARE INDEPENDENT OF ONE OTHER.

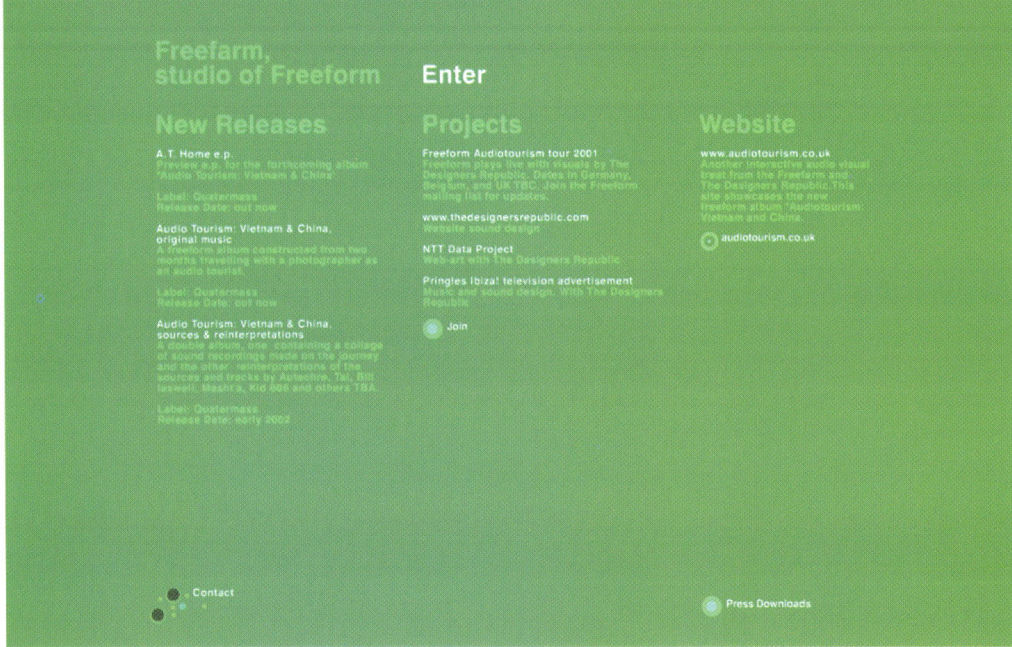

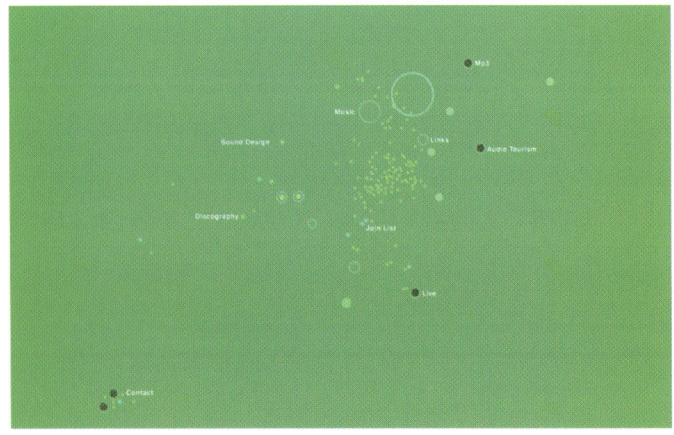

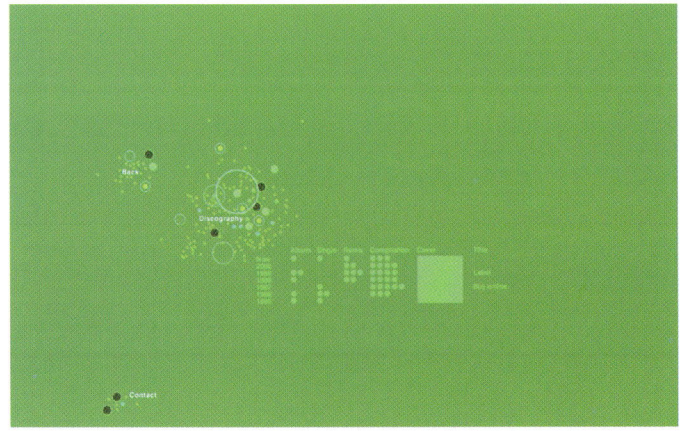

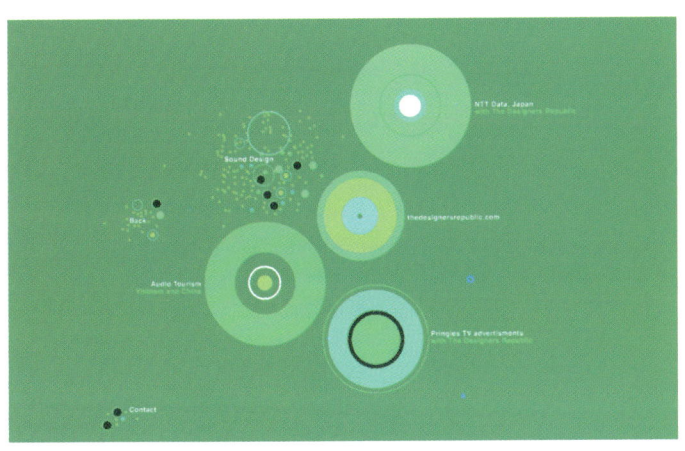

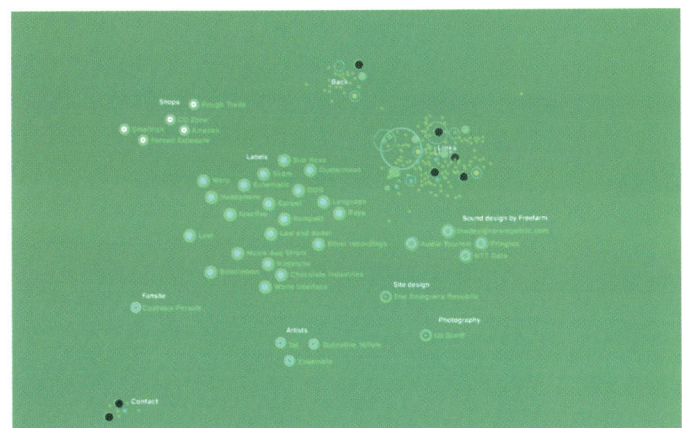

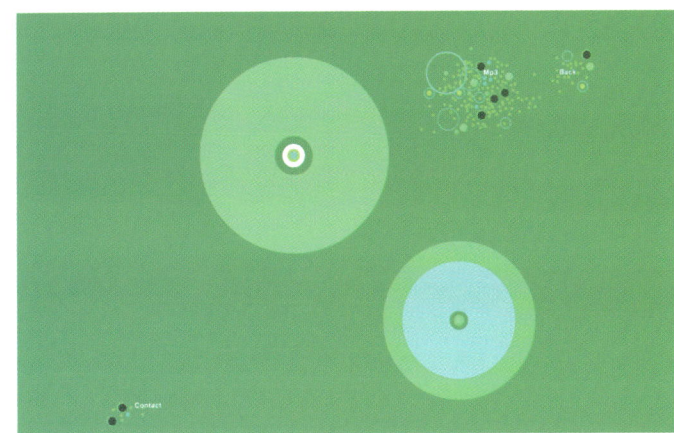

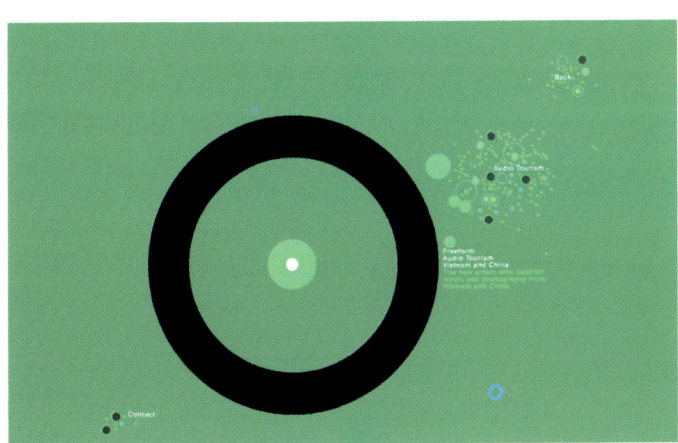

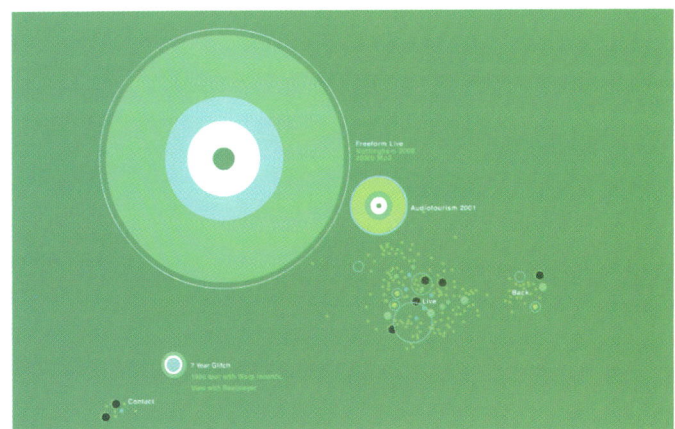

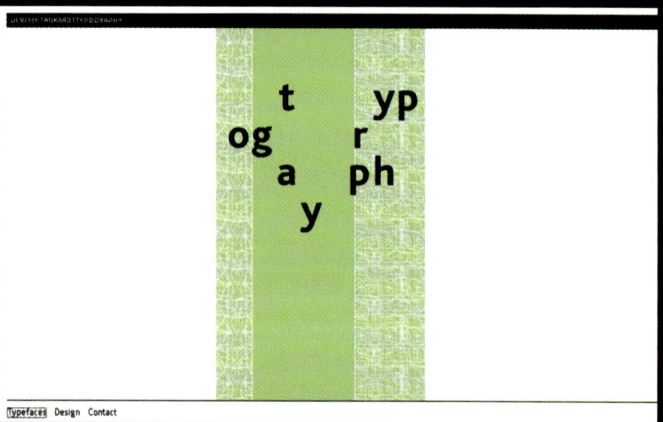

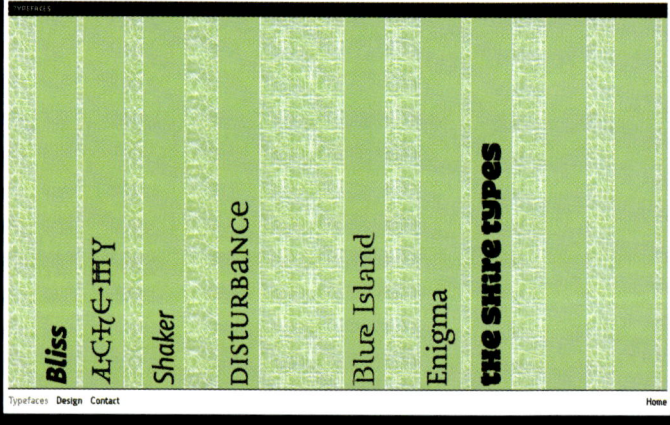

WWW.TYPOGRAPHY.NET

> NAME: JEREMY TANKARD, TYPOGRAPHY > SECTOR: TYPEFACE DESIGN > SPECS: FLASH, HTML > RATING: ORIGINALITY 😐 GRAPHICS 😐 INTERACTIVITY 🙁

LOGICALLY, THE THEME OF THIS WEBSITE LARGELY DICTATES THE DESIGN: TYPOGRAPHY BECOMES A GRAPHIC ELEMENT IN THE LAYOUT. DIFFERENT FONTS ARE USED AS EXAMPLES, THEREBY HIGHLIGHTING THE VALUE OF EACH LETTER. THE CHOICE OF COLOR SCHEME IS FAIRLY UNDERSTATED, SO AS NOT TO GET IN THE WAY. AN EQUAL VISUAL COMMUNICATION IS THEREBY ACHIEVED, IN A DESIGN WHICH AVOIDS CONFRONTATION.

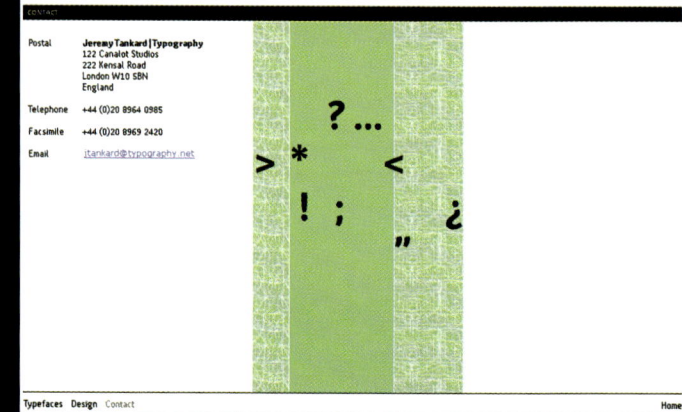

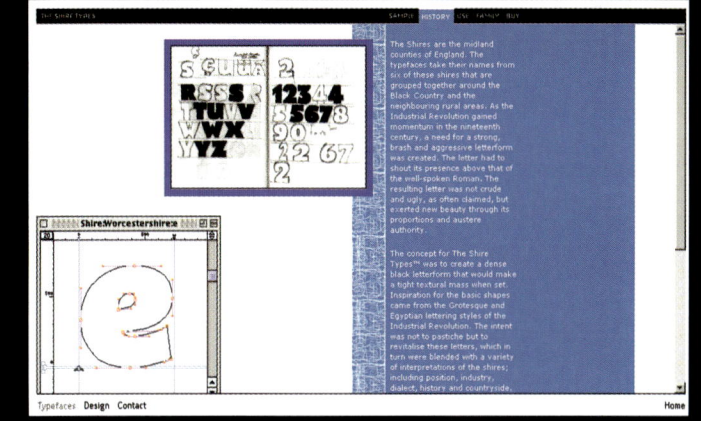

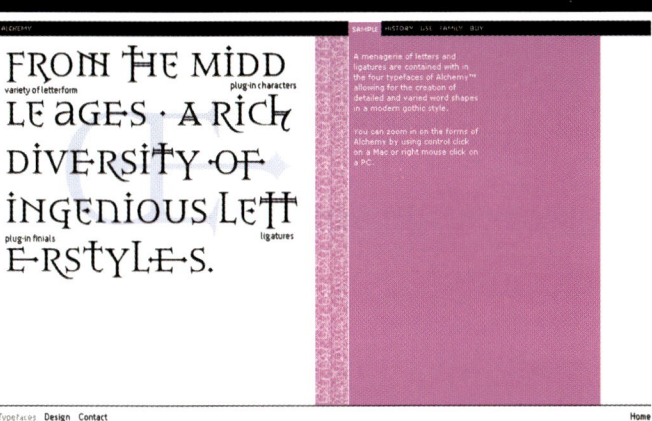

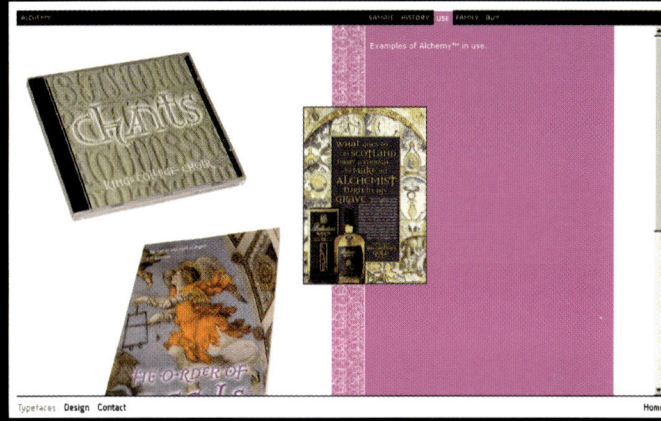

DESIGN

Jeremy Tankard MA(RCA)

Jeremy Tankard | Typography is based in London creating typographic design for a wide range of creative disciplines including advertising, corporate, graphic, publishing, television, digital, signage, environmental and architecture. Jeremy has worked with many companies around the world, co-ordinating, consulting and creating typographic images. He believes that the myriad qualities of typography are becoming more important as companies diversify across the increasing technologies.

He has designed several typefaces for FontShop International, Agfa Monotype and Adobe. See the typefaces section on this website for more information.

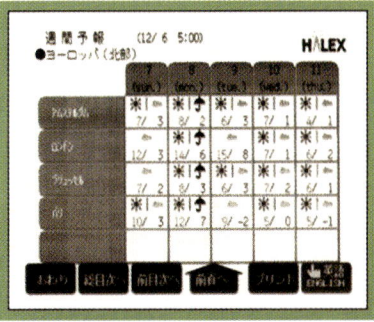

A variety of inspirations

WWW.DESIGN-MUSEUM.DE

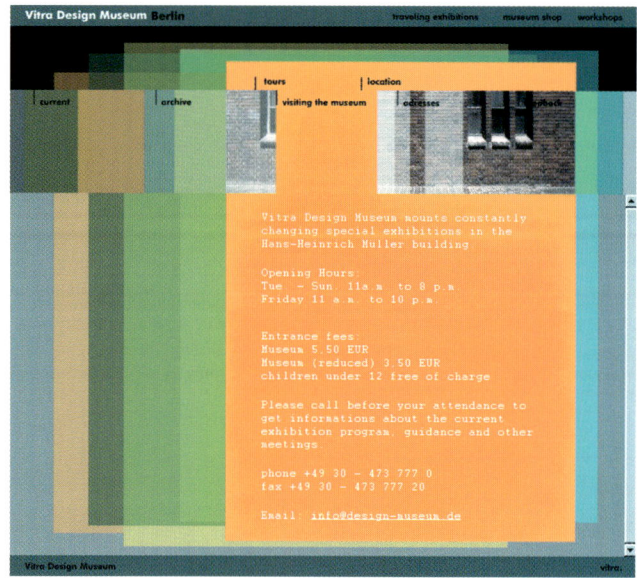

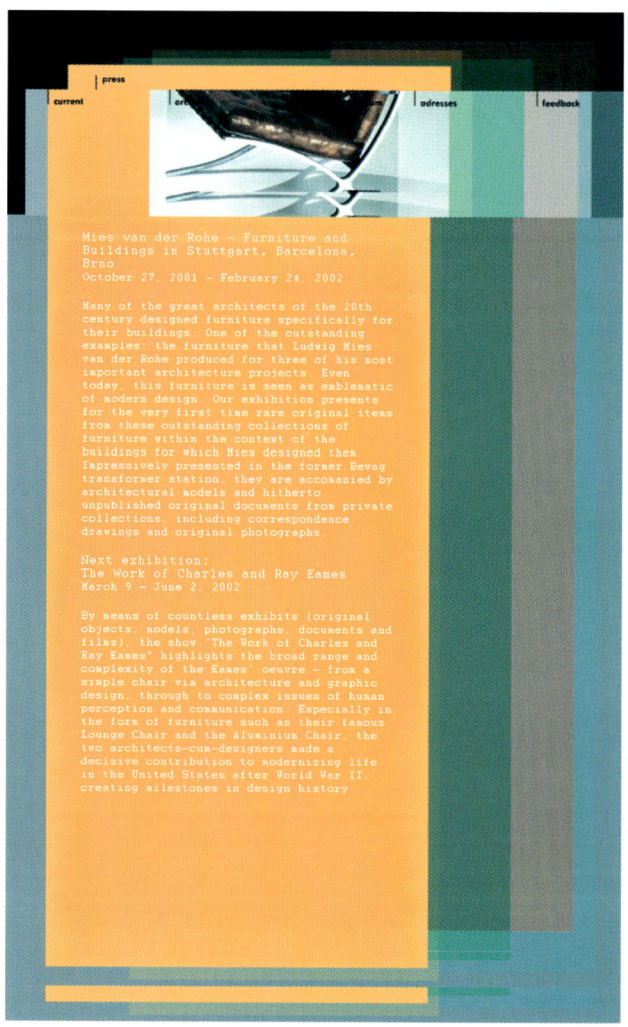

> NAME: VITRA DESIGN MUSEUM
> SECTOR: PROMOTION > SPECS:
FLASH, HTML > RATING: ORIGINALITY 😐
GRAPHICS 😐 INTERACTIVITY 😐

WIDE EXPANSES OF SCREEN SPACE
HAVE BEEN DEDICATED TO A SINGLE
COLOR, THE IDEA BEING TO STRUCTURE
SECTIONS ON THE BASIS OF ONE TONE
IN ORDER TO CLEARLY SEPARATE CON-
TENTS WITHOUT HEAVY RELIANCE ON
GRAPHICS OR CATCHY ICONS.

A FIXED MENU AT THE TOP PEEKS OUT
FROM BEHIND THE CONTENTS, WHICH,
BECAUSE OF THEIR LENGTH, REQUIRE
SCROLLING DOWN FOR FULL VIEWING.

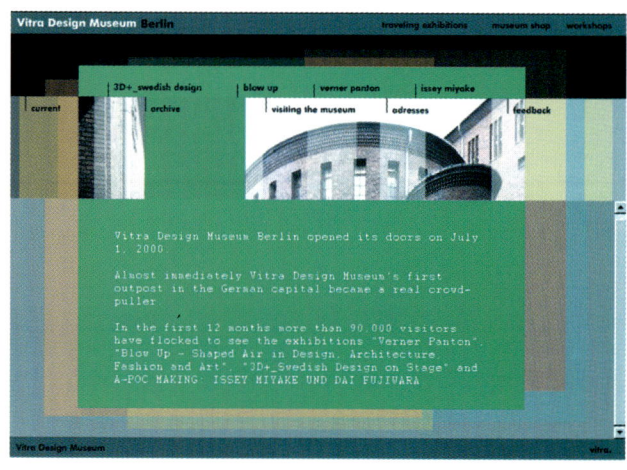

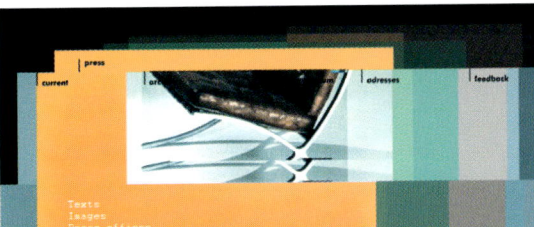

| press |
| current | art | adresses | feedback |

Texts
Images
Press offices

Mies van der Rohe - Architecture and
Design in Stuttgart, Barcelona, Brno

Vitra Design Museum Berlin,
October 27, 2001 - February 24, 2002

Alongside Le Corbusier, Frank Lloyd
Wright, and Walter Gropius, Ludwig Mies
van der Rohe (1886 - 1969) was one of the
most important and influential architects
of the 20th century. And this grand master
of Modernism created lasting exemplary
ideas not only in the field of
construction, but also in furniture
design. The exhibition "Mies van der Rohe
- Architecture and Design in Stuttgart,
Barcelona, Brno" brings all Mies van der
Rohe's furniture designs together for the
first time. Most of the exhibits are rare
original items dating from the first
production phases before 1935, including
not only his first cantilever chair dating
from 1927, the legendary Barcelona
armchair, and the Villa Tugendhat
furniture, but also prototypes and
individual pieces of furniture from the
designer's own estate. During the entire
exhibition period at Vitra Design Museum,
a comprehensive accompanying program of
lectures, symposia and special guided
tours conveys an idea of the importance of
Ludwig Mies van der Rohe as an architect
and his strong role for the city of
Berlin. A second exhibition of the Museum
of Modern Art New York entitled "Mies in
Berlin" shows the architectural oeuvre from
1907 through 1938 and will open in
December 2001 in the New Museum, Berlin.

textdownload

deutsch
english
francais

For further information please apply to
one of the following press offices.

For Vitra Germany, Switzerland, Spain,
Austria, Italy, etc
Gabriella Gianoli PR
Florastrasse 9
CH-3005 Bern
Tel. 031/3522454, Fax 031/3522456
e-mail: gianoli.pr@bluewin.ch

Vitra Design Museum Berlin
Britt Angelis
Kopenhagener Str. 58
D-10437 Berlin
Tel. +49 30 47377712
Fax +49 30 47377720
e-mail: britt.angelis@design-museum.de

For Vitra Portugal, Spain
Sheila Loewe
Plaza del Marqués de Salamanca n.10, 1
dcha
E-28006 Madrid
Tel. 91/4264565, Fax 91/5781217
e-mail: sheila.loewe@vitra.com

For Vitra France, Belgium
CS Communication
Chantal Senglier
177 rue de Lourmel
F-75015 Paris
Tel. 01/40600944, Fax 01/40600477
e-mail: senglier@easinet.fr

For Vitra Netherlands
Marianne van Dodeweerd
Tweede Weteringsdwarsstr. 65 A
NL-1017 ZV Amsterdam
Tel. 020/6249515, Fax 020/6208816
e-mail: mdodewe@interstroom.nl

For Vitra Great Britain
Articulate Communication
Hermine Newman
19A Air Street
GB-London W1R 5RJ
Tel. 0171/2871922, Fax 0171/7344992
e-mail: hnewman@articulate.co.uk

For Vitra USA
Andres Loukin
939 Union Street
USA-Brooklyn, NY 11215
Tel. 718-2308832, Fax 718-2308824
e-mail: andres.loukin@vitra.com

For inquiries from other countries
Elena Goarnecote

Vitra Design Museum Berlin   traveling exhibitions   museum shop   workshops

| current | | visiting the museum | adresses | feedback |

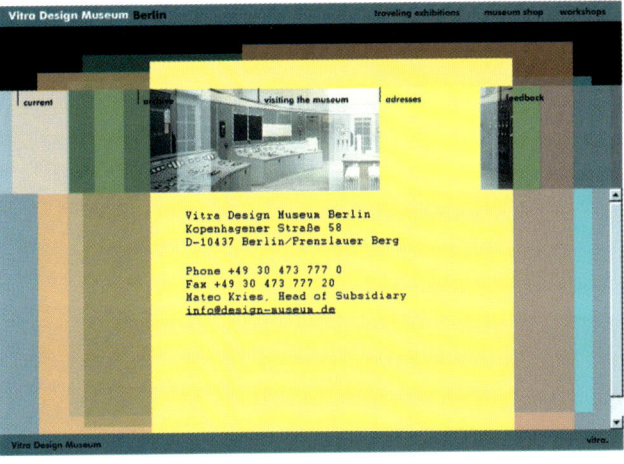

Vitra Design Museum Berlin
Kopenhagener Straße 58
D-10437 Berlin/Prenzlauer Berg

Phone +49 30 473 777 0
Fax +49 30 473 777 20
Mateo Kries, Head of Subsidiary
info@design-museum.de

Vitra Design Museum   vitra.

Vitra Design Museum Berlin   traveling exhibitions   museum shop   workshops

| sponsors |
| current | archive | visiting the museum | adresses | feedback |

Name:
Company:
E-mail:
Telephone:
Fax:
Street:
Postal Code:
City/State:
Country:
Comments:

Please send me information about:
☐ Opening Hours
☐ Guided Visits
☐ Workshops
☐ Friends
☐ Miniatures
☐ Publications
☐ Poster
☐ Special Edition

send

Vitra Design Museum   vitra.

>FF FF 00
>FF 99 00
>FF 00 00
>CC 33 66
>00 99 66
>00 CC 99

Viaduct
info@viaduct.co.uk

1-10 Summer's Street
London EC1R 5BD
United Kingdom

Tel +44 (0) 20 7278 8456
Fax +44 (0) 20 7278 2844

WWW.VIADUCT.CO.UK

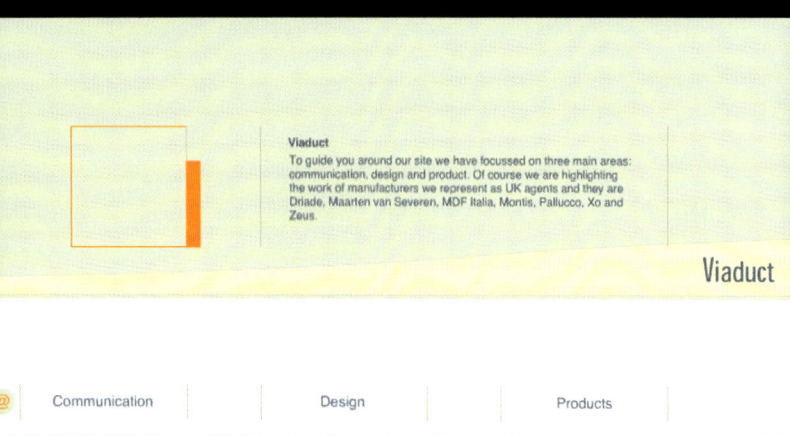

Viaduct
To guide you around our site we have focussed on three main areas:
communication, design and product. Of course we are highlighting
the work of manufacturers we represent as UK agents and they are
Driade, Maarten van Severen, MDF Italia, Montis, Pallucco, Xo and
Zeus.

Viaduct

Communication   Design   Products

Viaduct's showroom is a dramatic 1930's galleried industrial
space in Clerkenwell. A varied display is constantly
updated with the latest work from contemporary furniture and
lighting designers.

Viaduct aim to provide the specifier with a comprehensive
selection but also a high level of service from initial enquiry
through to delivery and installation.

Viaduct

Communication   Design   Products

> NAME: VIADUCT > SECTOR: INTE-
RIOR DESIGN > SPECS: FLASH,
HTML > RATING: ORIGINALITY ☺
GRAPHICS ☺ INTERACTIVITY ☺
> CREDITS: DEEPEND

THE MILDNESS OF GREEN AND YEL-
LOW COMBINE TO TRANSMIT A HARMO-
NIOUS BALANCE OF COLOR. THE
STRENGTH OF BLUE AND ORANGE
HAVE TAKEN THE PLACE OF TRADI-
TIONAL BLACK IN THE WRITTEN TEXTS,
ACHIEVING THE SAME EFFECTIVENESS.

THE GRAPHIC ELEMENTS ARE
DRAWINGS OF THE PRODUCTS
THEMSELVES.

THE REST OF THE INFORMATION IS
EXPRESSED THROUGH WORDS, WITH
CORRESPONDING LINKS BUILT INTO
THE TEXT.

A WAVE OF SORTS CURLING GENTLY
ACROSS THE BOTTOM OF THE PAGE,
ASSUMING A DIFFERENT SHAPE IN
EACH SECTION, HELPS AVOID VISUAL
MONOTONY.

A HORIZONTAL TREND IS MAIN-
TAINED THROUGHOUT THE SITE.
THE MENU AT THE BOTTOM IS ALSO
A CONSTANT ON EACH SUBSE-
QUENT PAGE, WHILE THE TOP POR-
TION CHANGES DEPENDING ON THE
CONTENTS.

WWW.ICONOGRAFICOS.COM

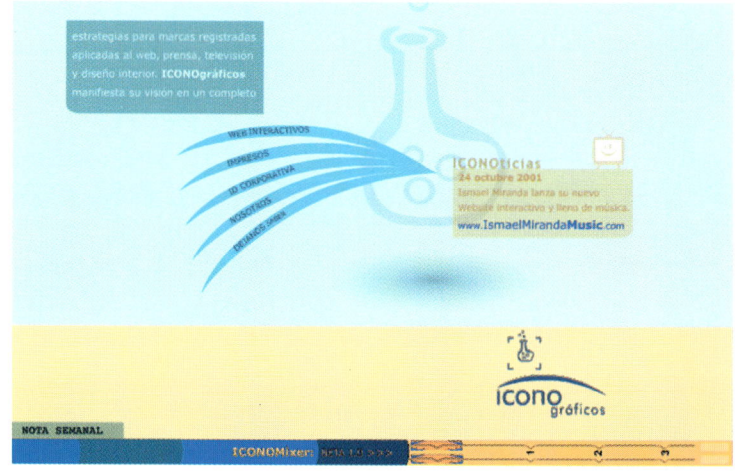

>NAME: ICONOGRÁFICOS > SEC-
TOR: DESIGN STUDIO > SPECS:
FLASH, HTML > RATING: ORIGI-
NALITY ☺ GRAPHICS ☺ INTER-
ACTIVITY ☹

THE SCREEN IS DIVIDED INTO TWO
HORIZONTAL RECTANGLES. ALL
OF THE CHANGES TAKE PLACE ON
THE TOP RECTANGLE, WHILE THE
ONE ON THE BOTTOM REMAINS
THE SAME. A SENSATION OF CON-
SONANCE AND BALANCE BETWEEN
THE TWO IS CREATED.

THE HOMEPAGE OFFERS VARIOUS
ILLUSTRATIONS FOR PERSONALIZ-
ING THE BACKGROUND OF SUBSE-
QUENT SECTIONS, THEREBY SUG-
GESTING THE NEED OF TAILORING
THE DESIGN TO THE TASTES OF
EACH USER.

IN KEEPING THE GRAPHIC IDENTITY
OF THE LOWER RECTANGLE, EACH
SECTION DISPLAYS A POLISHED DE-
SIGN CHARACTERISTIC: STROKES IN
GENTLE TONES OFFSET THE TEXTUAL
INFORMATION AND ARE INTEGRATED
IN A VISUALLY COHERENT WAY.

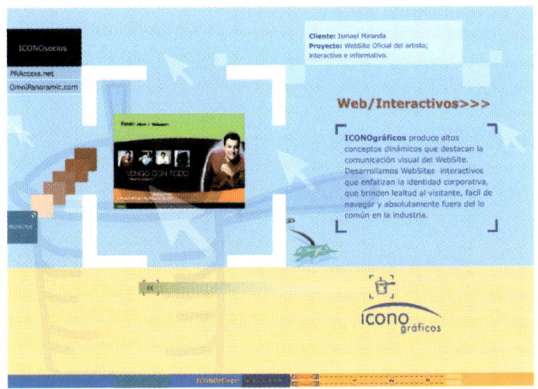

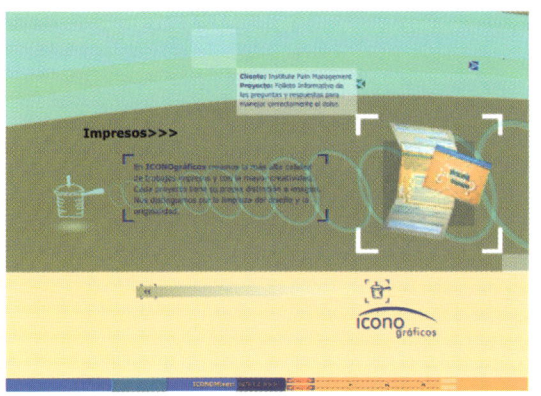

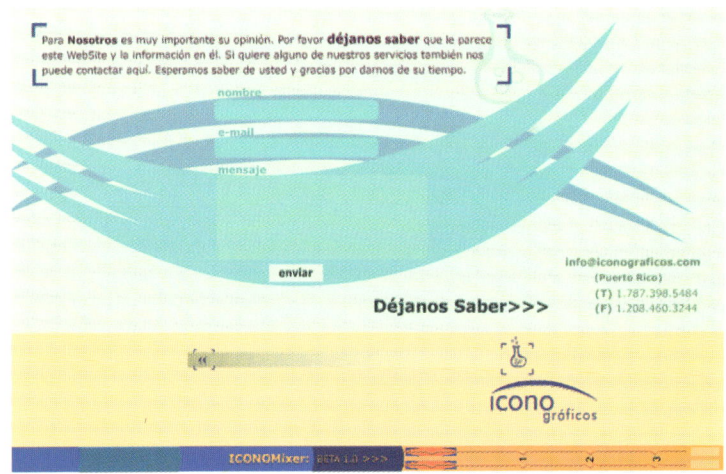

> NAME: 100% DESIGN > SECTOR: DESIGN > SPECS: FLASH, HTML > RATING: ORIGINALITY ☺ GRAPHICS ☺ INTERACTIVITY ☺ > CREDITS: LIPPA PEARCE DESIGN

THE TYPEFACE ACQUIRES A GREAT DEAL OF VISUAL STRENGTH IN THE DIFFERENT SECTIONS, TO THE POINT THEY FORM CENTRAL GRAPHIC ELEMENTS IN THE DESIGN ITSELF.

THIS PROJECT DISTRIBUTES THE NECESSARY INFORMATION AT THE TOP OF THE SCREEN, WITH A TENDENCY OF PLACING THE WEIGHT ON THE LEFT.

100%DESIGN

The exhibition   How to visit   How to exhibit   News   Press   Contact

Introduction   Exhibitor list   Events   Product launches   Floorplan

What is it?   Where is it?   When is it?   Who exhibits?

The UK's leading commercial contemporary interior design exhibition. Internationally recognised as one of the world's most influential design events, alongside Milan, Cologne and New York. In 8 years, 100%Design has grown by 500% making it one of the Uk's most successful exhibitions.

I would like to visit

100%DESIGN   close window

Furniture   Lighting   Accessories   Floorings   Kitchens & Bathrooms
Textiles   Fixtures & Fittings   Surface Finishes   All exhibitors

tbc

Contact: Lorna Bita
Stand No.: H37

Tel: 0207 267 5705
Fax: 0207 267 7086

Email:
lorna@isisdes.demon.co.uk
Web: http://tbc

Alva Lighting

4 Ella Mews
Cressy Road
London
United Kingdom
NW3 2NH

Below is a list of all exhibitors

100% Books
2 x 5 Interior AB
Aaronson Noon
Abet Limited
Abitare
ACID (Anti-copying in Design)
Addendum Collective Home
Aktiva
Alex Macdonald
Alison Cooke
Alivar - A. STUDIO SRL
Allermuir Ltd
Allgood Plc
Alma Home
Alpes Inox
Alternative Plans Ltd
Alva Lighting
Amat-3
Andrew Moor Associates
Andrew Muirhead & Son Ltd
Anne Kyyro Quinn
Annemette Beck
Annette Nix
Annie Sherburne Rugs
Anthony Stern Glass
AntiDiva
Apartment
Arc Creations Ltd
Arc Lighting Limited
Artcoustic by Danspeak
Artek oy ab
Asplund
Atrium
attic 2 (wales) ltd
Authentics
Authentics Ltd
Avad
Avante Bathroom Products
Avarte Oy
B Sweden
Babylon Design Ltd
Bakebean
Bald & Bang aps
Bankhead Products
Barnet Kitchen Design

100%DESIGN

26th-29th September 2002, Earls Court 2, London, UK   100info@reedexpo.com

Trade only: Thurs 26th Sept - 10am to 9pm, Fri 27th Sept - 10am to 7pm, Sat 28th Sept - 10am to 6pm
Trade and public: Sun 29th Sept - 10am to 6pm

The exhibition   How to visit?   How to exhibit   News   Press   Contact

100% Design 2001/2002

THE LUMINOSITY OF THE WHITE OF THE BACKGROUND IS MODIFIED BY USING BLUE AND GREEN FOR THE WRITTEN INFORMATION.

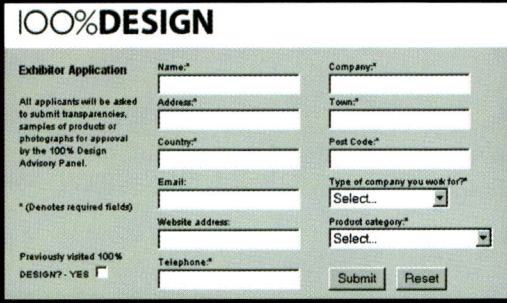

WE SPEND AN AVERAGE OF 39% SITTING DOWN

Lammhults Casus Chair by Johannes Foersom & Peter Hiort-Lorenzen

skip

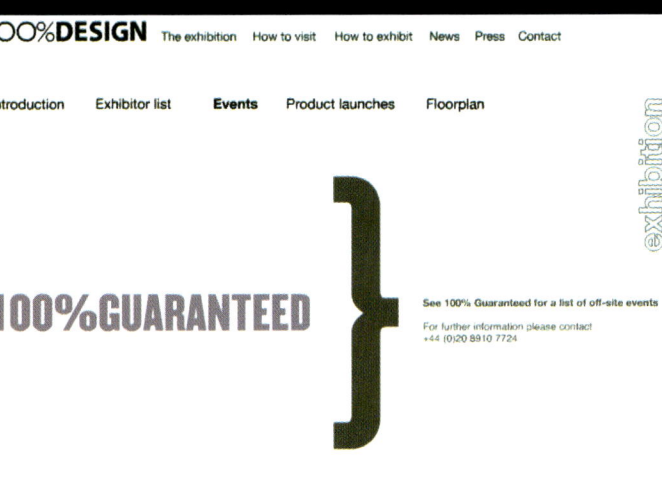

100%DESIGN — The exhibition · How to visit · How to exhibit · News · Press · Contact

Introduction · Exhibitor list · **Events** · Product launches · Floorplan

exhibition

100%GUARANTEED }

See 100% Guaranteed for a list of off-site events

For further information please contact
+44 (0)20 8910 7724

I would like to visit

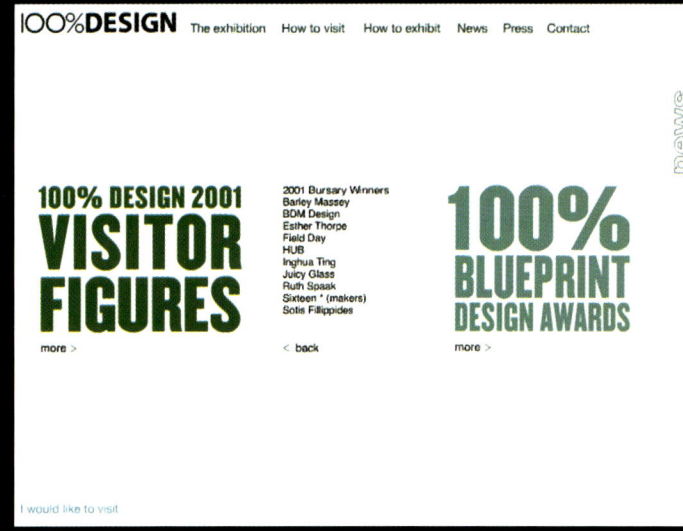

100%DESIGN — The exhibition · How to visit · How to exhibit · News · Press · Contact

news

100% DESIGN 2001
VISITOR FIGURES
more >

2001 Bursary Winners
Barley Massey
BDM Design
Esther Thorpe
Field Day
HUB
Inghua Ting
Juicy Glass
Ruth Spaak
Sixteen * (makers)
Sotis Fillippides
< back

100%
BLUEPRINT
DESIGN AWARDS
more >

I would like to visit

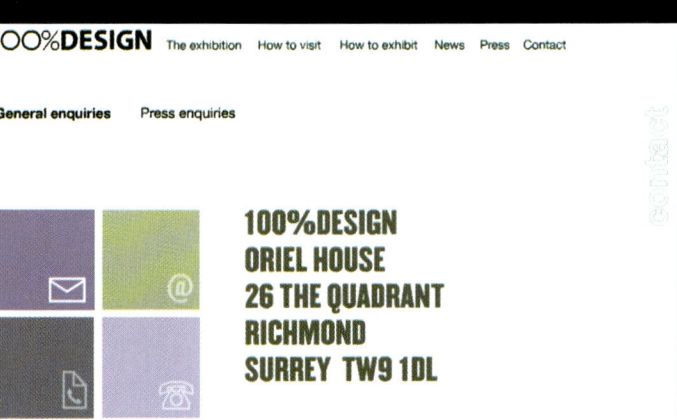

100%DESIGN — The exhibition · How to visit · How to exhibit · News · Press · Contact

General enquiries · Press enquiries

contact

100%DESIGN
ORIEL HOUSE
26 THE QUADRANT
RICHMOND
SURREY TW9 1DL

I would like to visit

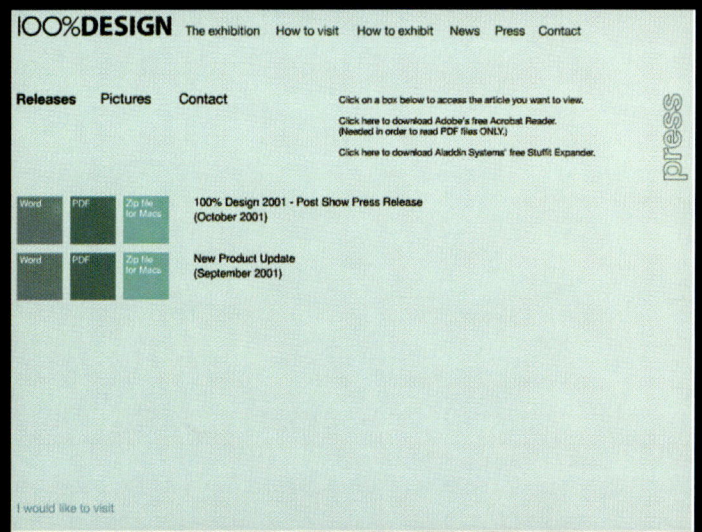

100%DESIGN — The exhibition · How to visit · How to exhibit · News · Press · Contact

Releases · Pictures · Contact

press

Click on a box below to access the article you want to view.

Click here to download Adobe's free Acrobat Reader.
(Needed in order to read PDF files ONLY.)

Click here to download Aladdin Systems' free Stuffit Expander.

| Word | PDF | Zip file for Macs |
100% Design 2001 - Post Show Press Release
(October 2001)

| Word | PDF | Zip file for Macs |
New Product Update
(September 2001)

I would like to visit

WWW.VOLUMEONE.COM

> NAME: VOLUME ONE > SECTOR: GRAPHIC DESIGN STUDIO > SPECS: FLASH, HTML > RATING: ORIGINALITY ☺ GRAPHICS ☺ INTERACTIVITY ☺

> CREDITS: MATT OWENS

THIS INNOVATIVE DESIGN NARRATIVE PLACES HIGH VALUE ON THE IMAGE AS A POWERFUL VEHICLE FOR CONVEYING SYMBOLISM AND ICONOGRAPHY. TEXT HERE PLAYS VERY LITTLE PART, IN AN OVERALL SCHEME THAT SEEKS INSTEAD TO ENCOURAGE AN INTUITIVE AND SYMBOLIC INTERPRETATION.

THE COLOR SCHEME IS MEANT TO BRING OUT THE SOMEWHAT ABSTRACT FORMS, CONFERRING ON THEM THEIR OWN READING. LIKEWISE, THE COLOR MARKS A CONTRAST BETWEEN THE BACKGROUND AND THE LINKS LYING ON ITS SURFACE.

THE ONLY WORDS TO BE FOUND ON NEARLY THE ENTIRETY OF THE PROJECT ARE LOCATED IN THIS SMALL WINDOW.

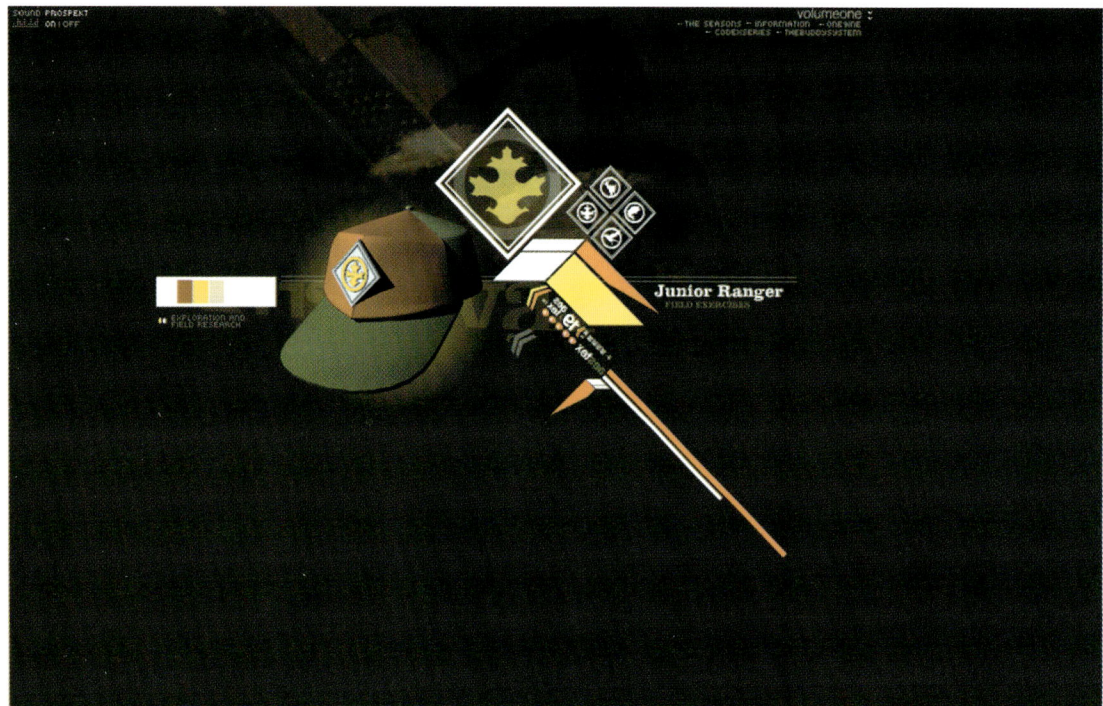

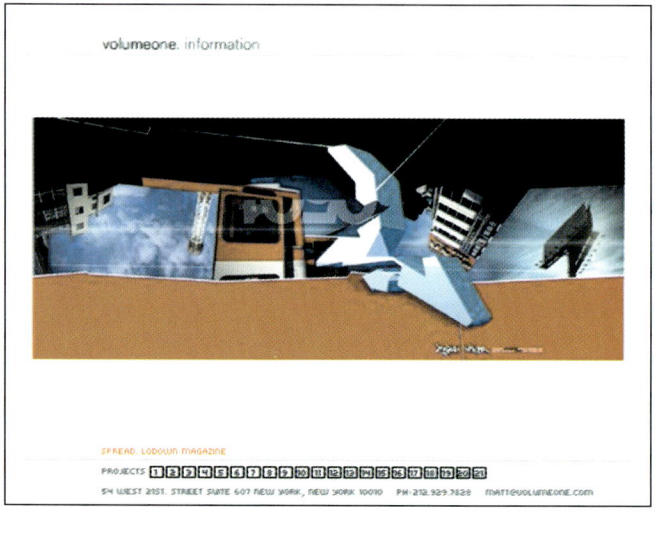

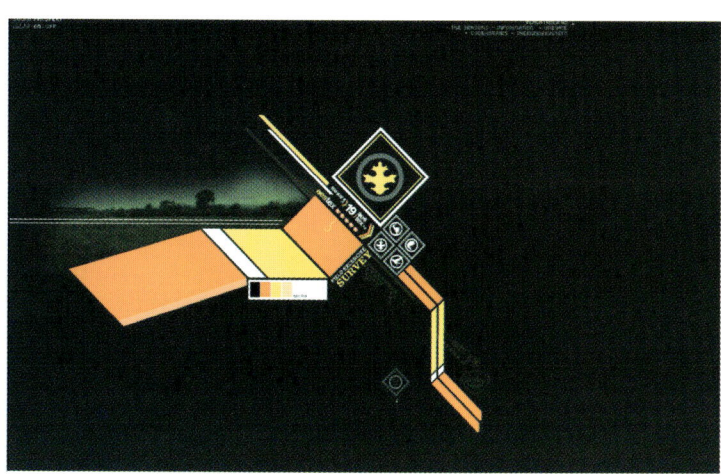
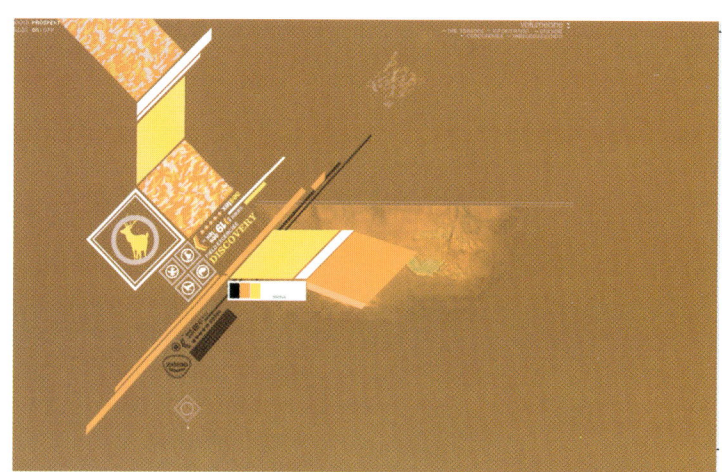

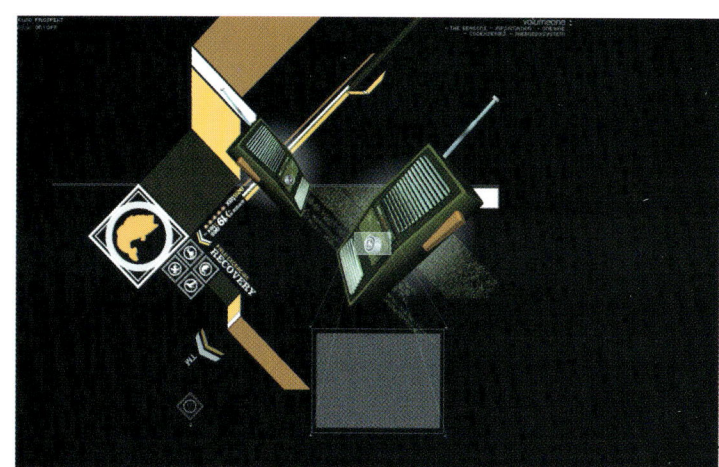
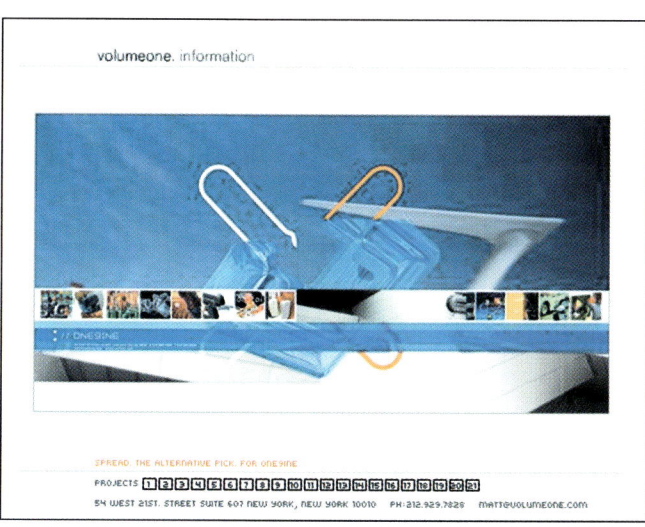
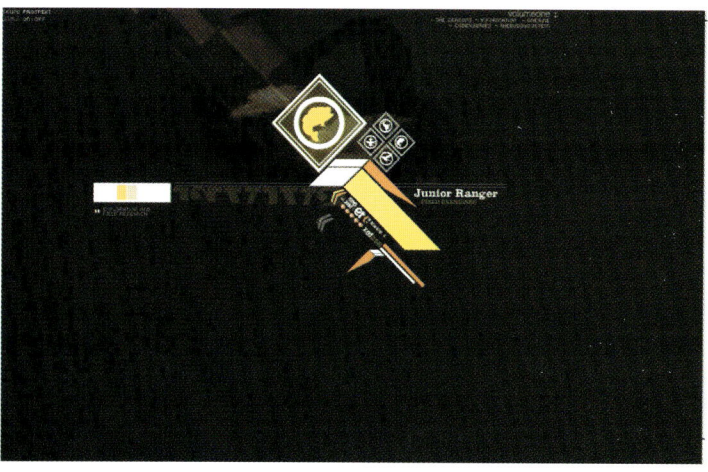

> NAME: MOMO HOME STORES > SECTOR: FURNITURE STORE > SPECS: FLASH, HTML > RATING: ORIGINALITY ☺ > GRAPHICS ☺ > INTERACTIVITY ☺

A FIXED WINDOW CONTAINS THE NARRATION AND DIFFERENT SECTIONS AVAILABLE FOR VIEWING. THESE SECTIONS DISPLAY THE STANDARD HORIZONTAL, SCREEN-WISE LAY-OUT. THE CONTENTS ARE DIVIDED INTO THREE SUBCATEGORIES, WHICH IN TURN SPLIT OFF IN OTHER DIRECTIONS.

ASIDE FROM THE LEFT TO RIGHT GRAPHIC LAY-OUT, SMALLER SUPERIMPOSED WINDOWS CONTAINING FURTHER INFORMATION OPEN UP AT A CLICK OF THE MOUSE.

WWW.MOMOHOME.COM

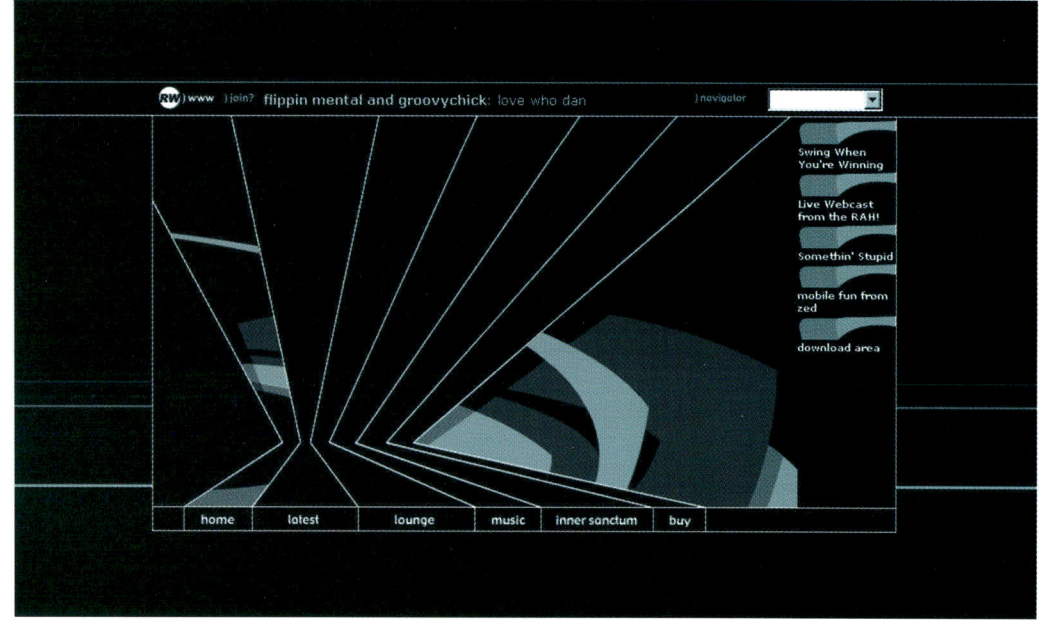

> NAME: ROBBIE WILLIAMS > SECTOR: PROMOTION > SPECS: HTML > RATING: ORIGINALITY ☺ GRAPHICS ☺ INTER- ACTIVITY ☺

WWW.ROBBIEWILLIAMS.COM

A CURSORY GLANCE REVEALS A HOMEPAGE CONTAINING, APPARENTLY, VERY LITTLE INFORMATION. THE OPPOSITE IS REVEALED ONLY WHEN THE CURSOR IS DRAGGED ACROSS THE PAGE, WITH NEW CONTENTS APPEARING IN ITS WAKE.

THUS, SIX INDEPENDENT SECTIONS, EACH WITH A WIDE RANGE OF COLOR AND ORIGINAL GRAPHICS, ARE CREATED. THE COLOR SCHEME PLAYS A CENTRAL ROLE, AS SEEN IN ITS CAPACITY TO HIGHLIGHT THE TEXTUAL INFORMATION.

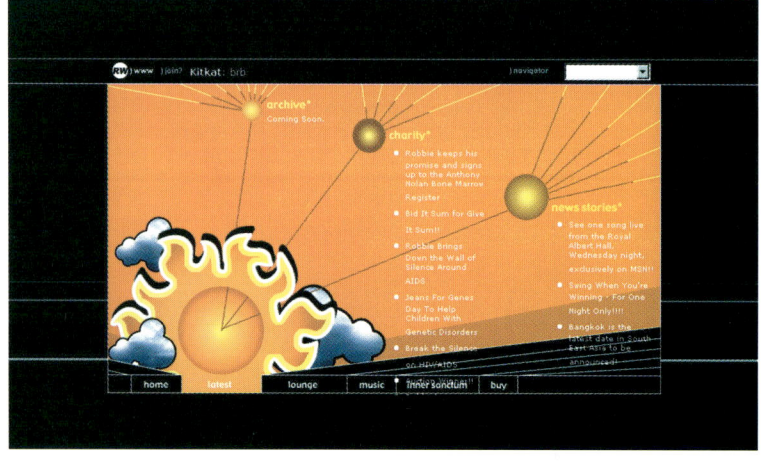

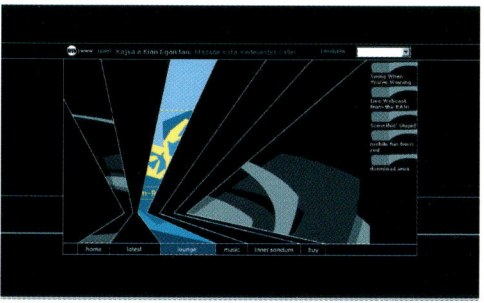

Navigation is unambiguous. The double menu, at the top and bottom, facilitates movement through the links, without users getting lost along the way. Each section is clearly indicated and we are constantly reminded of where we are.

>99
00
00

>FF
00
00

>00
CC
00

>66
99
CC

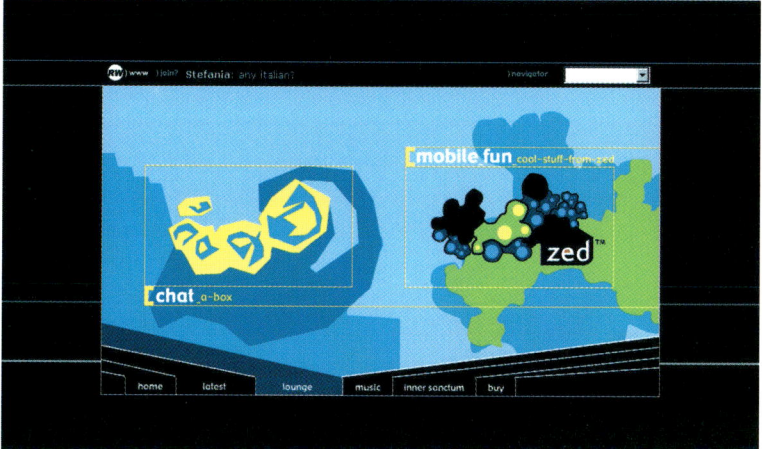

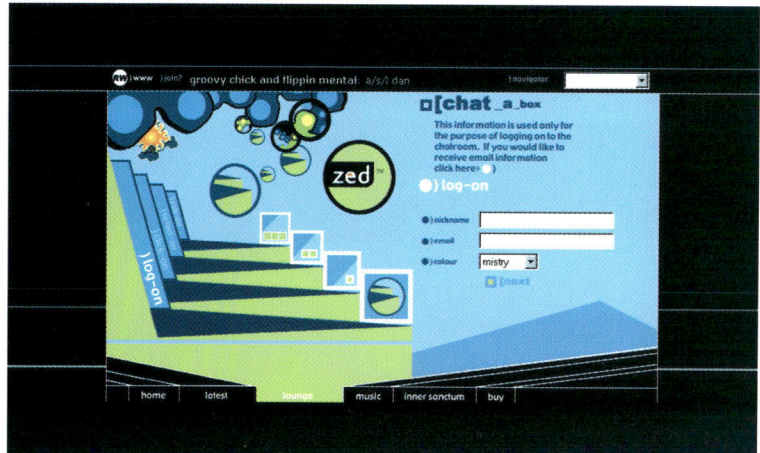

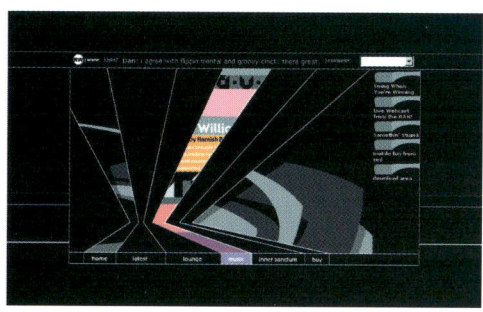

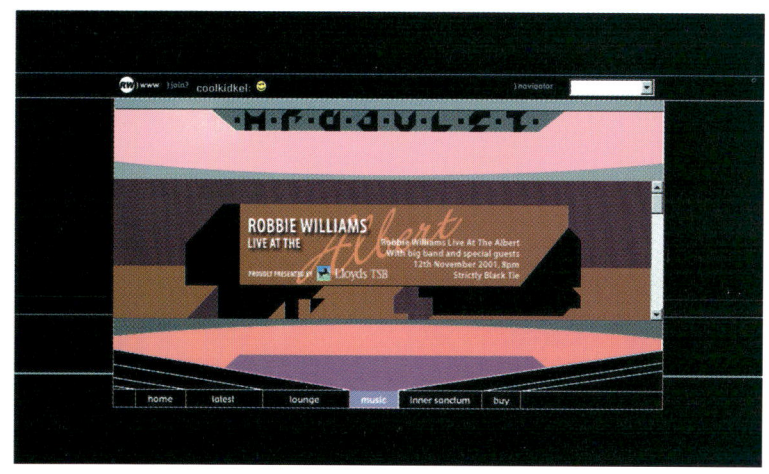

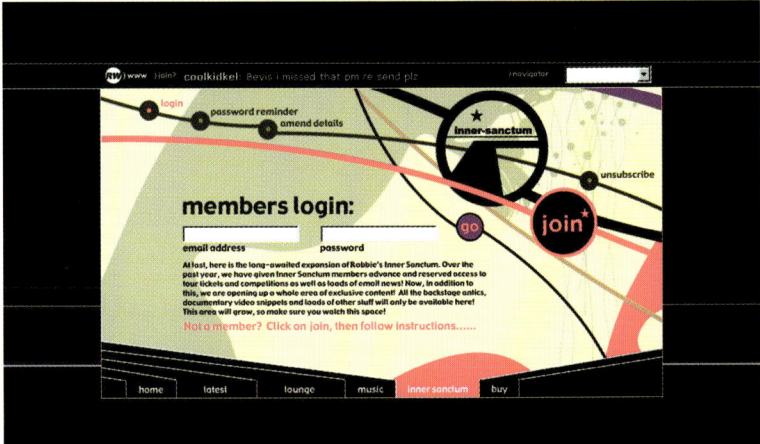

THE DISPLAY OF GRAPHICS AND COLOR IS VARIED. THERE IS NO HOMOGENEITY OF CRITERIA FOR THE DESIGN OF THE ILLUSTRATIONS. ON THE CONTRARY, GRAPHICS AS VERSATILE AS THE TOPIC OF THE WEBSITE SEEM TO HAVE BEEN THE GOAL.

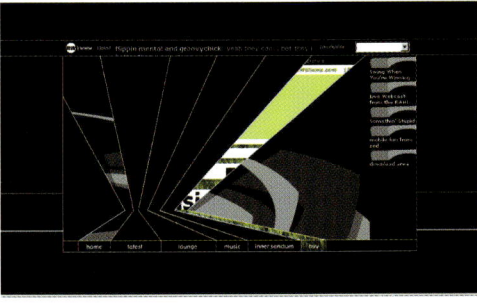

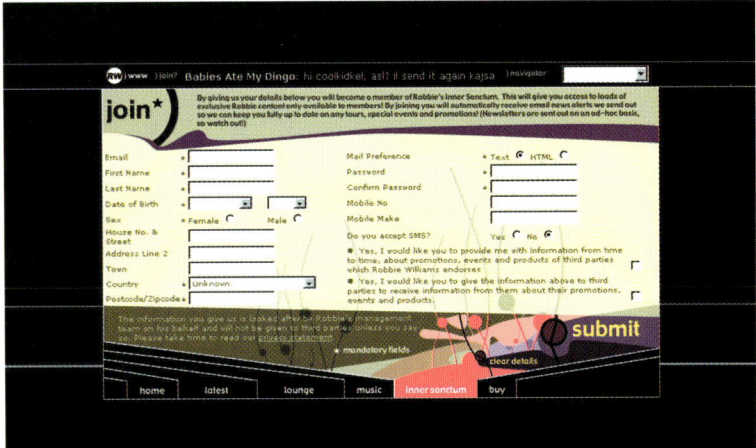

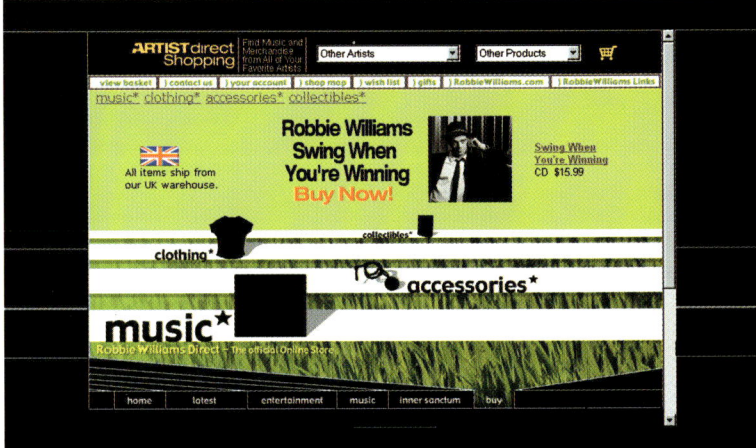

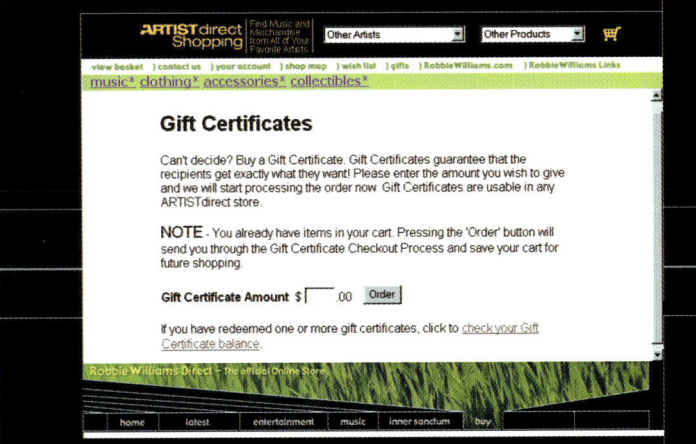

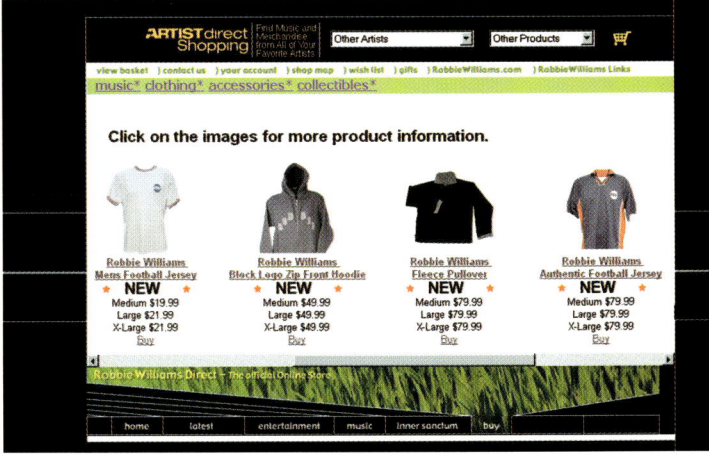

A COHERENT WHOLE HAS BEEN CON-
STRUCTED USING FEW GRAPHICS. THE
BASIC DESIGN CONSISTS OF SIMPLE
IMAGES, OPPOSING COLORS AND
EASY NAVIGATION.

OVERALL, THIS SITE LACKS ANY ONE
DEFINING ELEMENT WHICH WOULD
CAPTURE AND HOLD USER ATTENTION.

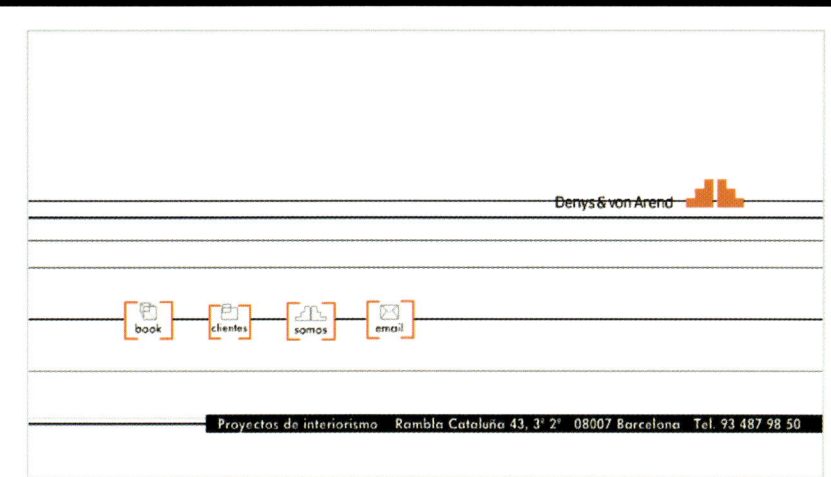

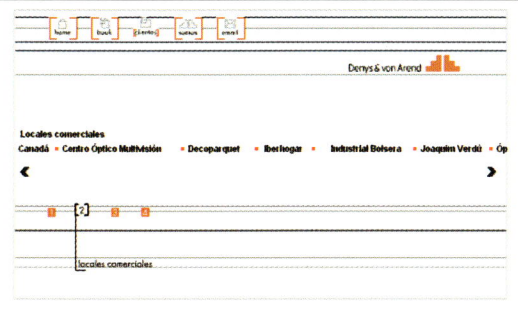

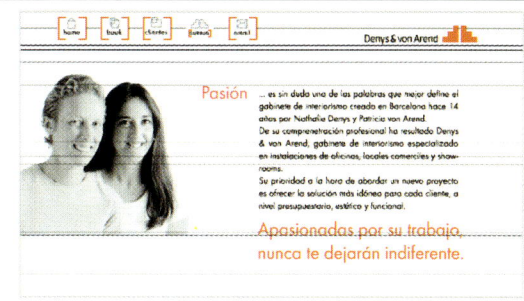

WWW.ODDCAST.COM

> NAME: ODDCAST MEDIA TECHNOLOGIES > SECTOR: INTERACTIVE MEDIA SOLUTIONS > SPECS: FLASH, HTML > RATING: ORIGINALITY ☺ GRAPHICS ☺ INTERACTIVIDAD ☺ > CREDITS: ODDCAST, INC.

BOLD ORANGE FRAMES A COMPLEX PROJECT, WITH A NUMBER OF LINKS-RICH SUBSECTIONS. THIS IS AN AMBITIOUS DESIGN, WHICH CONSTANTLY REQUIRES THE USER'S PARTICIPATION.

THE MAIN MENU IS DIVIDED INTO THREE GENERAL SECTIONS, WHICH IN TURN GENERATE NEW LINKS OF THEIR OWN.

THERE IS A GREAT DEAL OF WRITTEN TEXT AND THE GRAPHICS ARE USED TO SUPPORT AND EMPHASIZE EACH SECTION. THEREFORE, EACH LINK ENJOYS ITS OWN UNIQUE IDENTITY, WHILE MAINTAINING THE SAME BASIC STRUCTURE: ICON TO THE LEFT, WITH INFORMATION IN THE CENTER, UNFOLDING TOWARD THE BOTTOM OF THE SCREEN.

THE ANIMATED FIGURES DISPLAY A VIBRANT COLOR SCHEME. THE EVER-PRESENT ORANGE HIGHLIGHTS EACH SECTION, BUT IN QUANTITIES WHICH KEEP IT FROM BEING AN EYESORE.

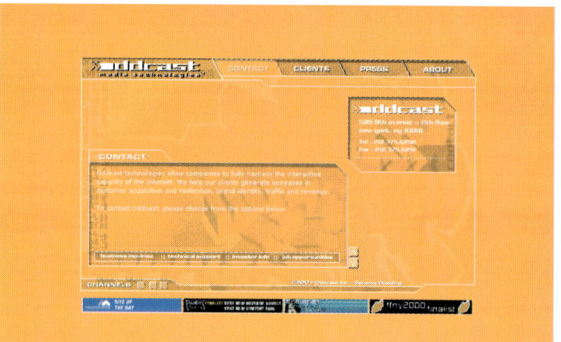

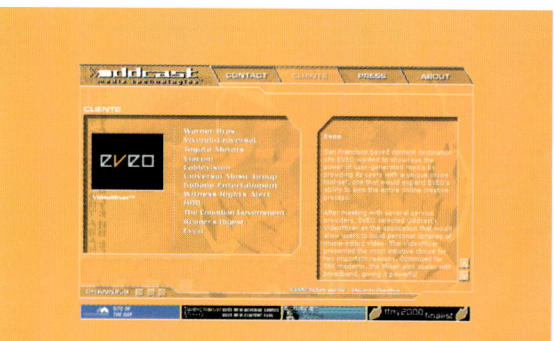

virtual host ™

back home

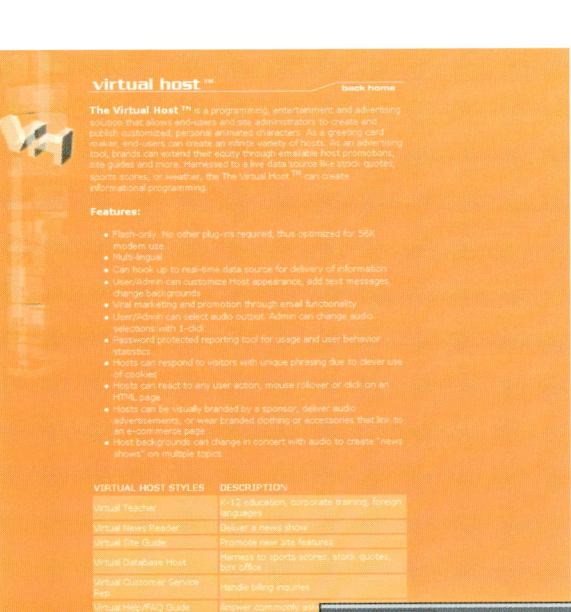

The Virtual Host ™ is a programming, entertainment and advertising solution that allows end-users and site administrators to develop and publish customized, personal animated characters. As a greeting card maker, end-users can create an infinite variety of hosts. As an advertising tool, brands can extend their equity through enslavable host promotions, site guides and more. Harnessed to a live data source like stock quotes, sports scores, or weather, the The Virtual Host ™ can create informational programming.

Features:

- Flash-only. No other plug-in's required, thus optimized for 56K modem use
- Multi-lingual
- Can hook up to real-time data source for delivery of information
- User/Admin can customize Host appearance, add text messages, change backgrounds
- Viral marketing and promotion through email functionality
- User/Admin can select audio output. Admin can change audio selections with 1-click
- Password protected reporting tool for usage and user behavior statistics
- Hosts can respond to visitors with unique phrasing due to clever use of cookies
- Hosts can react to any user action, mouse rollover or click on an HTML page
- Hosts can be visually branded by a sponsor, deliver audio advertisements, or wear branded clothing or accessories that link to an e-commerce page
- Host backgrounds can change in concert with audio to create "news shows" on multiple topics

VIRTUAL HOST STYLES	DESCRIPTION
Virtual Teacher	K-12 education, corporate training, foreign languages
Virtual News Reader	Deliver a news show
Virtual Site Guide	Promote new site features
Virtual Database Host	Harness to sports scores, stock quotes, box office
Virtual Customer Service Rep	Handle billing inquiries
Virtual Help/FAQ Guide	Answer commonly asked questions
Virtual E-Cards	Host-based e-cards for ... etc
Virtual Fashion Mannequin	Showcase apparel
Virtual Museum/Record Promoter	Promote a new release
Virtual Actor/Film Promoter	Market a new film
Virtual Comedian	Joke machine
Virtual E-Commerce Assistant	Assist with e-commerce

videomixer ™

back home

VideoMixer™ is the web's preeminent consumer level editing tool. It puts users in the editor's chair, allowing them to make shot-by-shot decisions to create custom music videos or narrative, dialogue driven movies. Ideal for the music, film and television industries, the application is also a perfect vehicle for marketing a brand through an entertaining user experience. Robust, easy to use administration tools allow for community management, content management, monitoring and reporting.

Features:

- Transitions: Users edit with cinematic transitions like cut, dissolve, and wipe
- Email: Completed videos can be emailed to multiple recipients
- Publishing: Completed emails can be saved to a site, syndicated to other sites, entered into contests, or broadcast on TV using Oddcast's Playback-on-TV™ product
- Title Workshop: Users can create personal title pages
- Drag and Drop Interface: Consumer friendly interaction
- Asset Library: Users select from a theoretically unlimited media library
- Uploads: VideoMixer™ supports optional upload of media
- Personal Video Locker: Users can store media in their personal locker for future retrieval
- Sponsorship: Supports and reports for banner ads, interstitials, logo on audio ads, and next generation product placement
- E-Commerce: The applications can link to an e-commerce page
- Administration: Webmasters can upload assets, preview and approve uploads, create contests and use monitoring and reporting tools that capture real time user behavior statistics
- Data Mining: Webmasters can determine asset popularity, viral success, overall usership, time online and much more

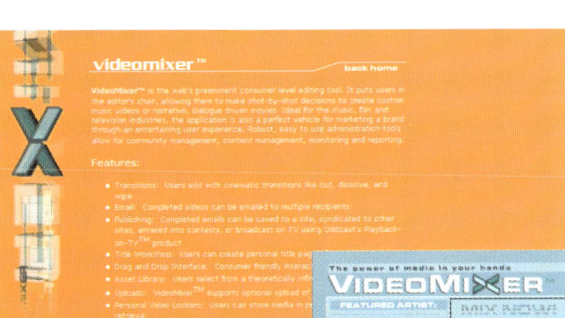

playback on tv ™

back home

Playback-on-TV™ is a powerful convergence tool that facilitates the marriage of the web and television. The application allows broadcasters to enable their viewers to create TV programming through narrow-band, consumer level web browsers. Built on Oddcast's flagship platform, VideoMixer, Playback-on-TV™ empowers television networks to select any Web-generated VideoMixer clip and create a broadcast quality version.

Playback-to-TV™ speaks to the current trend in reality-based television by giving viewers the opportunity to easily create and participate in media programming. Optimized for today's dial-up world, Playback-on-TV™ is designed to drive usership to both on and off-line media, and represents the best new weapon in the broadcaster's arsenal to monetize on Web-TV convergence.

Features:

- Uses VideoMixer's Web-based, consumer level editing interface for end users
- Delivers the simple assembly of Web-to-broadcast quality video clips
- Provides advanced content, community, and editorial management tools that allow for the easy creation of compelling promotions, and simple, in-depth harvesting of user/viewer data

back home

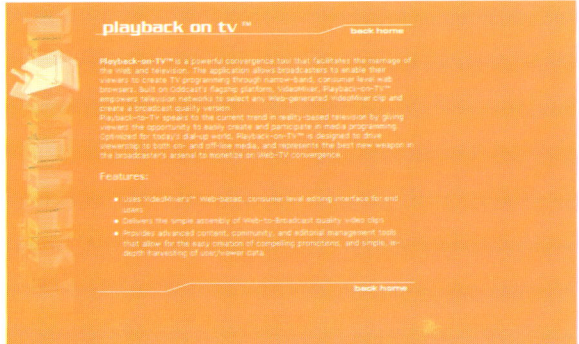

karaoke ™

back home

Karaoke Station™ invites consumers to sing, record and share their recordings of their favorite songs. The first in-browser karaoke application that allows users to do this, Karaoke Station™ is a powerful tool for record labels, music destinations, advertisers, portals and consumer brands. The application increases exposure to a musician, a site or product by exploiting the pervasiveness of music in our daily lives.

Features:

- Flash only. No downloads required, thus optimized for 56k modem users
- Plays on any flash enabled device including hand held, PS2 and set top boxes
- Synchronous text display provides users with song lyrics
- Live voice recording and instant playback
- Users can save, email and rank performances
- User can search by artist, track or performance
- Dynamic, e-commerce, label and artist links
- Reporting and monitoring tools provide up to the minute statistics and detailed usage reports
- Content management tools offer state of the art creative administration, allowing site editors to easily highlight outstanding performances, manage content and conduct extensive community management tasks

photo mixer ™

back home

The PhotoMixer™, the web's premiere search and play/multimedia engine, allows users to create dynamic slide shows of personal and web based photos to the beat of any audio file. PhotoMixer™ is ideal for music sites, consumer brands looking to add interactivity to their marketing efforts, and photo, family, and event sites looking to gain more mileage from their visual content.

Features:

- Search and play: Dynamic retrieval and display of web photos according to user inserted keywords
- Photo-upload: Users can combine their own images with images from the network
- Dynamic text insertion: A user created text layer animates according to the beat of the music
- Special visual effects and transitions: Split screen mosaic, jitter, zoom and other effects are applied to the visuals according to the beat of the music
- Email Functionality: Finished PhotoMixer™ clips are available
- Administration tool: The administration tool allows site editors to add/delete audio files for user selection, and data mine for keyword, audio and visual asset popularity, viral success, time online and more

beat sensor ™

back home

The BeatSensor™, a powerful music visualization tool, delivering eye-popping visual creations, edited to the beat of any audio. Ideal for the music industry, BeatSensor™ is also a perfect tool for promoting a brand through music entertainment. Using Flash and a proprietary algorithm, BeatSensor™ harnesses the power of real time audio-visual feedback to allow users to edit, live and on the fly, any animation to the beat of an audio track.

Features:

- Live Mix Feedback: Whatever choices the user makes, the BeatSensor™ creates an exciting, unique video
- Visual Assets: Animated figures, background animations, textures and tints
- Special Effects: Split Screen, Cloning, Extreme Zoom, Inversion and Background Masking
- Text Work Shop: Users can mix in personal text messages throughout the song
- E-mail: Users can email friends with settings and personalization
- Sponsorship: Supports banners, interstitials, next generation product placement
- E-Commerce: The applications can link to an e-commerce page
- Administration: Webmasters can upload assets
- Data Mining: Webmasters can determine asset popularity, viral success, overall usership, time online and much more

> NAME: THE DESIGNERS REPUBLIC
> SECTOR: FORUM FOR DISCUSSION
> SPECS: FLASH, HTML > RATING:
ORIGINALITY ☺ GRAPHICS ☹
INTERACTIVITY ☻

AN EXCESSIVELY LARGE ICON CENTERS ATTENTION ON THE HOME PAGE. THE WORDS THEMSELVES HERE BECOME GRAPHIC RESOURCES, WHICH LEAD TO SUBSEQUENT PAGES.

BLACK, AN EXPANSE OF WHITE AND, TO A LESSER DEGREE, RED CONVERGE TO COMPRISE AN ALMOST COLORLESS DESIGN, WHERE THE TEXT HAS THE LAST WORD.

Website.
Phase one.
RGB.
mitDR.

Angryman:

The Designers Republic.
See below for more info.
485,421,439 and counting
Population: 34,266

Join.

Work.
Archive.
Retail.

Speak.
Discuss.

Website.
Phase one.
RGB.
mitDR.

Discuss:

The Designers Republic ltd.
Sheffield. Soyo. North of Nowhere.
Brain Aided Design.

mitDR is a division of Pho-Ku Corp.
Tokyo. Japan. Buy Nothing. Pay Now.

Start the discussion.
Your call will be monitored.

Talk.

The Designers Republic.
See below for more info.
485,421,483 and counting
Population: 34,266

Join.

Work.
Archive.
Retail.

Speak.
Discuss.

Website.
Phase one.
BGB.
☐miTDR.

The Designers Republic.
See below for more info.

485,421,561 and counting
Population: 34,266

Neue.DR.　　**Add message.** -　　**Discuss:** -　　**Join.**

Subject:　**Who:**　**Date:**　**Size:**

Graffiti Rules.　　　　　　TrainFucker　30/11/01　10
"gravity keeps my head down"　dux　30/11/01　13
%Đ Ð   QUOTES ON CREATIV　Francis　30/11/01　2
What are the 4 basic principles　Woolhouse　30/11/01　18
nike or adidas?　　　liquidHAIR　30/11/01　26
darwin talks shite　　rep　30/11/01　15
flash 6 beta>>???　　Charlie　30/11/01　3
EVERY ONE READ　Max　30/11/01　92
creative freedom　　oli　30/11/01　2
FORHEAD????　　　Bocha　30/11/01　1
me likes you likes　　floorless　30/11/01　1
ATTIK RULES - tDR SUKS ASS　K.Jens　30/11/01　46
scize?　　　　　　fulk　30/11/01　9
Wipeout Disappointment　Rich L　30/11/01　7

Forward.　　**Back.**

Messages.

Subject:　　　**Who:**　　　**Date:**

Graffiti Rules.　　　TrainFucker　30/11 02:52
Re: Graffiti Rules.　　at　　30/11 02:55
Fuck Up More Trains　TrainFucker　30/11 03:02
Re: Fuck Up More Trains　eichHoernchen　30/11 06:57
Re: Graffiti Rules.　　allan simonsen　30/11 07:26
Re: Graffiti Rules.　　elph　30/11 12:24
Re: Fuck Up More Trains　bitterman　30/11 14:10
Re: Graffiti Rules.　　qwerty　30/11 14:12
Graff: Good and Bad　Ghetto Bastard　30/11 17:13
Trainfucker/Good Links　Ghetto Bastard　30/11 17:24

Help. -　　-　　-

They say:

Posted by TrainFucker
30/11/01 02:52:58 GMT
Graffiti Rules.

In the history of arts there is no
other kind of art that took so many
souls like graffiti.

Respond.

Work.
Archive.
Retail.

Speak.
Discuss.

> F F
☐☐
☐☐

Website.
Phase one.
BGB.
☐miTDR.

The Designers Republic.
See below for more info.

485,421,713 and counting
Population: 34,266

Mailing List.　　**You are:** -　　**Join.**

Receive the truth, lies
and disinformation from
The Designers Republic.

Email. -　　**Work.**
Archive.
Retail.

Use me. -　　**Speak.**
Discuss.

-　　-　　-

Finding your way through the
sections is something of a chal-
lenge, with new contents revealed at every step. This sort
of layout is designed to lead
users deeper into the site.

Website.
Phase one.
BGB.
☐miTDR.

The Designers Republic.
See below for more info.

485,421,796 and counting
Population: 34,266

Client.　　**Name.** -　　**Time remaining.** -　　**Archive.**
The Designers Republic　TDR-Corporate ID　349,860,942 seconds

Location.　　**Format.**　　**Date.**
Soyo, UK　　Image　　01/01/00

The Designers Republic
→ Customized Terror
→ Customized Terror A3

-　　-　　-

Website.
Phase one.
BGB.
☐miTDR.

The Designers Republic.
See below for more info.

485,421,772 and counting
Population: 34,266

Client.　　**Name.** -　　**Time remaining.** -　　**Archive.**
The Designers Republic　TDR-Corporate ID　349,860,966 seconds

Location.　　**Format.**　　**Date.**
Soyo, UK　　Image　　01/01/00

The Designers Republic ltd.
The Workstation, 15 Paternoster Row
Sheffield S1 2BX United Kingdom.
E:dr@thedesignersrepublic.com
URL:www.thedesignersrepublic.com
T:+44 [0] 114 275 4982. F:+44 [0] 114 275 9127.
ISDN:+44 [0] 114 276 6339.

TDR is a division of Pho-Ku Corp.
L 6 3F Daikanyama-cho Shibuya-ku
Tokyo 150-0034 Japan.
〒150-0034 東京都渋谷区代官山町1-6 3F

The Designers Republic
→ Customized Terror
→ Customized Terror A3
→ DR M-Art Exhibition
→ DR M-Art Poster
→ TDR-Corporate ID
→ Cathode-Ray Propaganda
→ 100 x Neo.DR T-Shirts
The Peoples Bureau

-　　-　　-

Return.

> NAME: BECOMING HUMAN

> SECTOR: DIVULGACIÓN > SPECS: FLASH, HTML > RATING: ORIGINALITY ☺ GRAPHICS ☺ INTERACTIVITY ☺

> DESIGNED BY: A TEAM DIRECTED BY BART MARABLE, TERRA INCOGNITA INTERACTIVE MEDIA AND NEONSKY CREATIVE MEDIA

BLACK BEARS THE VISUAL WEIGHT OF THE CENTRAL WINDOW, WHERE THE CONTENTS ARE DISPLAYED. THE PHOTOGRAPHS AND VARIETY OF SHADES FLUCTUATE AMIDST ABUNDANT INFORMATION. ON THE OTHER HAND, THE COLOR IS NOT WHAT DRAWS ATTENTION IN THIS DESIGN. RATHER, THE SOBRIETY OF SHADES OF BLUE AND BROWN IMBUE THE DESIGN WITH A NOTE OF SERIOUSNESS.

WWW.BECOMINGHUMAN.ORG

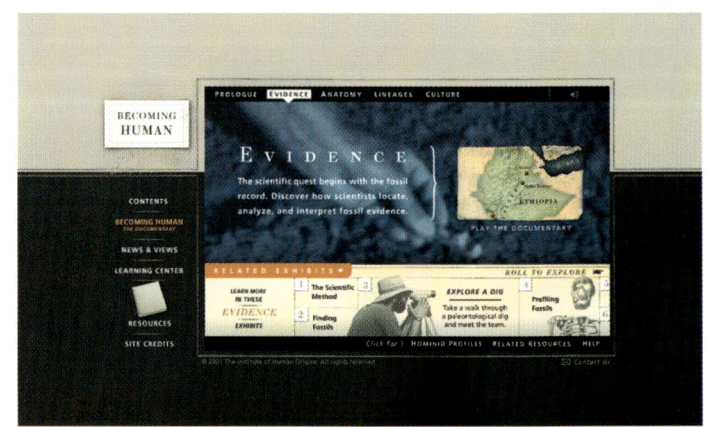

A VIDEO MAKES UP THE INTRODUCTORY SECTION, WHILE THERE IS A VARIED OFFERING OF DETAILED INFORMATION FILLING THE OTHER FOUR CATEGORIES.

TWO MENUS (ONE VERTICAL, THE OTHER HORIZONTAL) PROVIDE ACCESS TO THE INFORMATION, THEREBY ENSURING THOROUGH HYPERTEXTUAL NAVIGATION.

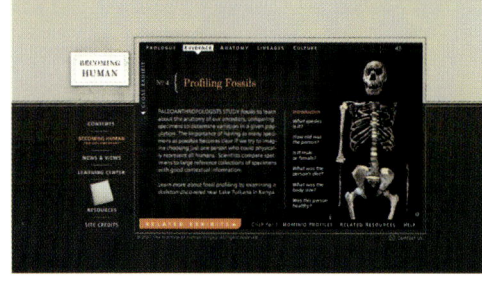

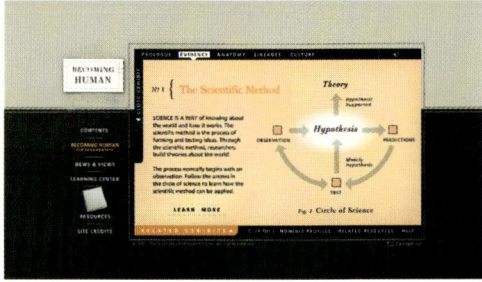

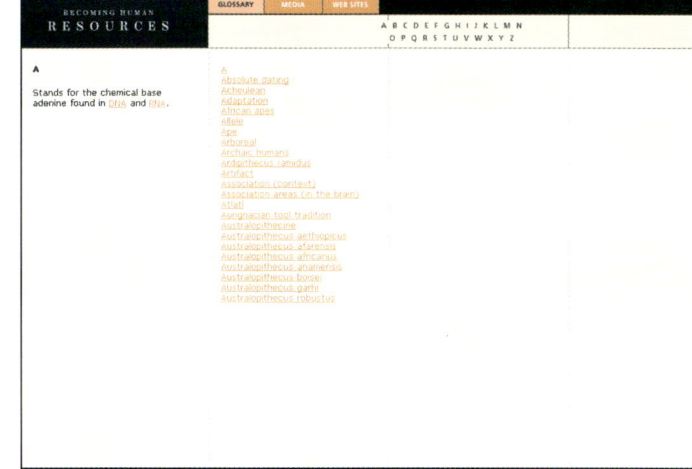
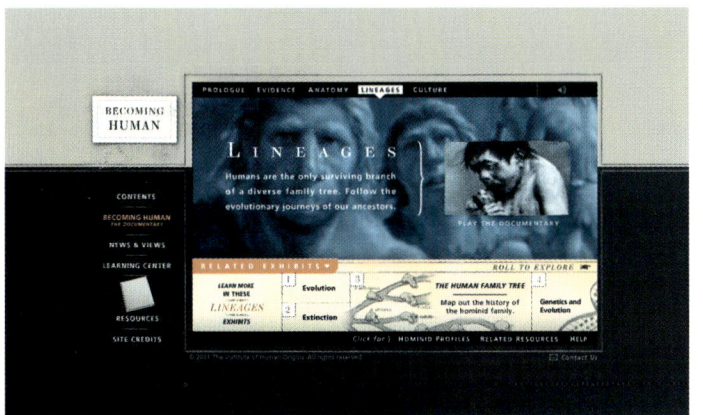
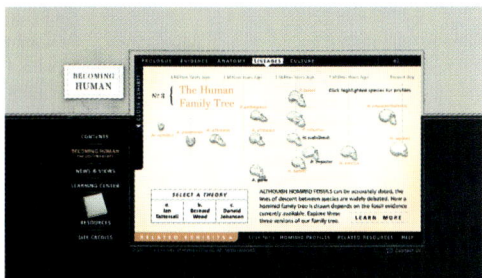

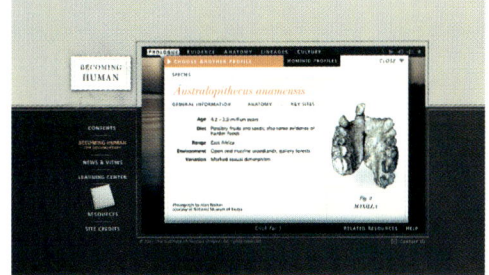
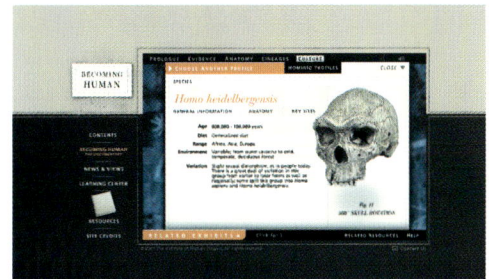
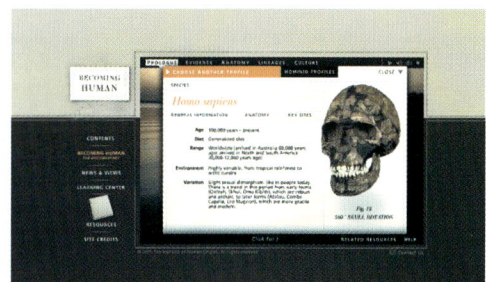
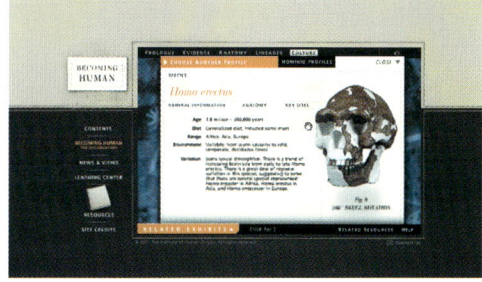

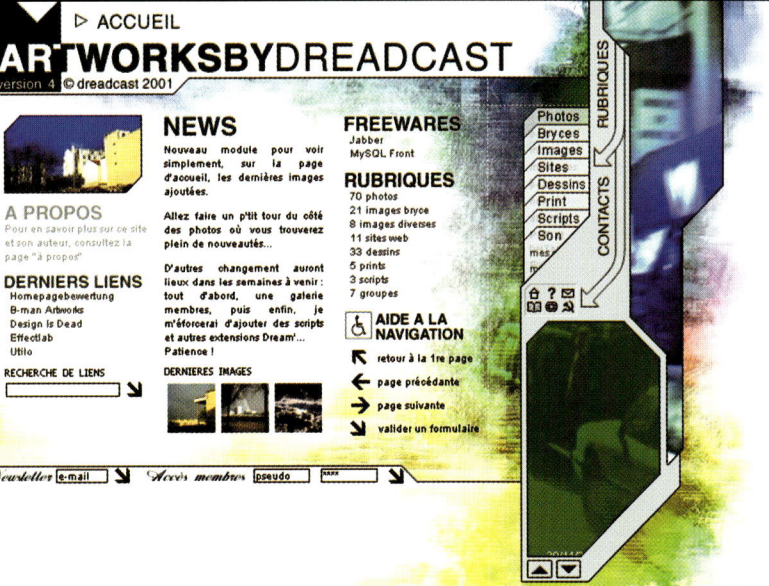

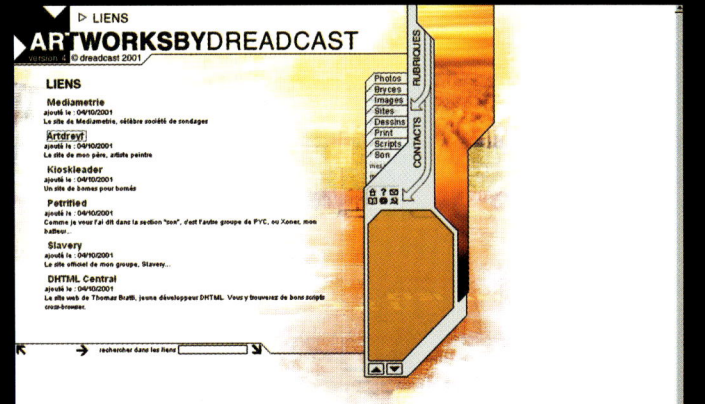

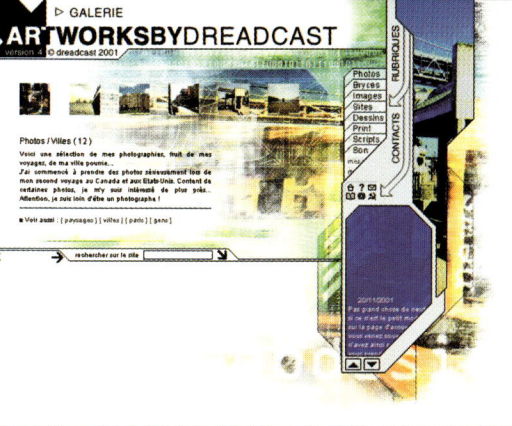

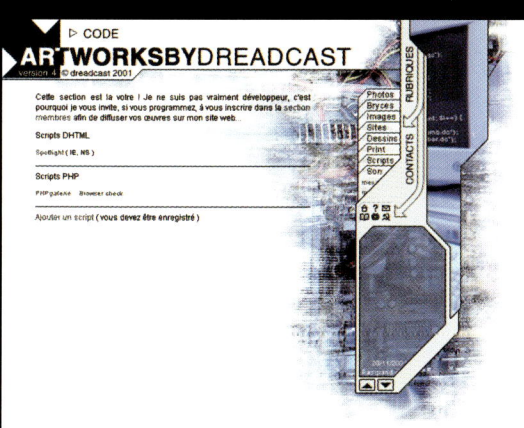
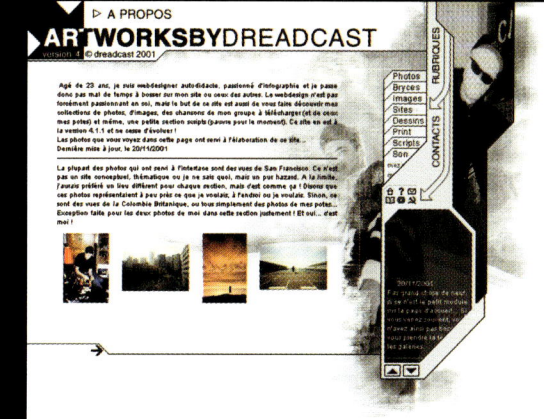
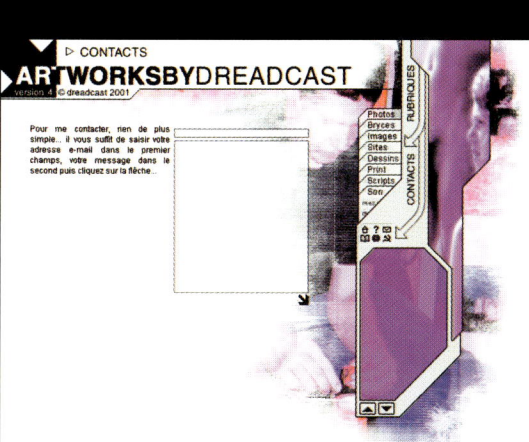
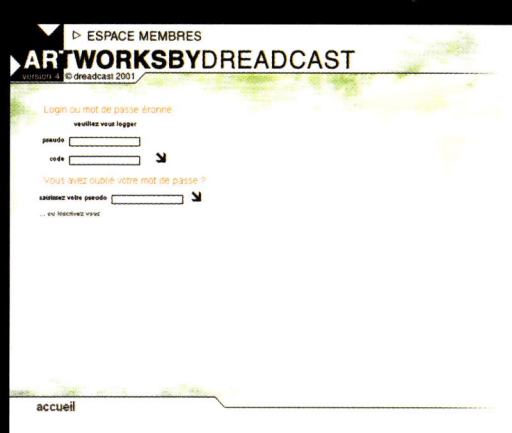

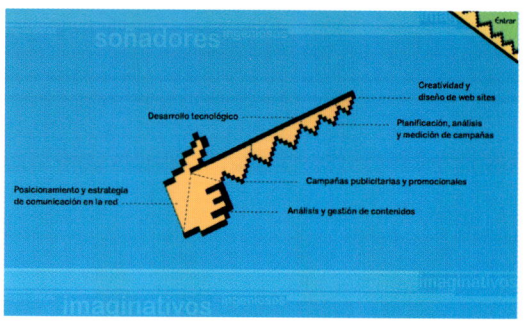

> NAME: MAS MADERA INTERACTIVE
> SECTOR: ADVERTISING AGENCY
> SPECS: FLASH, HTML > RATING:
ORIGINALITY ☺ GRAPHICS ☺
INTERACTIVITY ☺ > DESIGNED BY:
MAS MADERA INTERACTIVE

WWW.MASMADERA.NET

ONE ASPECT WHICH STANDS OUT ABOVE ALL OTHERS IN THE DESIGN OF THIS SITE IS THE ARRAY OF HUES WHICH SERVE AS THE BASIC STRUCTURE OF THE FOUR MAIN SECTIONS. HERE, IT IS THE COLOR SCHEME WHICH CARRIES THE WEIGHT OF CONVEYING AUTONOMY AND STRENGTH.

EACH SECTION HAS BEEN METICULOUSLY DEVELOPED, WHILE REMAINING TRUE TO THE UNDERLYING TONALITY, THEREBY RESPECTING THE LAYOUT'S OVERALL HOMOGENEITY.

ANOTHER EYE-CATCHING FEATURE IS THE VARIETY AND DEPTH OF THE INTRODUCTORY GRAPHICS. THIS IS AN ORIGINAL EXAMPLE OF HOW FLEXIBLE TEXT CAN BE, SHEDDING THE NORMS THAT WOULD OTHERWISE DICTATE A STATIC LOOK.

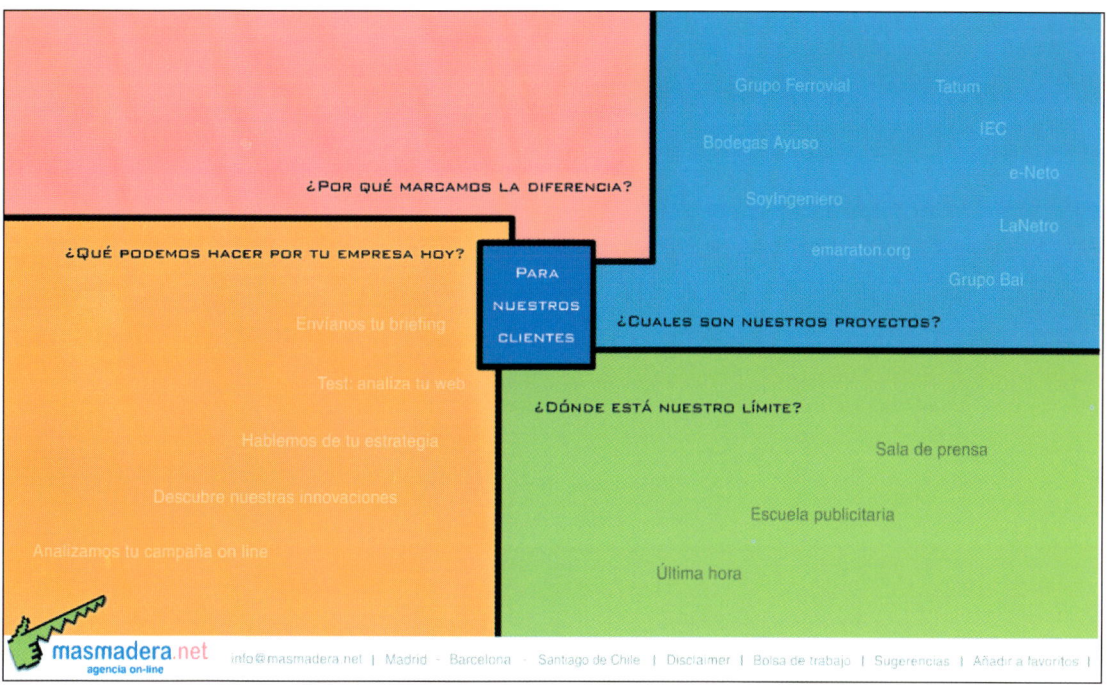

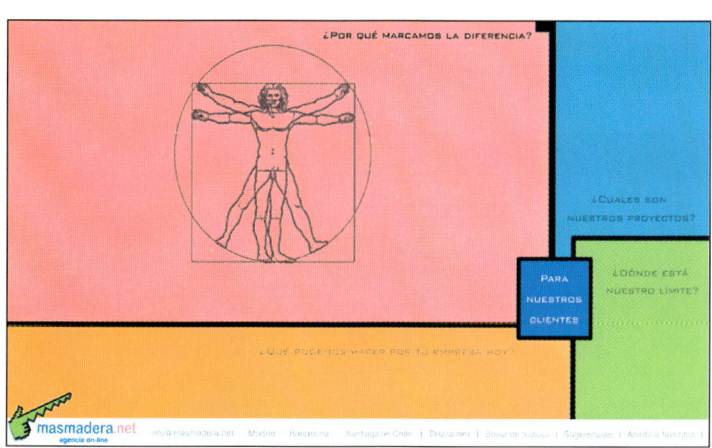

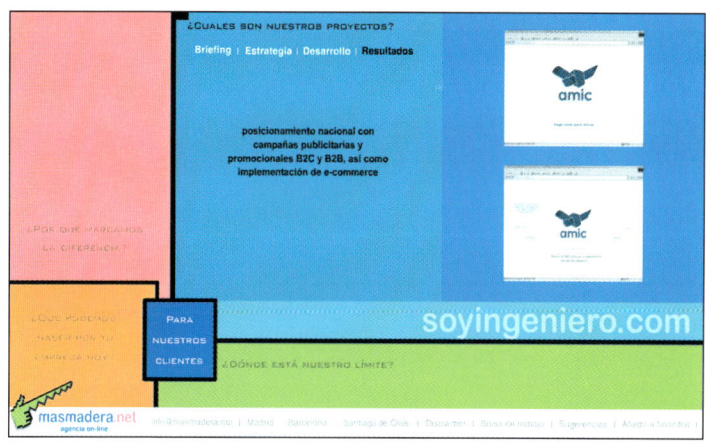

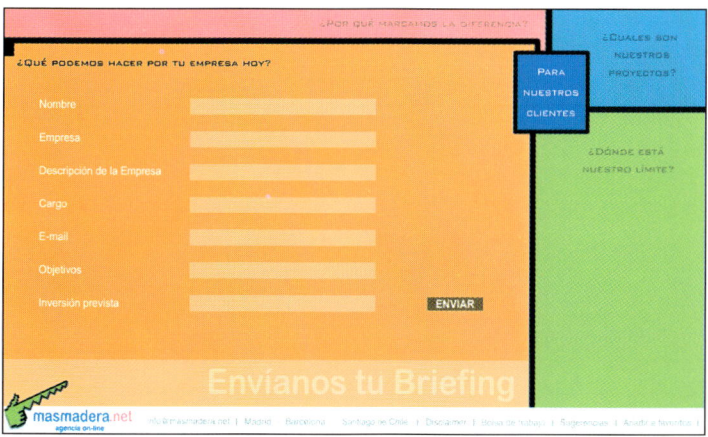

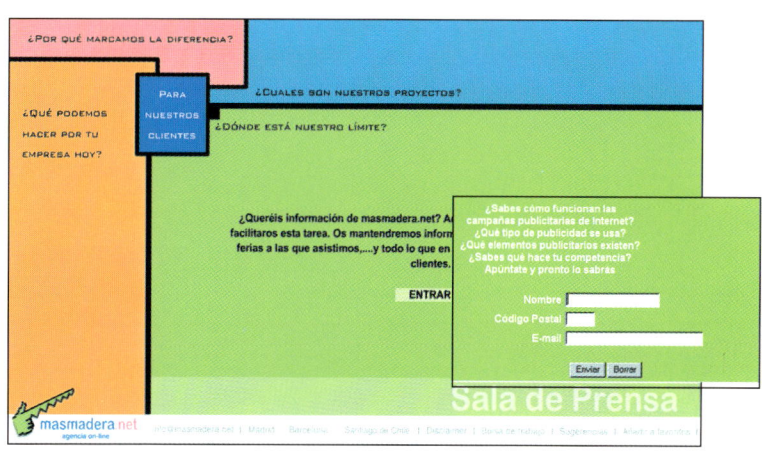

WWW.WMV.CO.UK

> NOMBRE: WINDERMERE MARINA VILLAGE > SECTOR: LAKESIDE RESORT > SPECIFICATIONS: HTML > RATING: ORIGINALITY ☹ GRAPHICS ☹ INTERACTIVITY 😐

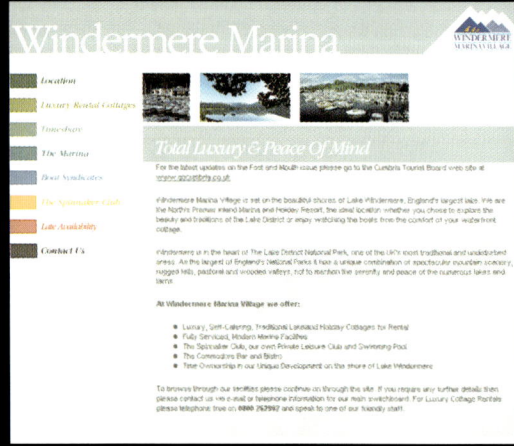

THE HOMEPAGE GIVES WAY TO A RIGID STRUCTURE WITH A VERTICAL MENU. EACH SECTION DISPLAYS THE SAME COHERENCY AND GRAPHIC DISTRIBUTION, MAKING NAVIGATION SIMPLE: NO UNWARRANTED SURPRISES HERE.

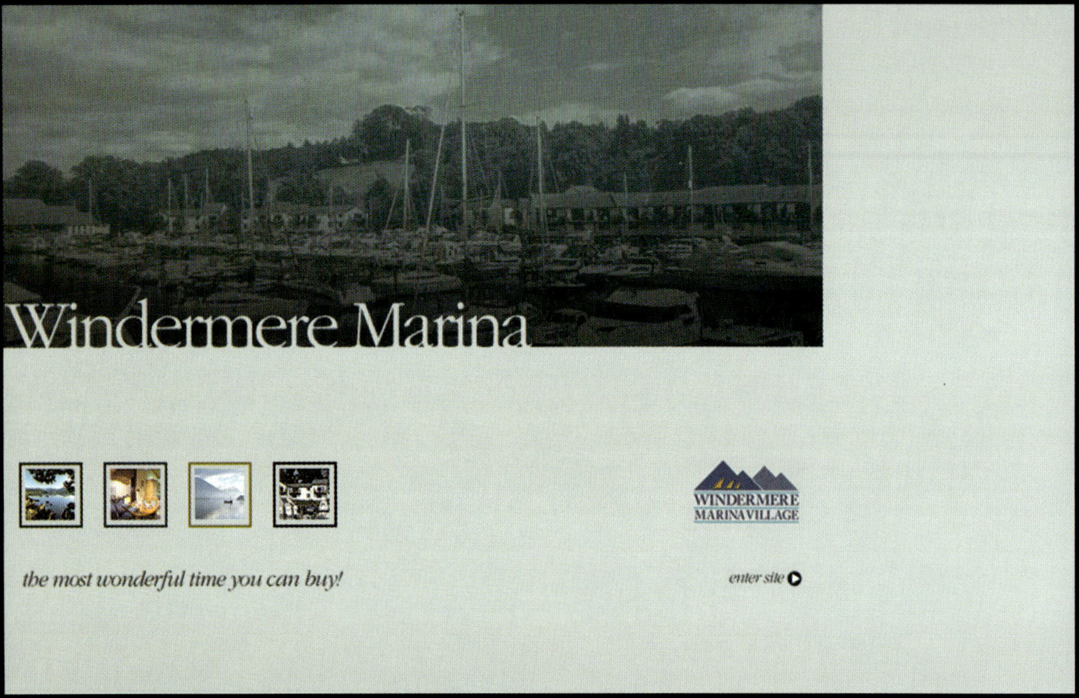

THE TEXTUAL INFORMATION PREVAILS IN IMPORTANCE OVER ALL OTHER GRAPHIC ELEMENTS. THIS IS, ABOVE ALL, A SITE MEANT TO INFORM, NOT DAZZLE.

ON THE OTHER HAND, A RANGE OF COLORS AND TONES CLEARLY DIFFERENTIATES EACH SECTION WITHOUT THE NEED FOR GIMICKY ICONS. THUS, THE USE OF COLOR FULFILLS THE ROLE OF SEPARATING THE CONTENTS.

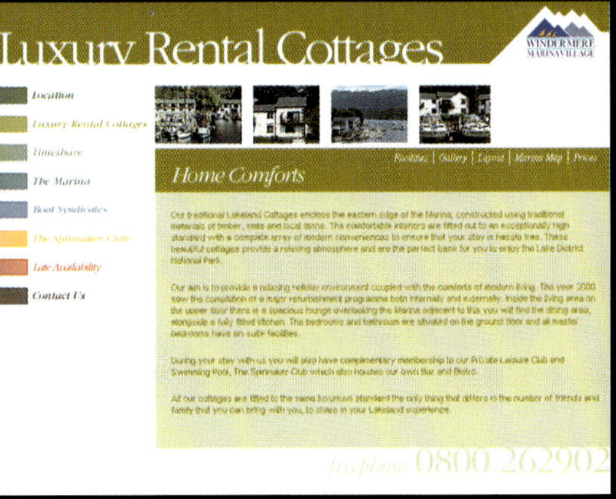

Luxury Rental Cottages

WINDERMERE MARINA VILLAGE

Location
Luxury Rental Cottages
Timeshare
The Marina
Boat Syndicates
The Spinnaker Club
Late Availability
Contact Us

Facilities | Gallery | Layout | Marina Map | Prices

Home Comforts

Our traditional Lakeland Cottages enclose the eastern edge of the Marina, constructed using traditional materials of timber, slate and local stone. The comfortable interiors are fitted out to an exceptionally high standard with a complete array of modern conveniences to ensure that your stay is hassle free. These beautiful cottages provide a relaxing atmosphere and are the perfect base for you to enjoy the Lake District National Park.

Our aim is to provide a relaxing holiday environment coupled with the comforts of modern living. This year 2000 saw the completion of a major refurbishment programme both internally and externally. Inside the living area on the upper floor there is a spacious lounge overlooking the Marina adjacent to this you will find the dining area, alongside a fully fitted kitchen. The bedrooms and bathroom are situated on the ground floor and all master bedrooms have en-suite facilities.

During your stay with us you will also have complimentary membership to our Private Leisure Club and Swimming Pool, The Spinnaker Club which also houses our own Bar and Bistro.

All our cottages are fitted to the same luxurious standard the only thing that differs is the number of friends and family that you can bring with you, to share in your Lakeland experience.

freephone 0800 262902

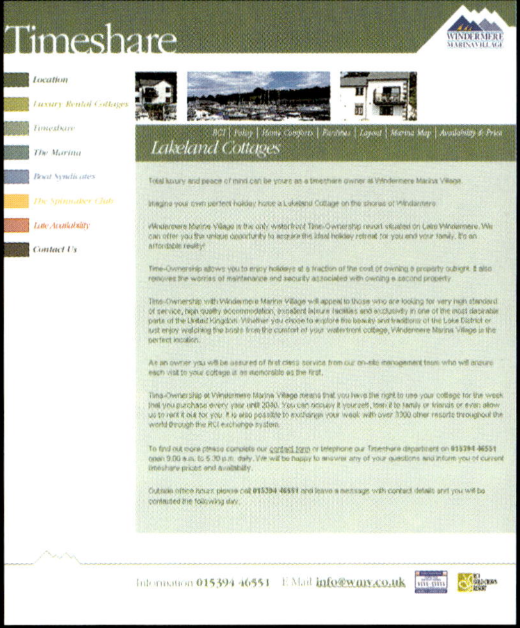

Timeshare

WINDERMERE MARINA VILLAGE

Location
Luxury Rental Cottages
Timeshare
The Marina
Boat Syndicates
The Spinnaker Club
Late Availability
Contact Us

RCI | Policy | Home Comforts | Facilities | Layout | Marina Map | Availability & Price

Lakeland Cottages

Total luxury and peace of mind can be yours as a timeshare owner at Windermere Marina Village.

Imagine your own perfect holiday home a Lakeland Cottage on the shores of Windermere.

Windermere Marina Village is the only waterfront Time-Ownership resort situated on Lake Windermere. We can offer you the unique opportunity to acquire the ideal holiday retreat for you and your family. It's an affordable reality!

Time-Ownership allows you to enjoy holidays at a fraction of the cost of owning a property outright. It also removes the worries of maintenance and security associated with owning a second property.

Time-Ownership with Windermere Marina Village will appeal to those who are looking for very high standard of service, high quality accommodation, excellent leisure facilities and exclusivity in one of the most desirable parts of the United Kingdom. Whether you chose to explore the beauty and traditions of the Lake District or just enjoy watching the boats from the comfort of your waterfront cottage, Windermere Marina Village is the perfect location.

As an owner you will be assured of first class service from our on-site management team who will assure each visit to your cottage is as memorable as the first.

Time-Ownership at Windermere Marina Village means that you have the right to use your cottage for the week that you purchase every year until 2040. You can occupy it yourself, loan it to family or friends or even allow us to rent it out for you. It is also possible to exchange your week with over 3700 other resorts throughout the world through the RCI exchange system.

To find out more please complete our contact form or telephone our Timeshare department on 015394 46551 open 9.00 a.m. to 5.30 p.m. daily. We will be happy to answer any of your questions and inform you of current timeshare prices and availability.

Outside office hours please call 015394 46551 and leave a message with contact details and you will be contacted the following day.

Information 015394 46551 E-Mail info@wmv.co.uk

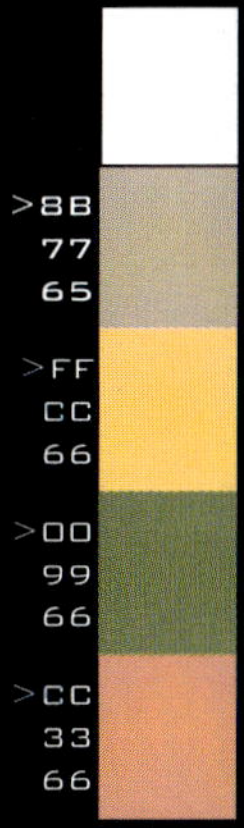

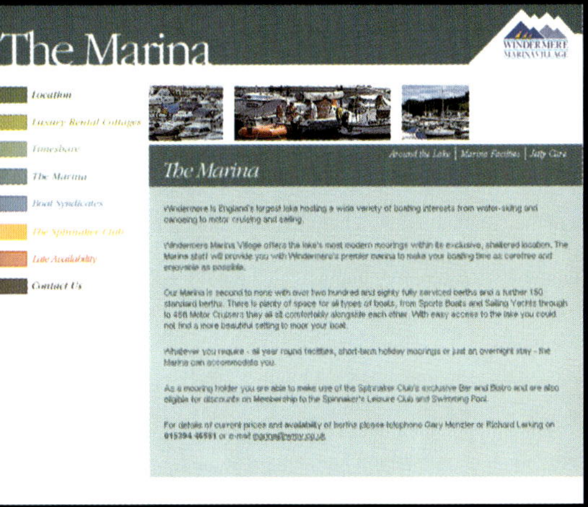

The Marina

WINDERMERE MARINA VILLAGE

Location
Luxury Rental Cottages
Timeshare
The Marina
Boat Syndicates
The Spinnaker Club
Late Availability
Contact Us

Around the Lake | Marina Facilities | Jetty Cars

The Marina

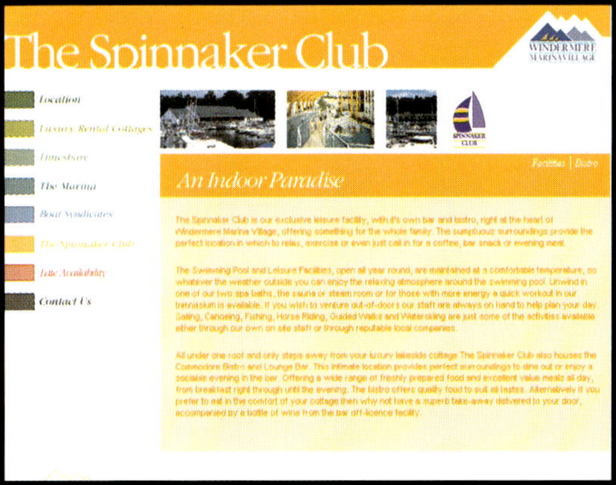

Windermere is England's largest lake hosting a wide variety of boating interests from water-skiing and canoeing to motor cruising and sailing.

Windermere Marina Village offers the lake's most modern moorings within its exclusive, sheltered location. The Marina staff will provide you with Windermere's premier marina to make your boating time as carefree and enjoyable as possible.

Our Marina is second to none with over two hundred and eighty fully serviced berths and a further 150 standard berths. There is plenty of space for all types of boats, from Sports Boats and Sailing Yachts through to 48ft Motor Cruisers they sit all comfortably alongside each other. With easy access to the lake you could not find a more beautiful setting to moor your boat.

Whatever you require - all year round facilities, short-term holiday moorings or just an overnight stay - the Marina can accommodate you.

As a mooring holder you are able to make use of the Spinnaker Club's exclusive Bar and Bistro and are also eligible for discounts on Membership to the Spinnaker's Leisure Club and Swimming Pool.

For details of current prices and availability of berths please telephone Gary Metcalfe or Richard Larking on 015394 46551 or e-mail marina@wmv.co.uk.

The Spinnaker Club

WINDERMERE MARINA VILLAGE

Location
Luxury Rental Cottages
Timeshare
The Marina
Boat Syndicates
The Spinnaker Club
Late Availability
Contact Us

Facilities | Bistro

An Indoor Paradise

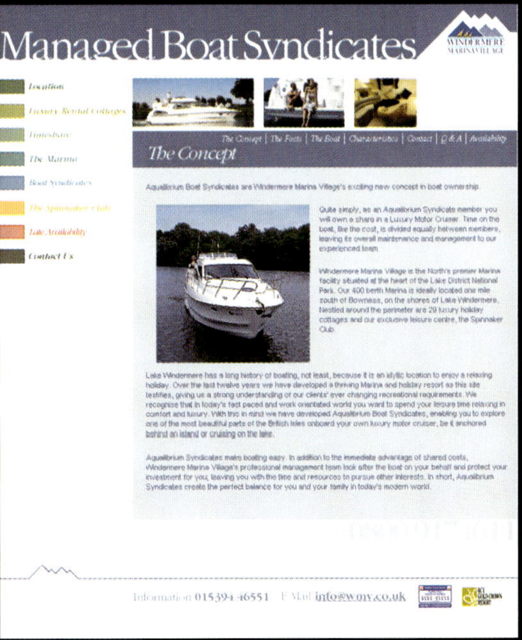

The Spinnaker Club is our exclusive leisure facility, with its own bar and bistro, right at the heart of Windermere Marina Village, offering something for the whole family. The sumptuous surroundings provide the perfect location in which to relax, exercise or even just call in for a coffee, bar snack or evening meal.

The Swimming Pool and Leisure Facilities, open all year round, are maintained at a comfortable temperature, so whatever the weather outside you can enjoy the relaxing atmosphere around the swimming pool. Unwind in one of our two spa baths, the sauna or steam room or for those with more energy a quick workout in our gymnasium is available. If you wish to venture out-of-doors our staff are always on hand to help plan your day. Sailing, Canoeing, Fishing, Horse Riding, Guided Visits and Water-skiing are just some of the activities available either through our own on-site staff or through reputable local companies.

All under one roof and only steps away from our luxury lakeside cottage The Spinnaker Club also houses the Commodore Bistro and Lounge Bar. This intimate location provides perfect surroundings to dine out or enjoy a sociable evening in the bar. Offering a wide range of freshly prepared food and excellent value meals all day, from breakfast right through until the evening. The bistro offers quality food to suit all tastes. Alternatively if you prefer to eat in the comfort of your cottage then why not have a superb take-away delivered to your door, accompanied by a bottle of wine from the bar off-licence facility.

Managed Boat Syndicates

WINDERMERE MARINA VILLAGE

Location
Luxury Rental Cottages
Timeshare
The Marina
Boat Syndicates
The Spinnaker Club
Late Availability
Contact Us

The Concept | The Facts | The Boat | Characteristics | Contact | Q & A | Availability

The Concept

Aqualibrium Boat Syndicates are Windermere Marina Village's exciting new concept in boat ownership.

Quite simply, as an Aqualibrium Syndicate member you will own a share in a Luxury Motor Cruiser. Time on the boat, like the cost, is divided equally between members, leaving its overall maintenance and management to our experienced team.

Windermere Marina Village is the North's premier Marina facility situated at the heart of the Lake District National Park. Our 400 berth Marina is ideally located one mile south of Bowness, on the shores of Lake Windermere. Nestled around the perimeter are 29 luxury holiday cottages and our exclusive leisure centre, the Spinnaker Club.

Lake Windermere has a long history of boating, not least, because it is an idyllic location to enjoy a relaxing holiday. Over the last twelve years we have developed a thriving Marina and luxury resort so this site testifies, giving us a strong understanding of our clients' ever changing recreational requirements. We recognise that in today's fast paced and work orientated world you want to spend your leisure time relaxing in comfort and luxury. With this in mind we have developed Aqualibrium Boat Syndicates, enabling you to explore one of the most beautiful parts of the British Isles onboard your own luxury motor cruiser, be it anchored behind an island or cruising on the lake.

Aqualibrium Syndicates make boating easy. In addition to the immediate advantage of shared costs, Windermere Marina Village's professional management team look after the boat on your behalf and protect your investment for you, leaving you with the time and resources to pursue other interests. In short, Aqualibrium Syndicates create the perfect balance for you and your family in today's modern world.

Information 015394 46551 E-Mail info@wmv.co.uk

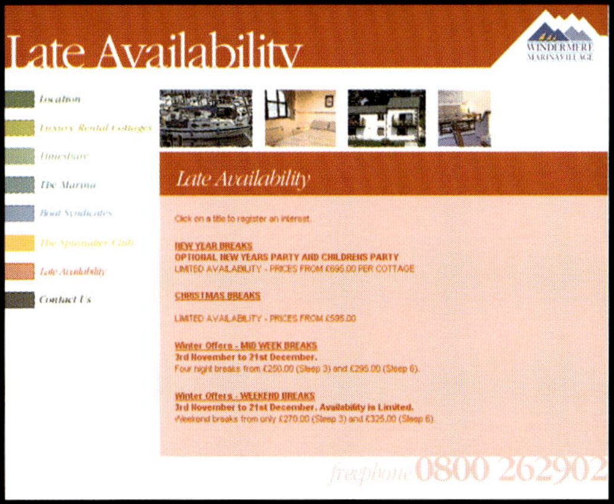

Late Availability

WINDERMERE MARINA VILLAGE

Location
Luxury Rental Cottages
Timeshare
The Marina
Boat Syndicates
The Spinnaker Club
Late Availability
Contact Us

Late Availability

Click on a title to register an interest.

NEW YEAR BREAKS
OPTIONAL NEW YEARS PARTY AND CHILDRENS PARTY
LIMITED AVAILABILITY - PRICES FROM £695.00 PER COTTAGE

CHRISTMAS BREAKS
LIMITED AVAILABILITY - PRICES FROM £595.00

Winter Offers - MID WEEK BREAKS
3rd November to 21st December.
Four night breaks from £250.00 (Sleep 3) and £295.00 (Sleep 6).

Winter Offers - WEEKEND BREAKS
3rd November to 21st December. Availability is Limited.
Weekend breaks from only £270.00 (Sleep 3) and £325.00 (Sleep 6).

freephone 0800 262902

> NAME: PROBE3 > SECTOR: PER-
SONAL PORTFOLIO > SPECS: FLASH,
HTML > RATING: ORIGINALITY ☺
GRAPHICS ☺ INTERACTIVITY ☹
> CREDITS: MARK WISNIOWSKI

THE PHOTOGRAPHS AND ANIMATION,
DENOTING SENSITIVITY, MASTERY OF
THE MEDIUM AND THE DESIRE TO
CREATE A CUTTING EDGE DESIGN,
ARE SURELY THE FIRST THINGS THAT
THE EYE IS DRAWN TO.

FINDING YOUR WAY AROUND THE SITE
IS FAIRLY STRAIGHTFORWARD. THE
MAIN MENU PROVIDES AN INITIAL SE-
LECTION, WITH NEW OPTIONS OPEN-
ING UP ON THE SECOND SCREEN.

WWW.PROBE3.COM

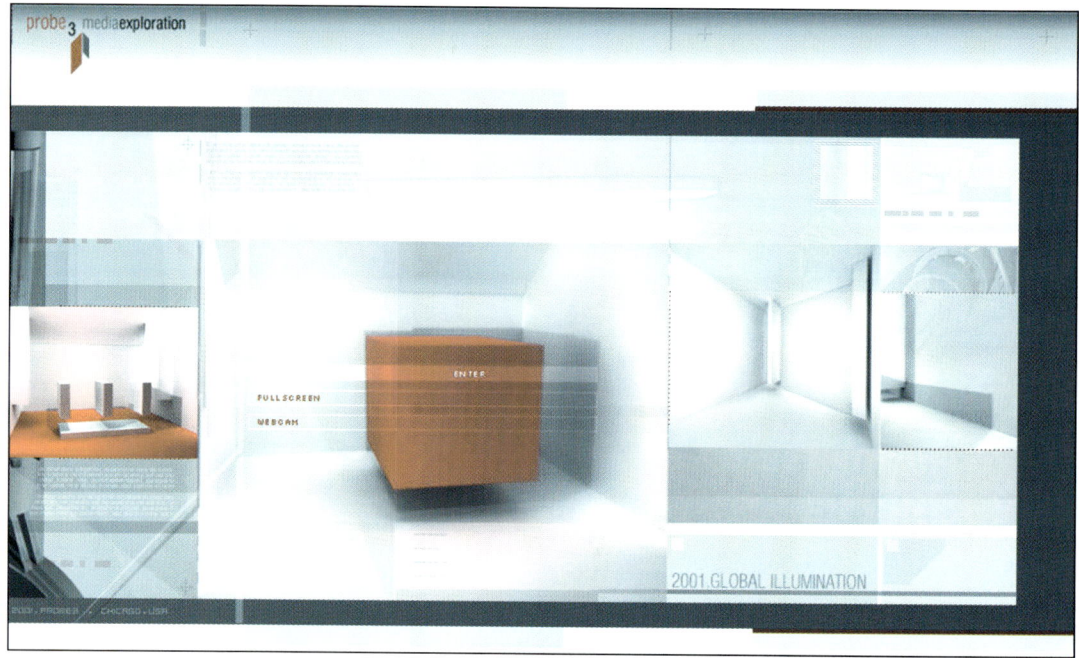

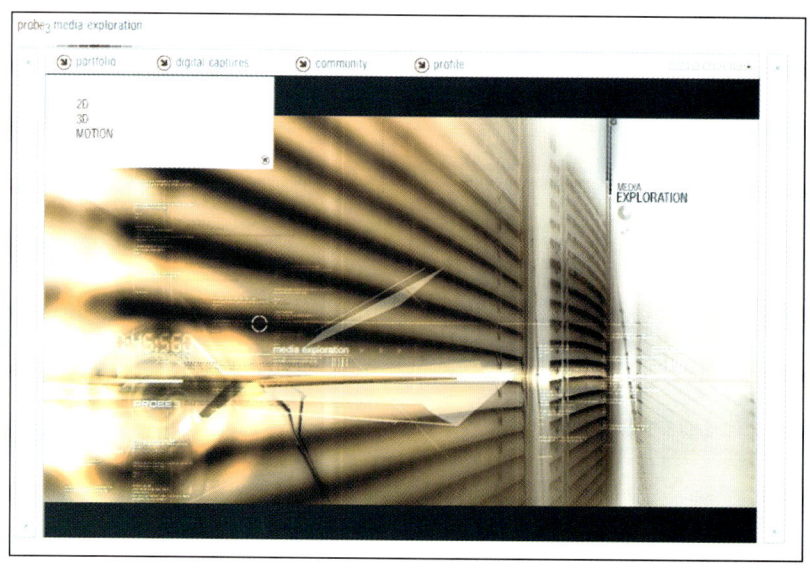

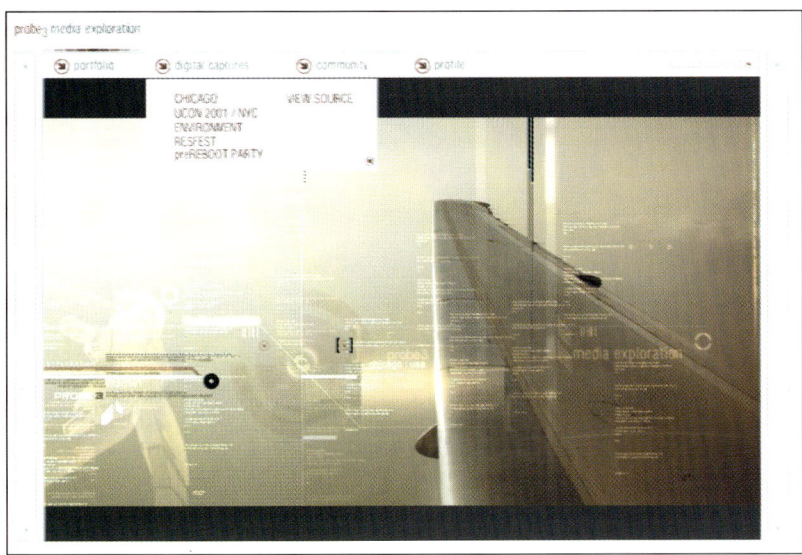

THE SYNTHETIC IMAGES ARE INTRIGU-
ING, SOMEHOW WEIGHTLESS, VIRTUAL
LANDSCAPES. THE FOUR SECTIONS
HAVE BEEN CONSTRUCTED AS INDE-
PENDENT UNITS, ALL TIED TOGETHER
BY THE RECURRING MENU AT THE TOP
OF THE PAGE.

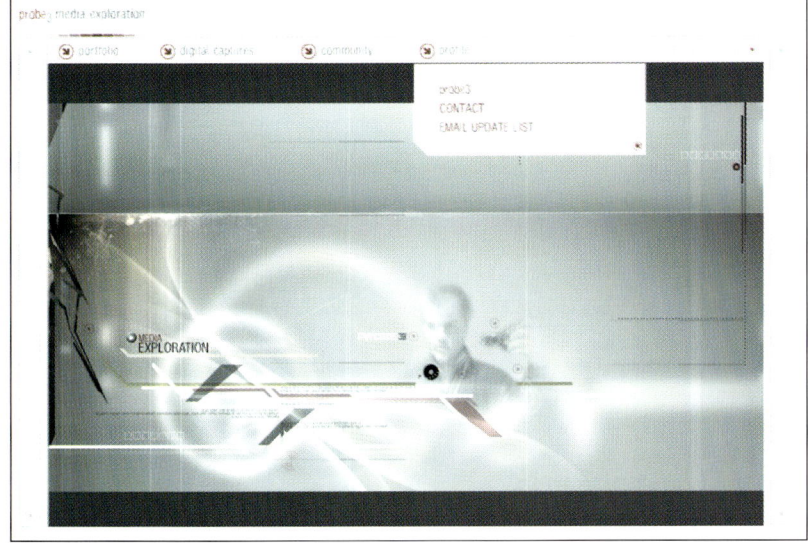

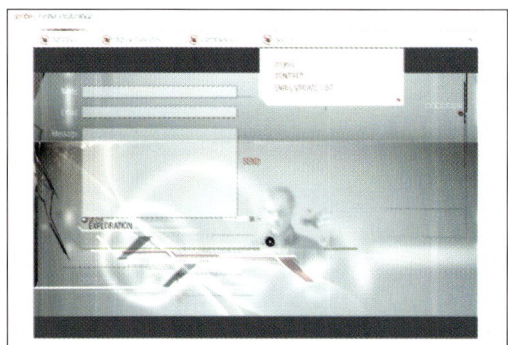

> NAME: TOPOREK.COM > SECTOR: GRAPHIC DESIGN > SPECS: FLASH, HTML > RATING: ORIGINALITY ☺ GRAPHICS ☺ INTERACTIVITY ☺ > CREDITS: SERGIO TOPOREK

The menu is in constant flux, its forms mutating, capable of taking on any number of shapes in any given section. Such versatility in an apparently static element puts this design in a class of its own.

As the element which grants strength to the contents, the color scheme is a highly important part of this central icon.

WWW.TOPOREK.COM

Bienvenido a Toporek.com

Un sitio enfocado en el arte, el diseño gráfico, la información, y su relación con la industria de la música.

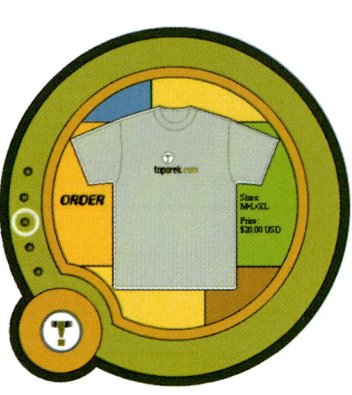

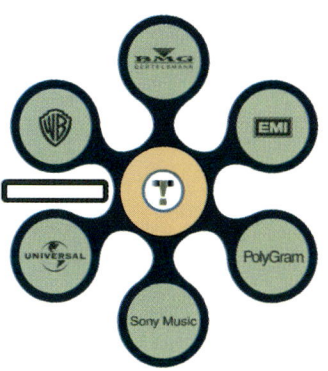

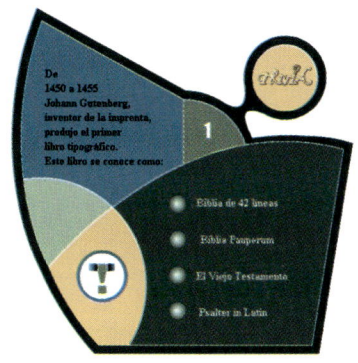

De
1450 a 1455
Johann Gutenberg,
inventor de la imprenta,
produjo el primer
libro tipográfico.
Esto libro se conoce como:

1

• Biblia de 42 líneas

• Biblia Pauperum

• El Viejo Testamento

• Psalter in Latin

Ven al OnLine
PressRoom de
Toporek.com

CANADA
128-5835 HAMPTON PLACE
VANCOUVER B.C. , V6T 2E2
TEL/FAX: (604) 224.6029
MOBILE: (604) 512.5646
MEXICO
AMSTERDAM 271 APT 402
COL. HIPODROMO CONDESA
06170, MEXICO D.F.
TEL/FAX (525) 564.2317
& (525) 564.2347
toporek@home.com

DOWNLOADS

ARTE Y DISEÑO / ART & DESIGN

MÚSICA / MUSIC

INTERESANTE / INTERESTING

WWW.FRANCOISE-HARDY.COM

> NAME: FRANÇOISE HARDY > SEC-
TOR: PERSONAL WEBSITE > SPECIFI-
CATIONS: FLASH > RATING: ORIGI-
NALITY ☺ GRAPHICS ☺ INTER-
ACTIVITY ☺ > DESIGNED BY: OEIL
POUR OEIL

A RICH BLACK BACKGROUND SERVES
TO ENHANCE AND HIGHLIGHT AN UN-
DERSTATED COLOR SCHEME, WHILE AL-
SO EMPHASIZING THE MENU. FIVE MAIN
SECTIONS FEATURE ON THE REVOLVING
HOMEPAGE MENU, EACH OF WHICH
CORRESPONDS TO A PHASE IN THE
WORK OF THIS SINGER-SONGWRITER
A DIVERGENCE FROM THE STANDARD,
STATIC MENU.

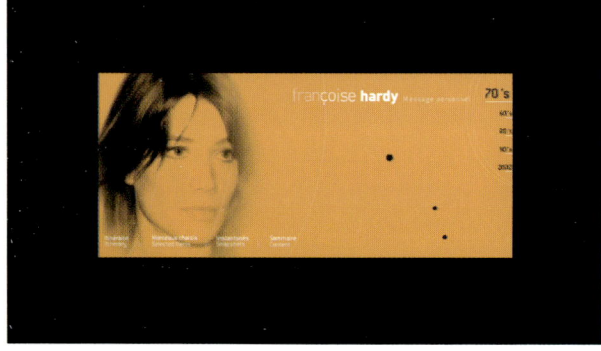

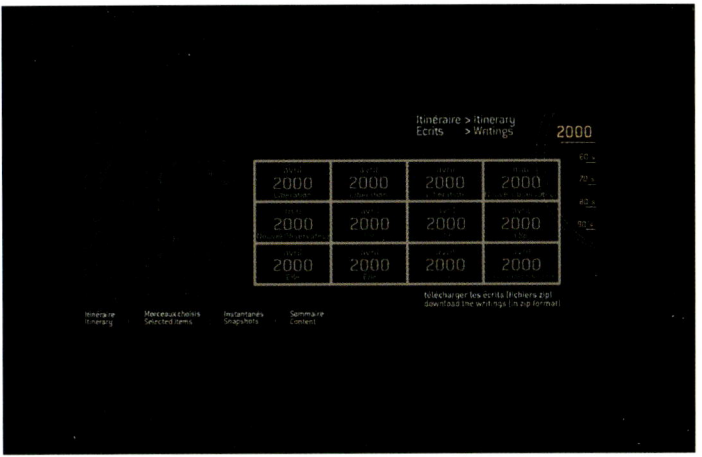

THE CONTENTS ARE CONTAINED WITH-
IN A CENTRAL RECTANGLE OCCUPYING
A MINIMUM OF SPACE ON THE
SCREEN. THERE IS NO NEED TO HUNT
AROUND FOR THE INFORMATION,
SCROLLING DOWN OR SHIFTING THE
PAGE FROM LEFT TO RIGHT, AS ALL
OF EACH PAGE'S INFORMATION IS DIS-
PLAYED ON A SINGLE SCREEN.

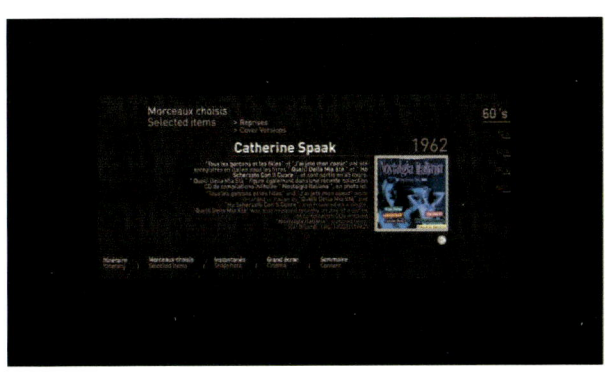

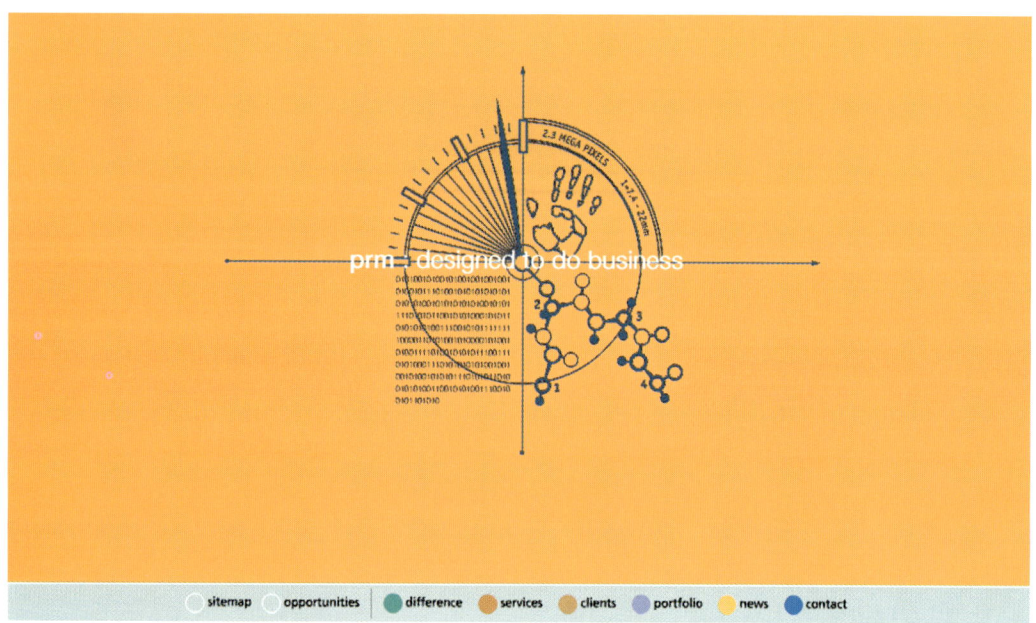

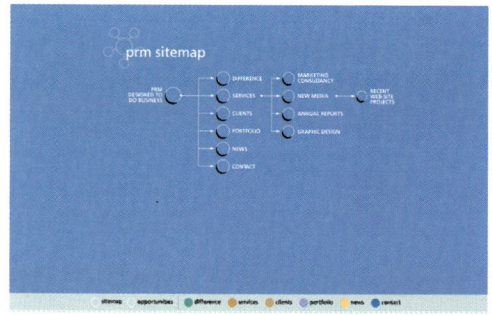

WWW.PRM.CO.UK

> NAME: PRM > SECTOR: ADVERTISING AGENCY
> SPECS: FLASH, HTML > RATING: ORIGINALITY 😐
> GRAPHICS 😐 > INTERACTIVITY 🙂

THE CAREFUL APPLICATION OF COLOR IS ALWAYS AN EFFECTIVE WAY OF DISCRIMINATING BETWEEN CONTENTS. A GRAPHIC COVER PAGE OF SORTS INTRODUCES EACH SUBSECTION, WHICH IS SUBTLY, YET CLEARLY, DIFFERENT FROM THE OTHERS. A HORIZONTAL MENU AT THE BOTTOM ORGANIZES ACCESS TO EACH LINK. THIS IS AN UNCHANGING ELEMENT, FOUND IN THE SAME SPOT THROUGHOUT THE SITE. TEXT HAS BEEN REMARKABLY CONDENSED SO THAT USERS CAN QUICKLY AND EASILY PULL UP INFORMATION, WITHOUT GETTING LOST IN A SEA OF WORDS - ONLY THE ESSENTIAL INFORMATION HAS BEEN INCLUDED.

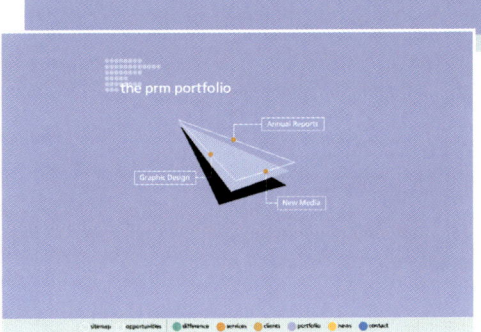

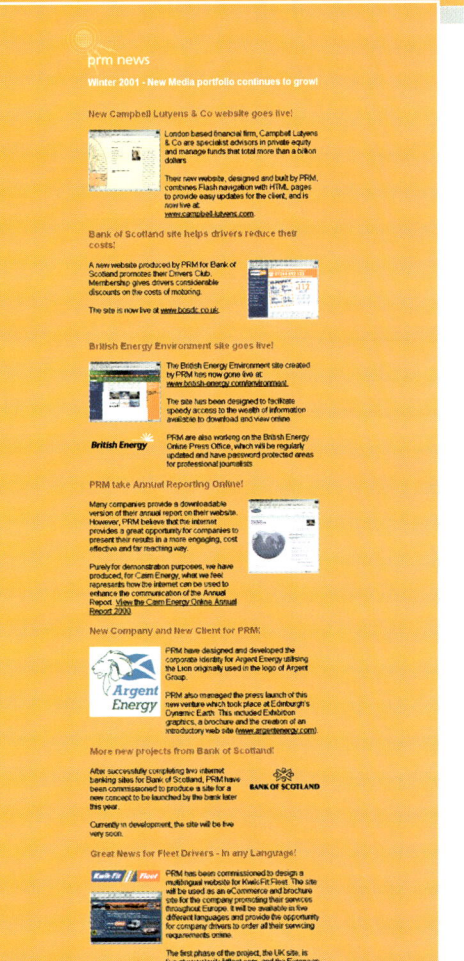

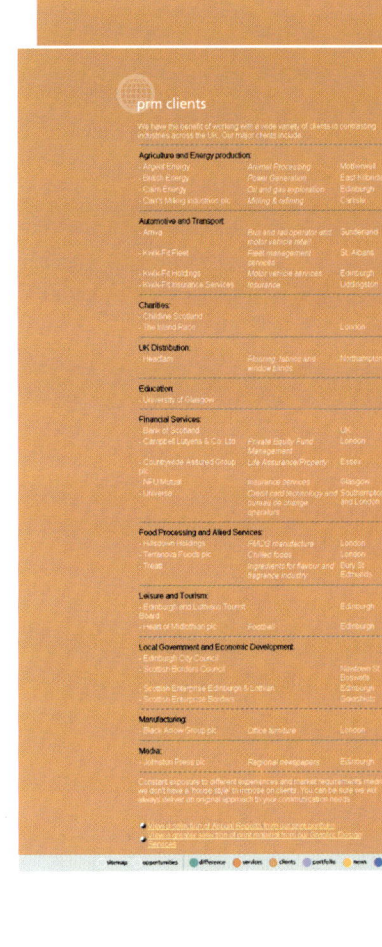

portfolio

news

clients

contact

>FF
99
00

>FF
00
00

>66
00
CC

>99
33
99

>00
99
99

the prm portfolio

Annual Reports

Graphic Design

New Media

sitemap opportunities difference services clients portfolio news contact

prm contact

Peter McGrail
PRM

Third Floor, 27/29 Berwick Street, London W1V 3RF
tel: 020 7336 0717   fax: 020 7287 8828

Slateford House, 53 Lanark Road, Edinburgh EH14 1TL
tel: 0131 455 7000   fax: 0131 455 8111

or email: peter@prm.co.uk

prm news

Winter 2001 - New Media portfolio continues to grow!

New Campbell Lutyens & Co website goes live!

London based financial firm, Campbell Lutyens & Co are specialist advisors in private equity and manage funds that total more than a billion dollars.

Their new website, designed and built by PRM, combines Flash navigation with HTML pages to provide easy updates for the client, and is now live at www.campbell-lutyens.com.

Bank of Scotland site helps drivers reduce their costs!

A new website produced by PRM for Bank of Scotland promotes their Drivers Club. Membership gives drivers considerable discounts on the costs of motoring.

The site is now live at www.bosdc.co.uk.

British Energy Environment site goes live!

The British Energy Environment site created by PRM has now gone live at: www.british-energy.com/environment/.

The site has been designed to facilitate speedy access to the wealth of information available to download and view online.

PRM are also working on the British Energy Online Press Office, which will be regularly updated and have password protected areas for professional journalists.

PRM take Annual Reporting Online!

Many companies provide a downloadable version of their annual report on their website. However, PRM believes that the internet provides a great opportunity for companies to present their results in a more engaging, cost effective and far reaching way.

Purely for demonstration purposes, we have produced, for Cairn Energy, what we feel represents how the internet can be used to enhance the communication of the Annual Report. View the Cairn Energy Online Annual Report 2000.

New Company and New Client for PRM!

PRM have designed and developed the corporate identity for Argent Energy utilising the Lion originally used in the logo of Argent Group.

PRM also managed the press launch of this new venture which took place at Edinburgh's Dynamic Earth. This included Exhibition graphics, a brochure and the creation of an introductory web site (www.argentenergy.com).

More new projects from Bank of Scotland!

After successfully completing two internet banking sites for Bank of Scotland, PRM have been commissioned to produce a site for a new concept to be launched by the bank later this year.

Currently in development, the site will be live very soon.

Great News for Fleet Drivers - in any Language!

PRM has been commissioned to design a multilingual website for Kwik-Fit Fleet. The site will be used as an eCommerce and brochure site for the company promoting their services throughout Europe. It will be available in five different languages and provide the opportunity for company drivers to order all their servicing requirements online.

The first phase of the project, the UK site, is live at www.kwik-fitfleet.com, and the European sites are due to be launched soon.

prm clients

We have the benefit of working with a wide variety of clients in contrasting industries across the UK. Our major clients include:

Agriculture and Energy production:		
Argent Energy	Animal Processing	Motherwell
British Energy	Power Generation	East Kilbride
Cairn Energy	Oil and gas exploration	Edinburgh
Castle Mining (dormition) plc	Milling & refining	Carlisle

Automotive and Transport:		
Arriva	Bus and rail operator and motor vehicle retail	Sunderland
Kwik-Fit Fleet	Fleet management services	St. Albans
Kwik-Fit Holdings	Motor vehicle services	Edinburgh
Kwik-Fit Insurance Services	Insurance	Uddingston

Charities:		
Chestline Scotland		
The Island Race		London

UK Distribution:		
Howdari	Awnings, fabrics and window blinds	Northampton

Education:		
University of Glasgow		

Financial Services:		
Bank of Scotland		UK
Campbell Lutyens & Co Ltd	Private Equity Fund Management	London
Countrywide Assured Group plc	Life Assurance/Property	Essex
NFU Mutual	Insurance Services	Glasgow
Universe	Credit card technology and bureau bill change operations	Southampton and London

Food Processing and Allied Services:		
	CO2 manufacture	London
Tenderoy Foods plc	Chilled foods	London
Treatt	Ingredients for flavour and fragrance industry	Bury St Edmunds

Leisure and Tourism:		
Edinburgh and Lothians Tourist Board		Edinburgh
Heart of Midlothian plc	Football	Edinburgh

Local Government and Economic Development:		
Edinburgh City Council		
Scottish Borders Council		Newtown St Boswells
Scottish Enterprise Edinburgh & Lothian		Edinburgh
Scottish Enterprise Borders		Galashiels

Manufacturing:		
Black Arrow Group plc	Office furniture	London

Media:		
Johnston Press plc	Regional newspapers	Edinburgh

Constant exposure to different experiences and market requirements mean we don't have a 'house style' to impose on clients. You can be sure we will always deliver an original approach to your communication needs.

sitemap opportunities difference services clients portfolio news contact

> NAME: PC.BASE > SECTOR: DESIGN STU-
DIO AND COMPUTER COURSES > SPECS:
FLASH, HTML > RATING: ORIGINALITY 😐
GRAPHICS 😐 INTERACTIVITY 😐 > CRED-
ITS: RICHARD KAMMERER

THIS PROJECT IS ACTUALLY TWO IN ONE, WITH
TWO DIFFERENT DESIGNS CORRESPONDING TO
DIFFERENT BRANCHES OF THE SAME COMPANY.
THE CONTENTS OF THE FIRST HALF ARE SUMMA-
RIZED IN A MENU AT THE TOP OF THE PAGE. THE
SECOND HALF WORKS WITH THE SIMPLICITY OF
WHITE AND A MINIMUM OF GRAPHICS AND TEXT,
WHICH ARE DISTRIBUTED ASYMMETRICALLY.

ONE OF THE LINKS STUBBORNLY MAINTAINS ITS
HORIZONTAL LAYOUT, WHICH OBLIGES USERS TO
SCROLL LENGTHWISE, ACROSS THE PAGE, TO
VIEW ALL OF THE CONTENTS. THIS IS A RE-
FRESHING DEPARTURE FROM THE STANDARD
PATTERN OF RUNNING CONTENTS DOWN THE
PAGE, A PRACTICE THAT PLACES LIMITS ON HOW
A PAGE CAN BE ARRANGED.

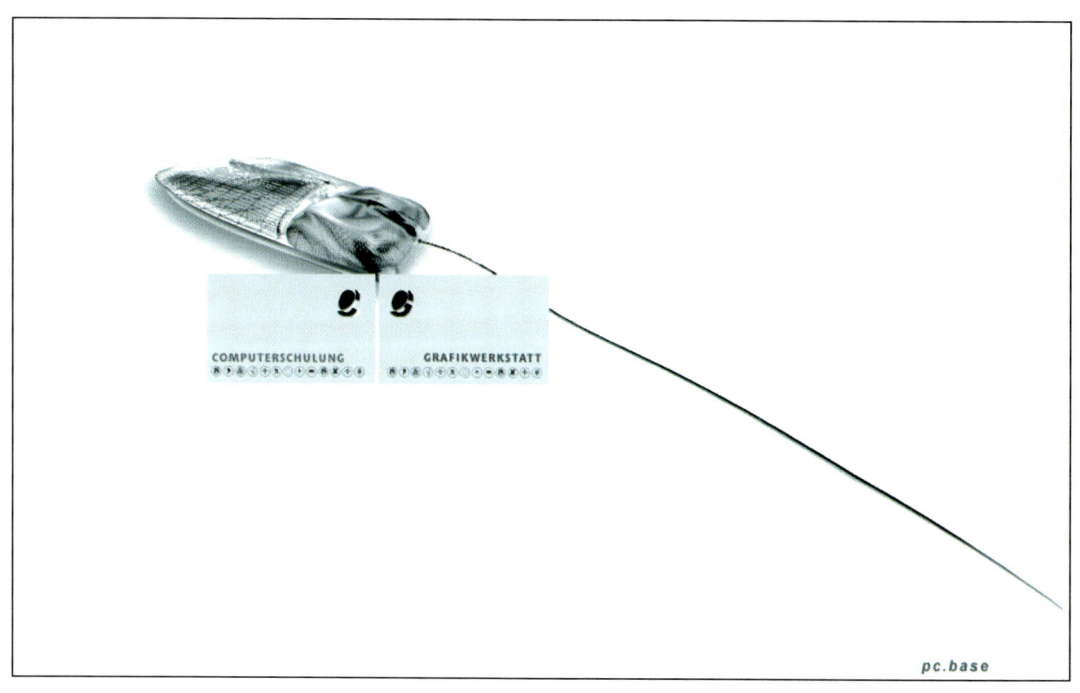

WWW.PC-BASE.COM

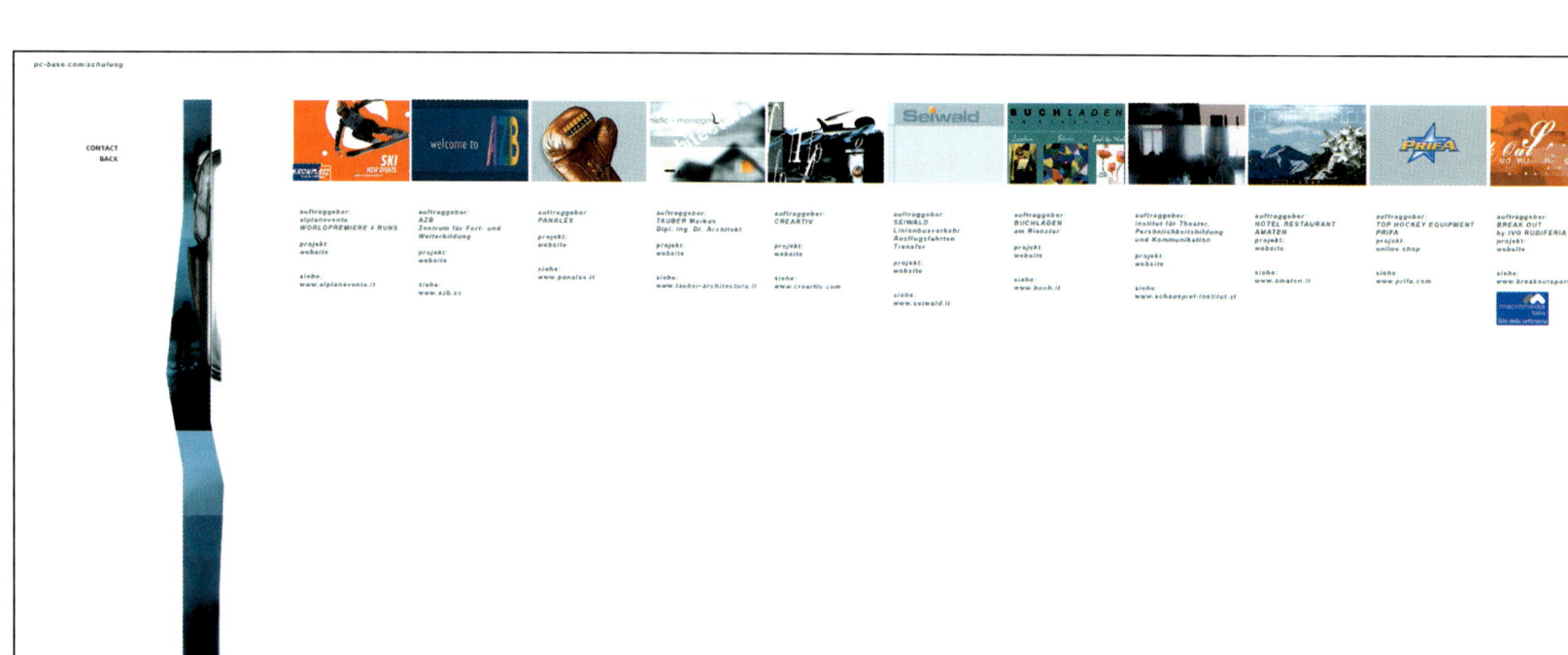

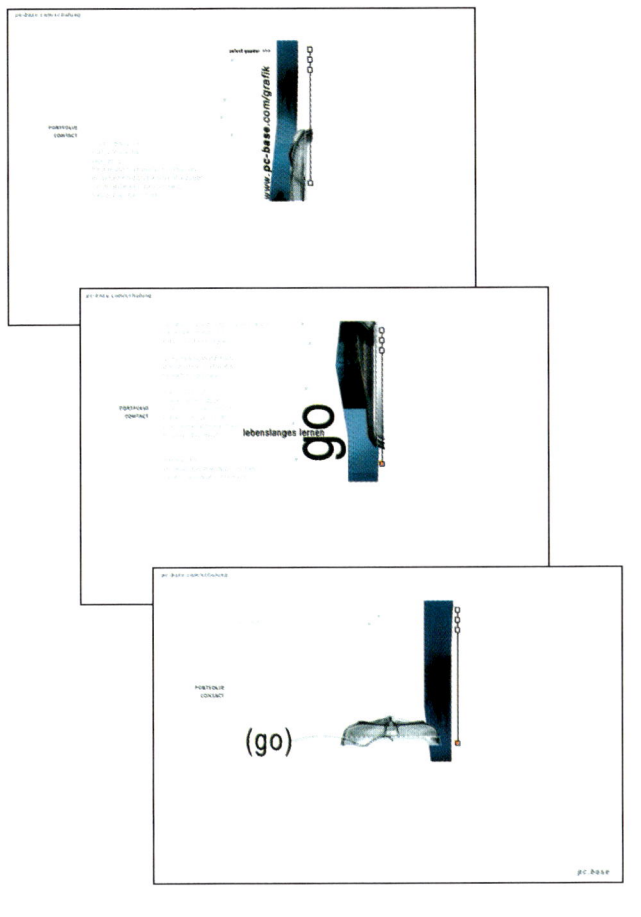

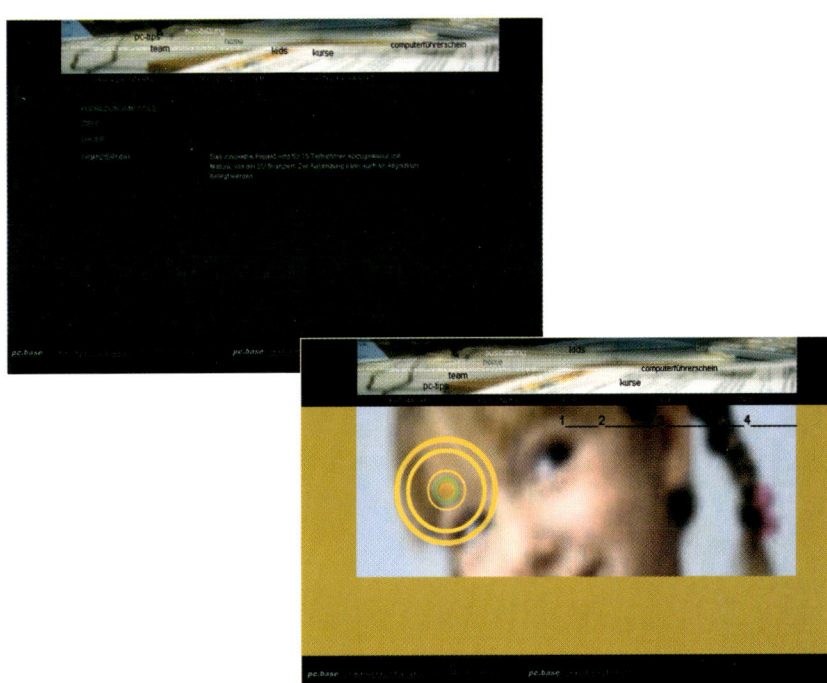

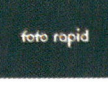

WWW.CPMMOBILEMARKETING.COM

> NAME: CPM MOBILE MARKETING

> SECTOR: MARKETING > SPECS:

FLASH, HTML > RATING: ORIGINALITY ☺

GRAPHICS ☺ INTERACTIVITY ☺

> CREDITS: ULTIMAGROUP

BELOW: SAMPLES OF THE INTRODUC-
TORY ANIMATION.

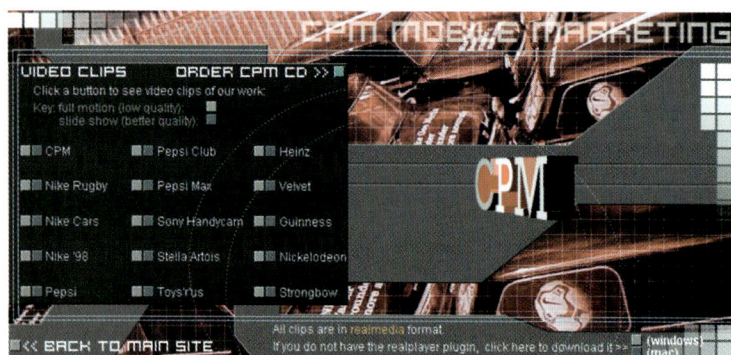

THE SOMEWHAT COLD, HARD GRAPH-
ICS AND SELECTION OF TONES GRANT
A SENSATION OF VERSATILITY IN A
SITE WHERE EACH SECTION EVOLVES
AND BECOMES MORE INDEPENDENT
FROM THE OTHERS. ALL INDICATIONS
AND SIGNALS ARE PERFECTLY COHER-
ENT AND RESPECT THE UNITY OF THE
OVERALL COMPOSITION.

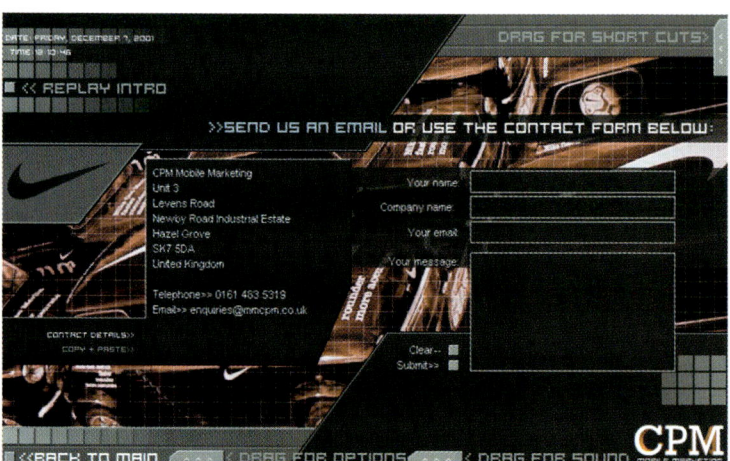

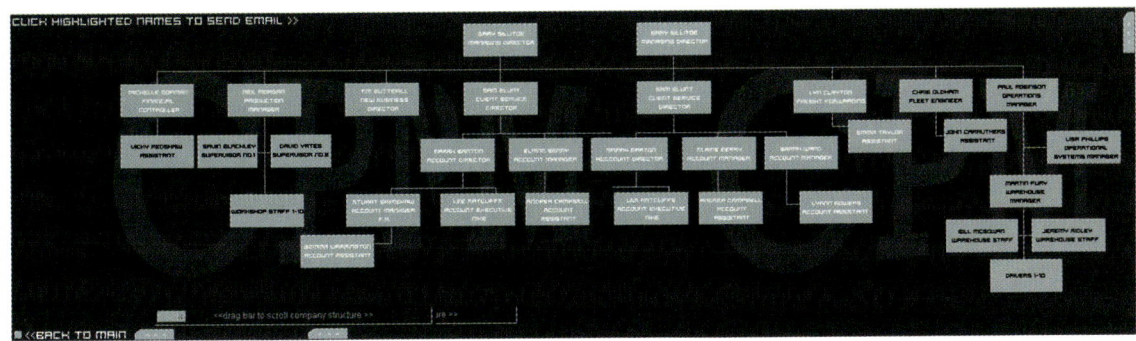

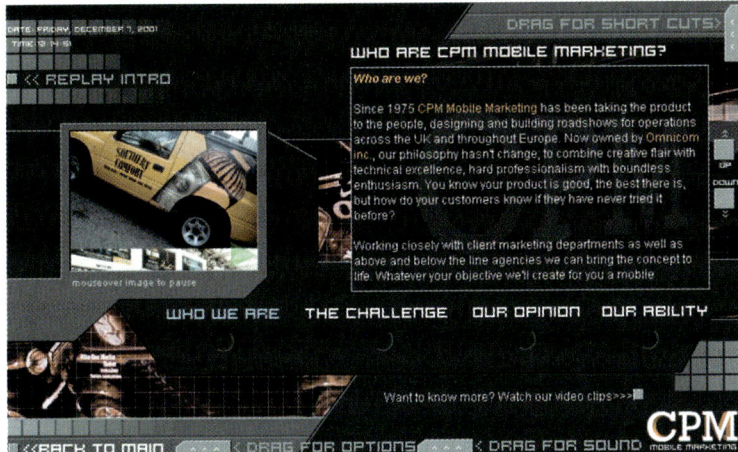

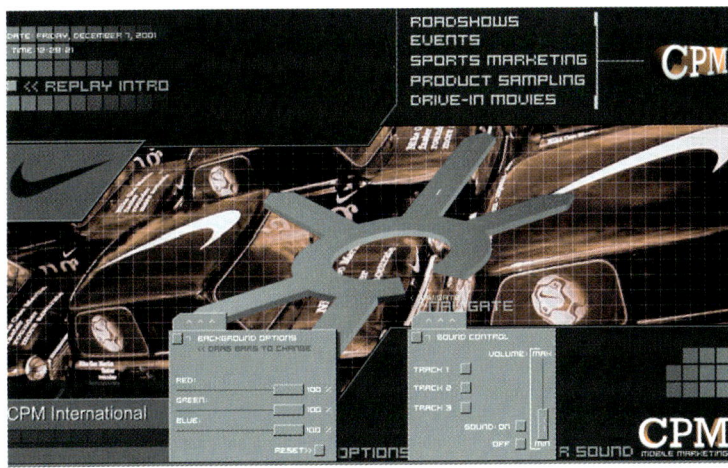

ABOVE, DETAILS OF TWO OF THE UN-
FOLDING PALETTES THAT PERSONAL-
IZE THE SOUND AND BACKGROUND
OF THE DESIGN.

WWW.MIRARCREATIVO.COM

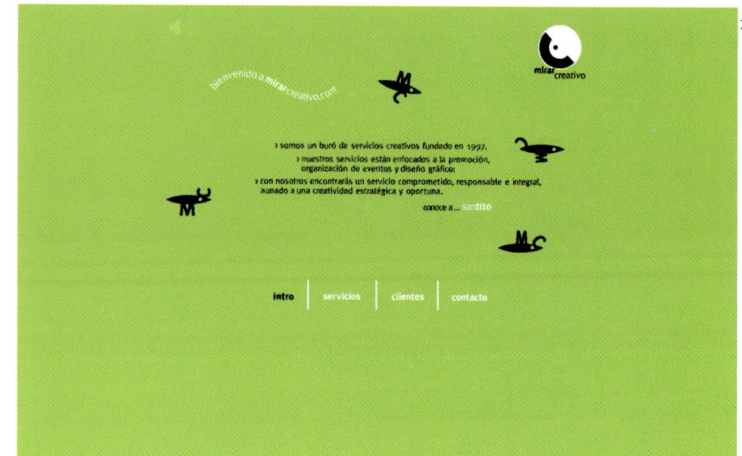

> NAME: MIRAR CREATIVO > SECTOR: DESIGN STUDIO > SPECS: FLASH, HTML > RATING: ORIGINALITY ☺ GRAPHICS ☺ INTERACTIVITY ☺ > CREDITS: GABRIEL RIVERA

INTERACTIVE ANIMATION IS, BEYOND DOUBT, THIS SITE'S SELLING POINT. HERE, A ROVING ICON SHOWS THE WAY AROUND EACH SECTION.

LIKEWISE, AN ENTERTAINING ICON HAS BEEN INCLUDED RIGHT FROM THE START AS A WAY OF PASSING THE TIME WHILE WAITING FOR THE SITE TO COME UP.

THESE FEATURES WORK WELL TO-GETHER IN THIS FRESH AND SIMPLE DESIGN, WHICH MAKES SPARING USE OF GRAPHICS AND INCORPORATES A SOOTHING GREEN FOR CAPTURING THE ATTENTION.

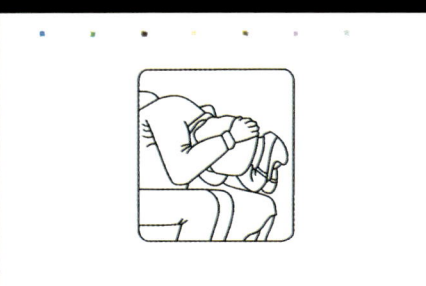

NAME: ENSEMBLE > SECTOR: MUSICAL GROUP > SPECS: FLASH > RATING: ORIGINALITY ☺ GRAPHICS ☺ INTER-ACTIVITY ☹ > CREDITS: FREESURF

The use of color is this site's key to clearly differentiating each section. Only a few pencilled strokes have been sufficient to change the tone of the expansive white background.

Likewise, icons and graphics were kept to a minimum when constructing this site. A central illustration becomes the menu, which is organized from top to bottom and quickly displays the site's limited contents.

info

"Ensembles album resonates powerfully with moods for daydreaming and introspection and is even at times heavy hearted. It illuminates intense emotions.Ensemble are an extroadinary new duo you should definitely keep an eye on ". (the guardian)

"Sublime and experimental electronica from French/English duo Ensemble, making 'sketch proposals' one of rephlex's most abstract yet strangely accessible releases in a long while. Each low and muted electronic track is taken over by a female voice,the beatific qualities nearly masking the fact that this is pretty extreme stuff ". (jockey slut)

"Ensemble représente une alternative mélodique a l'electronica expérimentale telle qu'on la conçoit en Grande-Bretagne du coté d'Autechre ou d'Oval en Allemagne. Ce qui n'est pas peu dire. En ajoutant un chant évanescent a leur musique cérébrale, Ensemble construit un univers extremement personnel tout en offrant de mystérieuse réminiscences a l'auditeur averti ". (coda magazine)

"Irgendwie haftet ihnen trotz Harddisk Manipulation immer noch dieses Homerecordingflair an, die Dichte im Sound, die sehr warm wirkt. Die Melodien (gesungen) stören sich überhaupt nicht an dem Geplockere und den funkegen Miniaturarrangements, sondern bilden einfach einen zweiten Layer. So eine Art Teletubbys für Erwachsene. Skurril, so halluziniert, dass es auch die Wirklichkeit sein könnte, versessen auf Wiederholungen, und dennoch immer sehr klar ". (de bug)

Ensemble was created in 1998 by Olivier Alary, his objective was to create a musical project which would combine avant-garde aesthetics / production systems with the harmonies of pop music.
The first album "sketch proposals", which could described as explorative pop music, was released in 2000 by rephlex records. Ensemble also released and remixed several tracks on multiple labels (sub-rosa, morr music)

Currently Ensemble is producing a new album as well as working on an interactive sound installation incorporating algorythmic computer programming. ▼

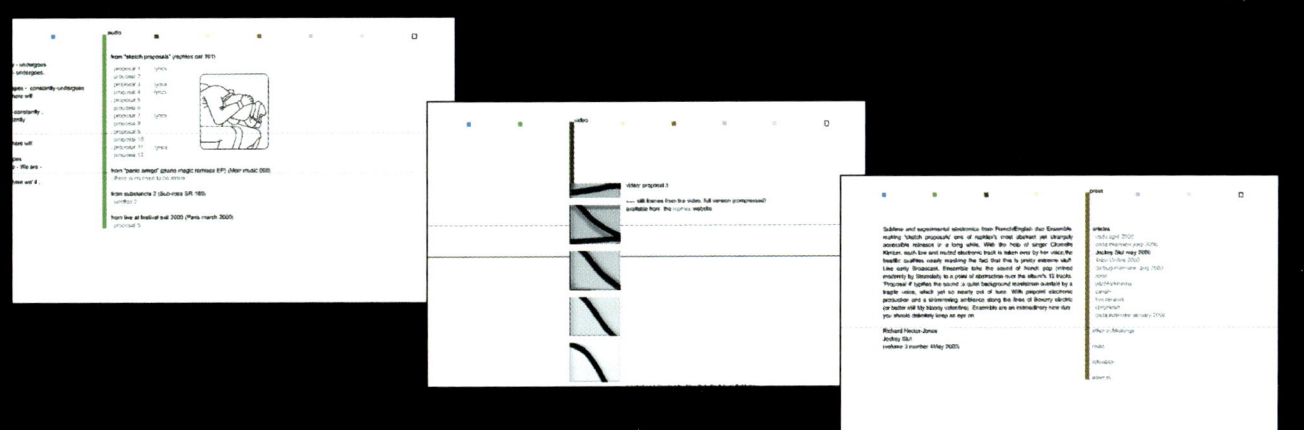

> NAME: RUBEN MEGIDO > SECTOR: PERSONAL PORTFOLIO > SPECIFICATIONS: HTML > RATING: ORIGINALITY ☺ GRAPHICS ☺ INTERACTIVITY ☺ > CREDITS: RUBEN MEGIDO

WWW.RUBENMEGIDO.COM/HTML/PAGINA_PRINCIPAL.HTM

THE USE OF SCHEMATIC GRAPHICS ACCOMPANIED BY VIBRANT COLORS DRAWS ATTENTION TO THE SIMPLICITY OF THE DRAWINGS, WHICH ARE ELEVATED TO THE LEVEL OF SYMBOLICALLY-LOADED ICONS.

A GENERAL MENU APPEARING ON THE LEFT SIDE OF THE HOMEPAGE MAKES ACCESS TO SUBSEQUENT PAGES EASY.

THE SAME GRAPHIC COMPOSITION IS REPEATED THROUGHOUT THE PROJECT, MAINTAINING AN OVERALL SENSE OF UNITY.

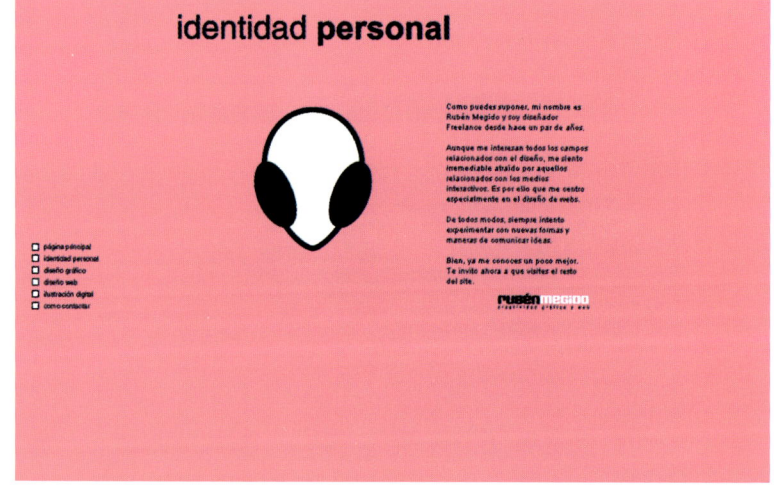

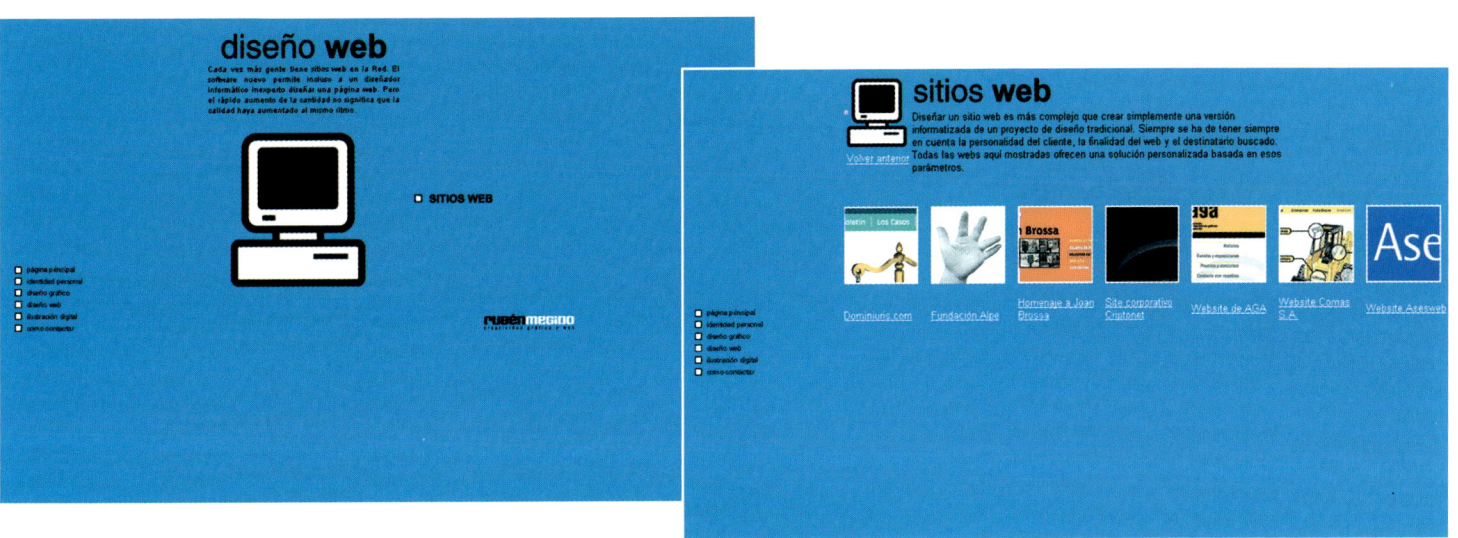

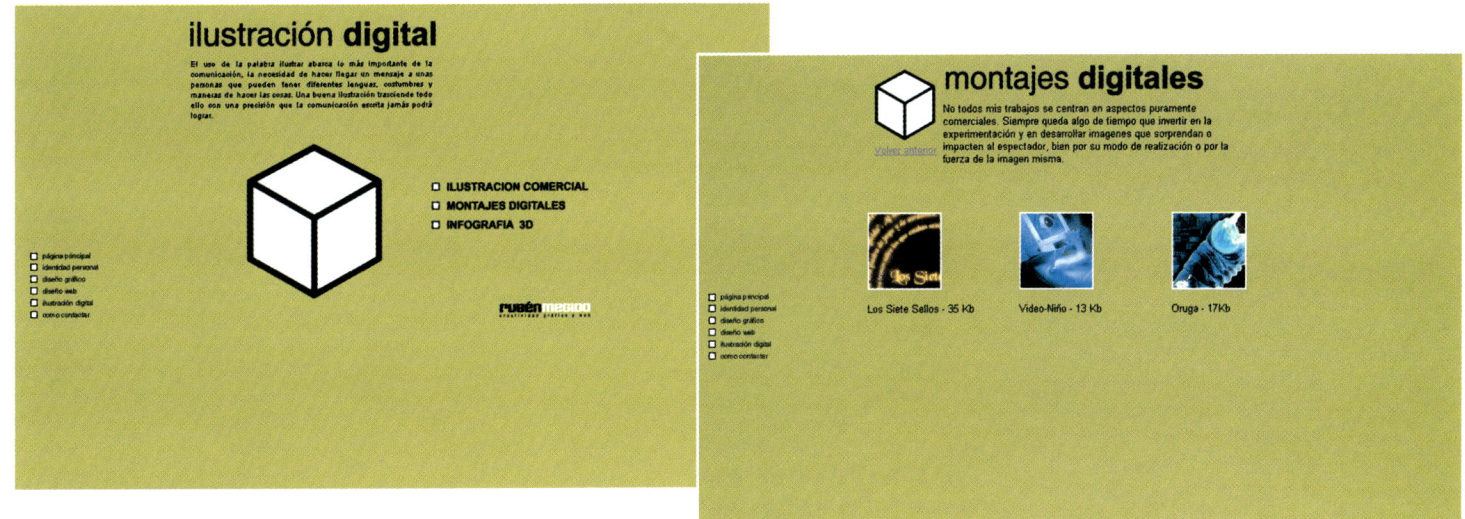

NY'S EMBLEMATIC COLORS, PREDOMI-
NATE ON THIS SITE. THE MAIN MENU
AND THE SEQUENCE OF PHOTO-
GRAPHS, BOTH HORIZONTAL, SHOW
UP ON ALL SUBSEQUENT PAGES. A
SECOND VERTICAL MENU EXPANDS
ON THE CONTENTS.
NAVIGATION IS FLUID AND UNAM-
BIGUOUS. ANY LINK CAN BE EASILY
ACCESSED, WITH NO COMPLICATIONS.

> NAME: HIGGINS HOMES > SEC-
TOR: REAL ESTATE > SPECS: FLASH,
HTML > RATING: ORIGINALITY 😐
GRAPHICSM 😐 INTERACTIVITY 😊
> CRÉDITOS: FRONTMEDIA

DEVELOPMENTS · LATEST NEWS · ABOUT HIGGINS HOMES · REGISTER · NHBC WARRANTY · CONTACT US · USEFUL LINKS

WELCOME TO HIGGINS HOMES

Latest news from Higgins:

- Higgins Homes launch cutting edge new homes website
- From Yuppies to Silver Surfers
- Higgins Homes win top web award

macromedia United Kingdom SITE OF THE WEEK

Welcome to the Higgins Homes Limited website. Please browse our easy to navigate site for details of all current, and future new homes developments and to see examples of the individual and distinctive homes already being enjoyed by our purchasers at some of the finest locations across Essex, Hertfordshire and London.

For your convenience, this interactive site carries up-to-the-minute information on the price & status of each property in a given development, along with floor plans, a site plan, a local area map, and full details on how to contact us.

WWW.HIGGINSHOMES.CO.UK

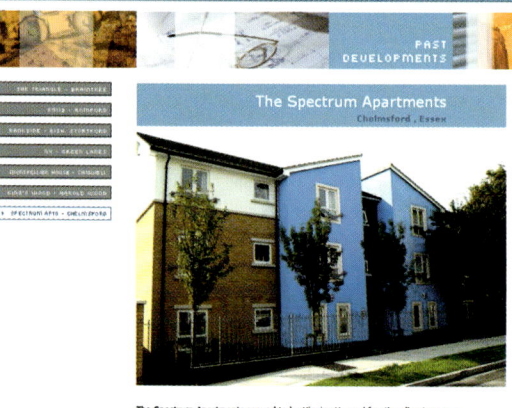

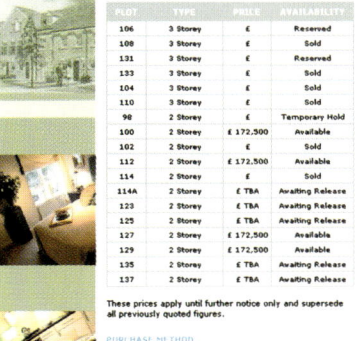

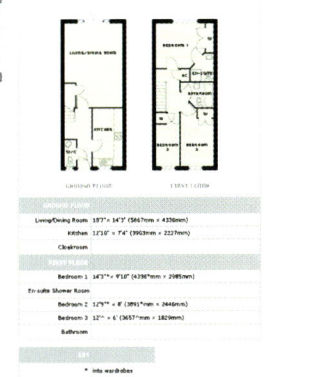
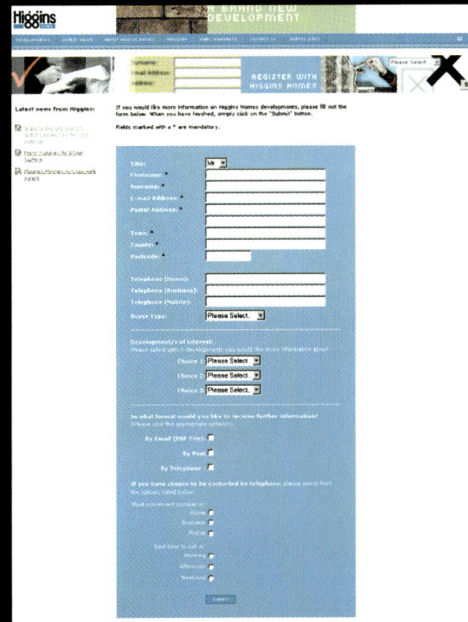
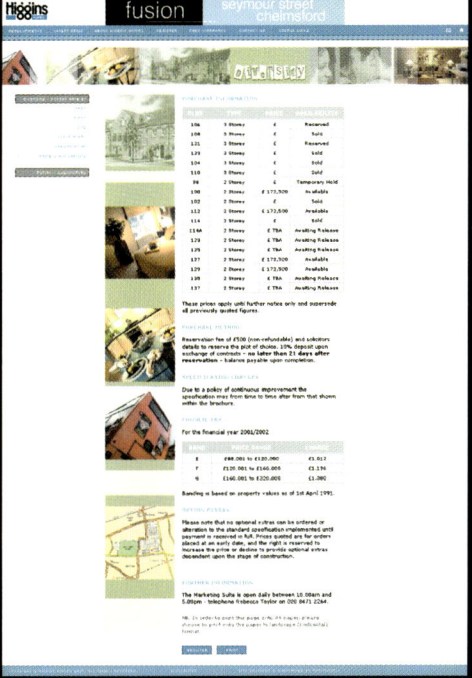

WWW.KOMASOLUTIONS.IT

> NAME: KOMASAULT > SECTOR: WEB DE-
SIGN > SPECIFICATIONS: FLASH, HTML
> RATING: ORIGINALITY 😐 GRAPHICS 😐
INTERACTIVITYC 🙂 > DESIGNED BY:
KOMASAULT

THE CONTENTS ON THIS SITE APPEAR
AND DISAPPEAR FROM THE CENTRAL
WINDOW AS AN ELEMENT RESEMBLING
THE SHUTTER OF A CAMERA SNAPS OPEN
AND SHUT.

GRAPHICALLY SPEAKING, THE SIDEBAR
MENU DISPLAYS A HOMOGENEOUS DE-
SIGN, CHANGING ONLY IN THE VARIOUS
SUB-SECTIONS.

THE USE OF COLOR HAS BEEN TIGHTLY RE-
STRICTED TO A RANGE OF GREY TONES
WHICH SEEM TO EMULATE LIGHT REFLECT-
ED FROM A SHEET OF WARPED METAL,
CREATING A FUTURISTIC FEEL.

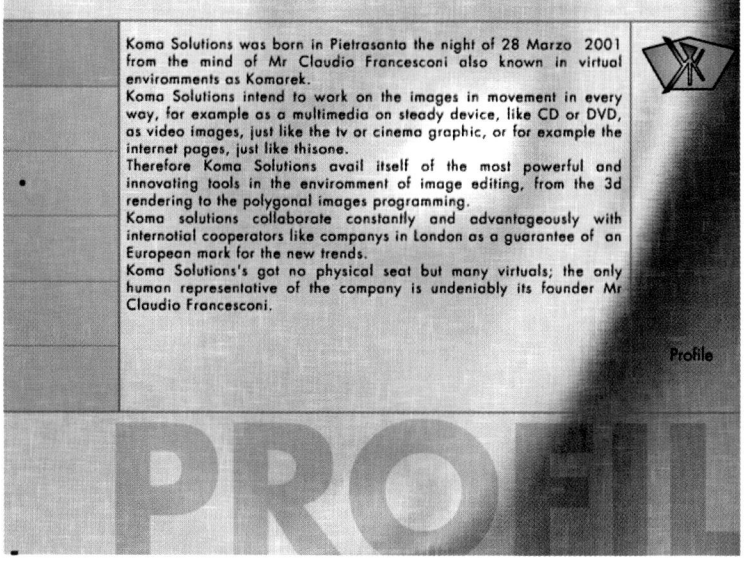

Quarta Group (Monaco)

visita il sito

Quarta Group e' un' agenzia internazionale di pubblicita' che si occupa di promuovere prodotti-eventi a tutti i livelli. Fra i vari clienti troviamo la British American Tobacco e la IP. Quarta Group ha sede a Montecarlo nel Principato di Monaco

Multimedia

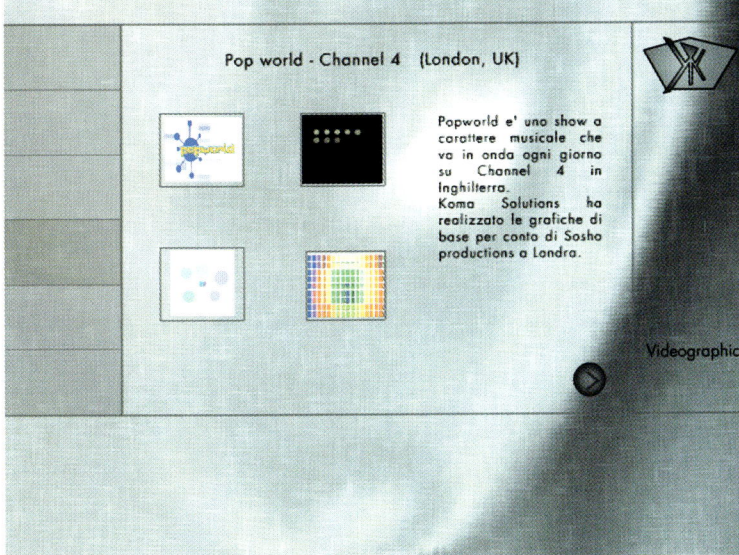

Pop world - Channel 4 (London, UK)

Popworld e' uno show a carattere musicale che va in onda ogni giorno su Channel 4 in Inghilterra.
Koma Solutions ha realizzato le grafiche di base per conto di Sosho productions a Londra.

Videographic

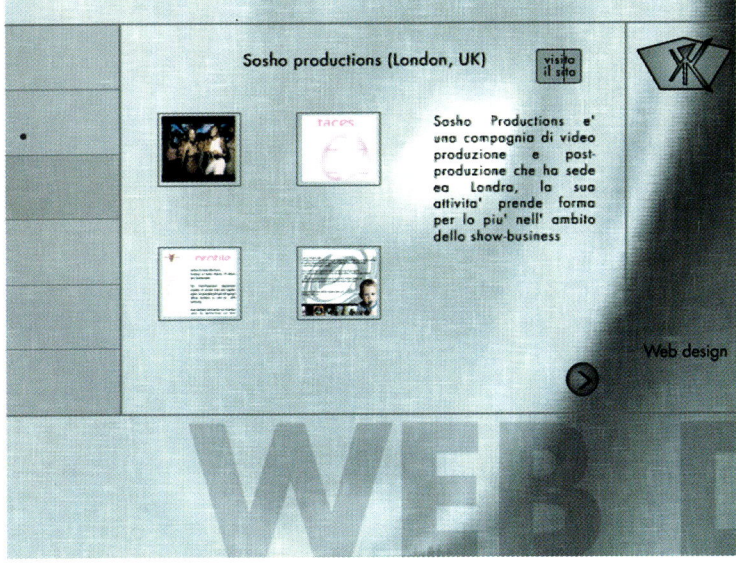

Sosho productions (London, UK)

visita il sito

Sosho Productions e' una compagnia di video produzione e post-produzione che ha sede ea Londra, la sua attivita' prende forma per lo piu' nell' ambito dello show-business

Web design

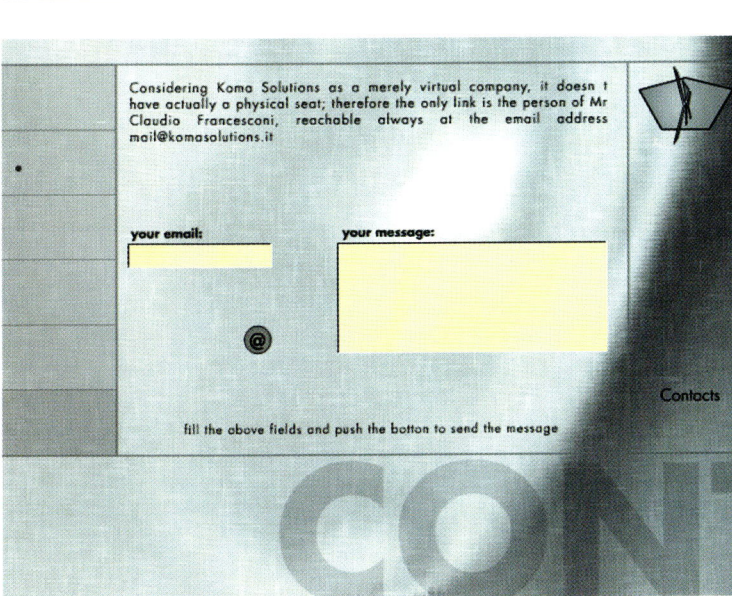

Considering Koma Solutions as a merely virtual company, it doesn t have actually a physical seat; therefore the only link is the person of Mr Claudio Francesconi, reachable always at the email address mail@komasolutions.it

your email:

your message:

@

fill the above fields and push the botton to send the message

Contacts

WWW.ONE9INE.COM

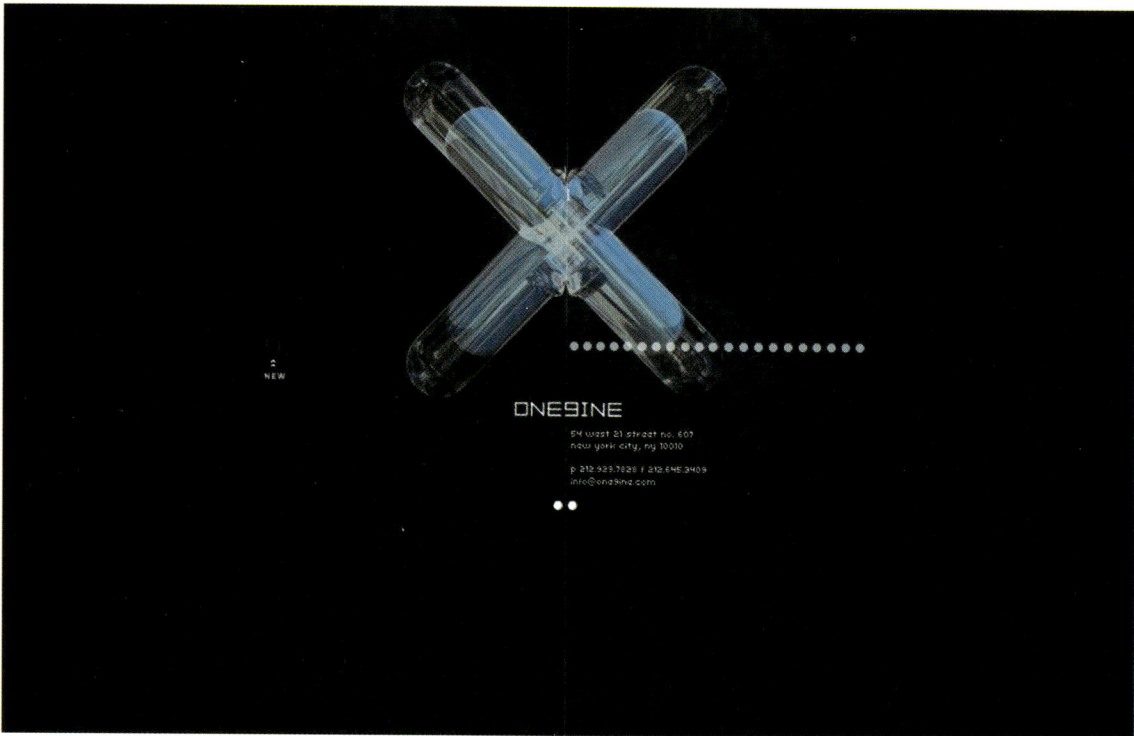

> NAME: ONE9INE > SECTOR: MULTI-MEDIA DESIGN STUDIO > SPECIFICATIONS: FLASH, HTML > RATING: ORIGINALITY ☺ GRAPHICS ☺ INTERACTIVITY ☺ > DESIGNED BY: ONE9INE

EACH PAGE OF THIS SITE FEATURES THE SAME BASIC LAYOUT, VARYING ONLY WITH THE INTRODUCTION OF NEW CONTENTS ON THE UPPER PART OF THE SCREEN. THUS, EACH NEW SCREEN DOES NOT MANAGE TO BREAK FREE FROM THE PREVIOUS ONE.

ASIDE FROM THE DIRECT LINKS, THERE ARE A NUMBER OF OTHERS WHICH GRANT A GREATER WEALTH OF VARIETY TO THE PROJECT.

The animation, placed front and center on the page, serves to visually structure the design. Its shape, dynamism and translucent colors make it an appealing and original piece.

Translucence is an inventive means of implying depth.

Likewise, impenetrable black serves as an excellent backdrop for strengthening the importance of the texts and graphics.

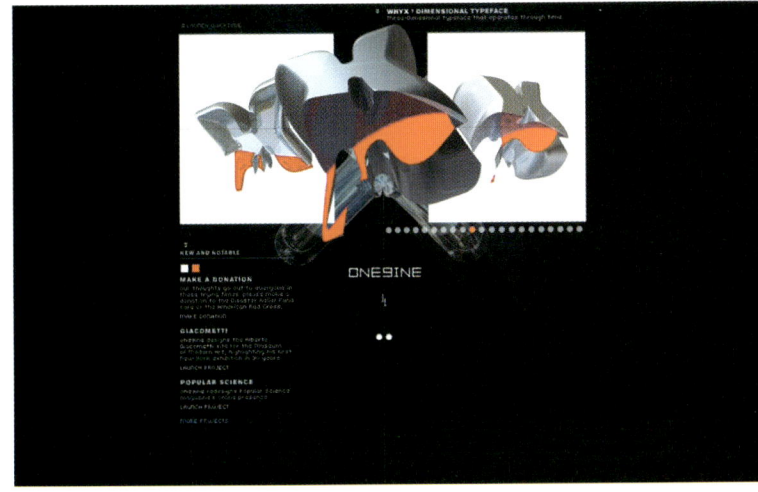

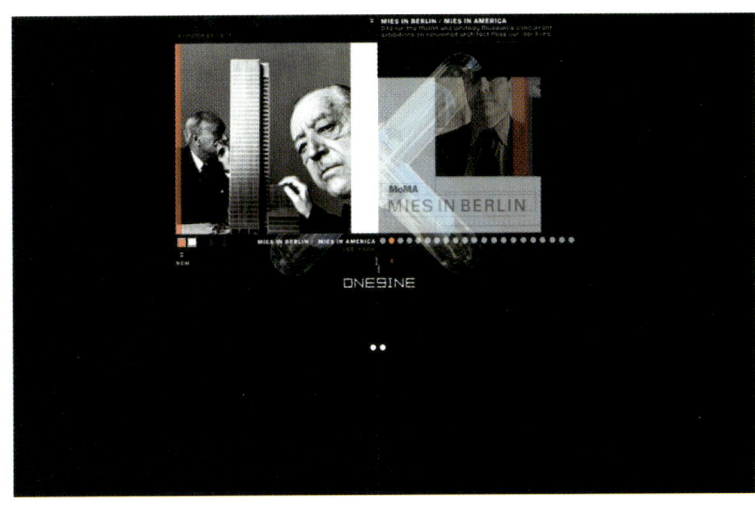

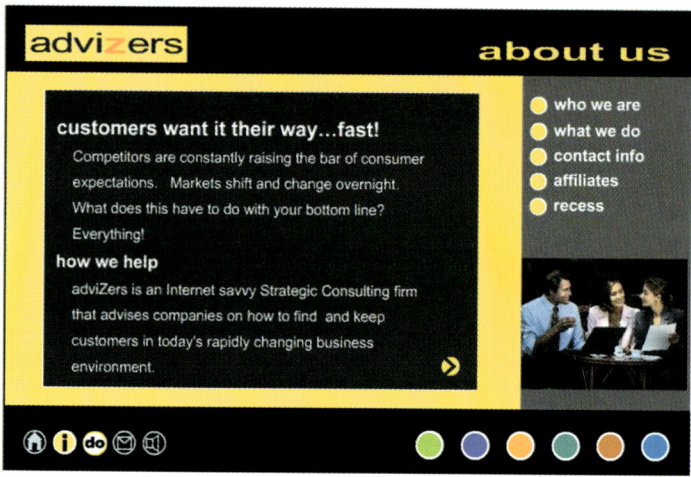

WWW.ADVIZERS.COM

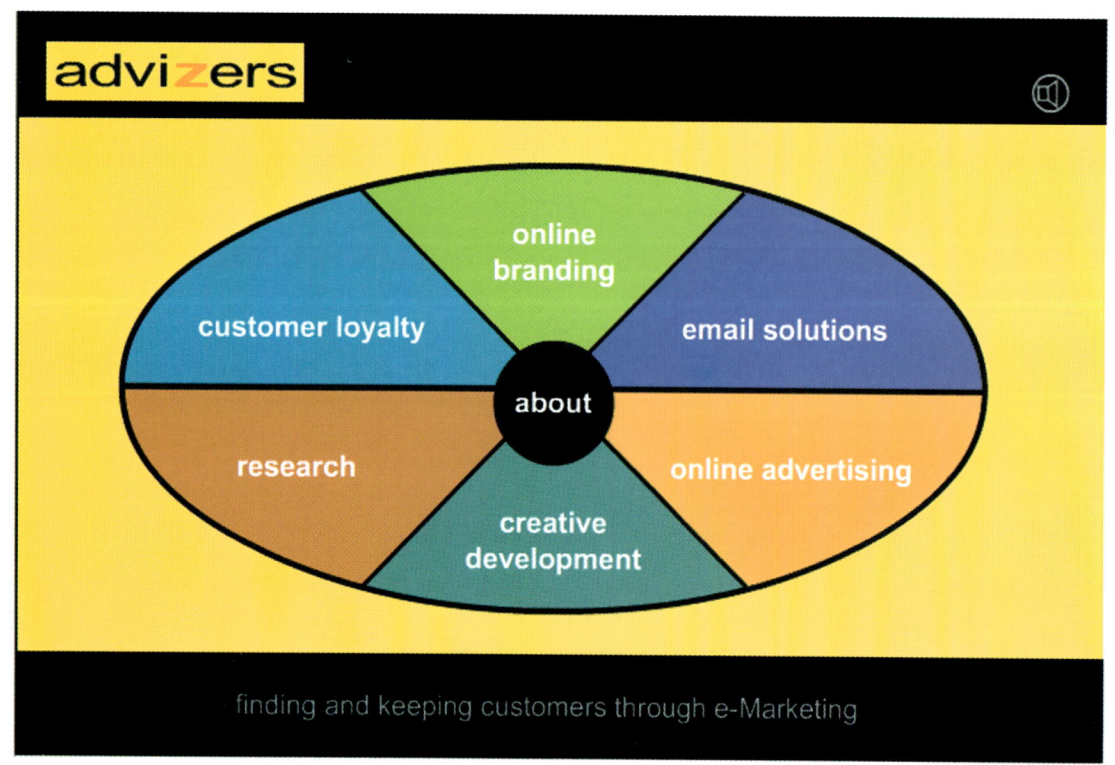

> NAME: ADVIZERS > SECTOR: MAR-KETING > SPECIFICATIONS: FLASH, HTML > RATING: ORIGINALITY 😐 GRAPHICS 😐 INTERACTIVITY 😊 > DESIGNED BY: NET STRATEGIES

THE MARKED CONTRAST IN COLORS CLEARLY EMPHASIZES THE VARIOUS LINKS FEATURED IN THIS WEB. THE PURITY OF PRIMARY AND SECONDARY COLORS ON A BLACK BACKGROUND SHOWS OFF THE CONTENTS.

HIGH VISIBILITY OF CLICKABLE GRAPHICS MAKES NAVIGATION EASY AND AVOIDS CONFUSION. BASIC IN-TUITION GUIDES THE USER THROUGH THESE PAGES.

STARTING FROM THE HOMEPAGE, THE DESIGN SCHEME IS CENTERED ON THE SAME PATTERN. THUS, DIF-FERENT SECTIONS DISPLAY THE SAME COHERENCY AND GRAPHIC CONTINUITY.

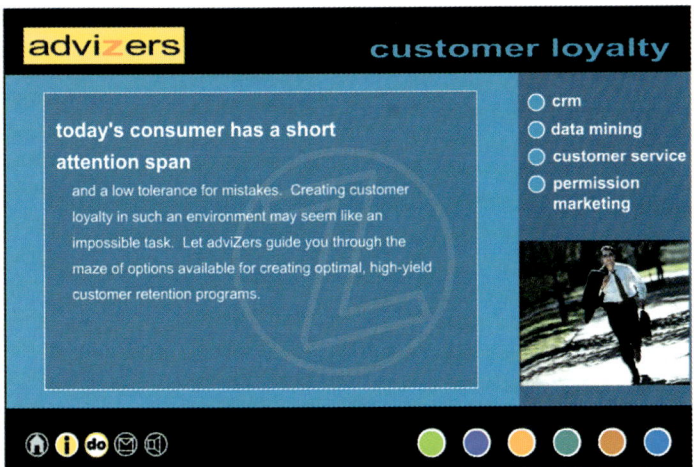
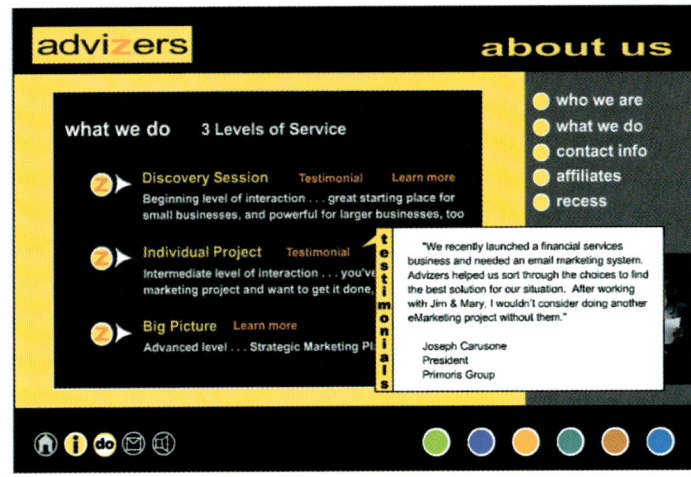
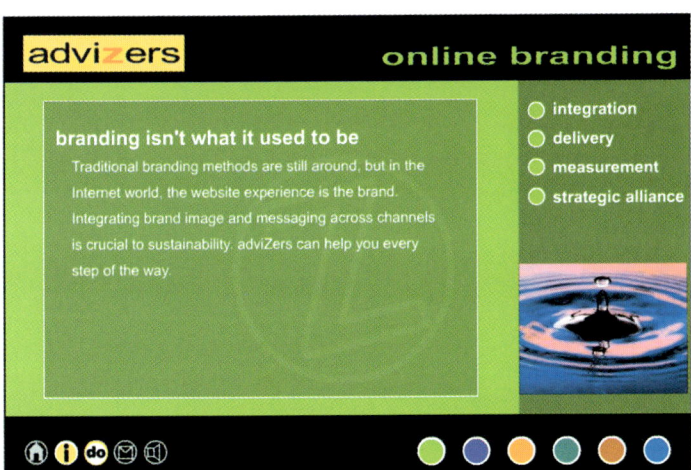
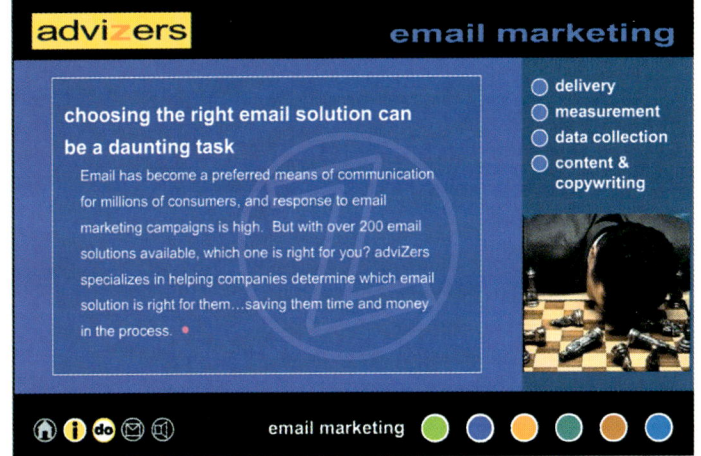
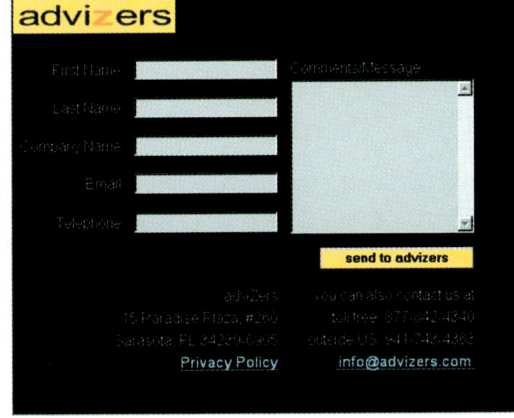

WWW.THUNKDESIGN.COM

> NAME: THUNK DESIGN

> SECTOR: ADVERTISING AGENCY

> SPECS: FLASH, HTML

> RATING: ORIGINALITY ☹

GRAPHICS ☹ INTERACTIVITY ☺

> CREDITS: FRONTMEDIA

THE DIFFERENT SHADES CHOSEN FUL-
FIL THE ROLE OF CLASSIFYING CON-
TENTS, AS SEEN ON THE SIMPLE, YET
EFFECTIVE, MENU AT THE TOP. MORE
THAN A NECESSARY FEATURE, THIS
MENU IS THE CENTRAL ELEMENT
WHICH DRAWS THE DESIGN TOGETHER.

A DIFFICULTY ARISES, HOWEVER, IN
THE FACT THAT NO SECTION STANDS
OUT ABOVE THE REST, MEANING THE
USER HAS TO WANDER AIMLESSLY
THROUGH ANY NUMBER OF PAGES BE-
FORE FINDING THE DESIRED CONTENT.

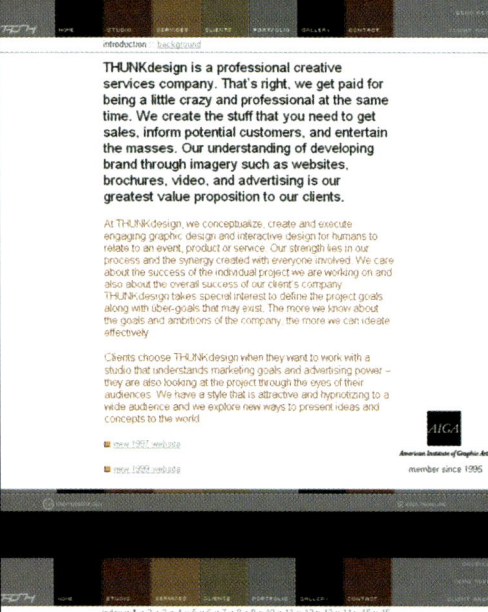

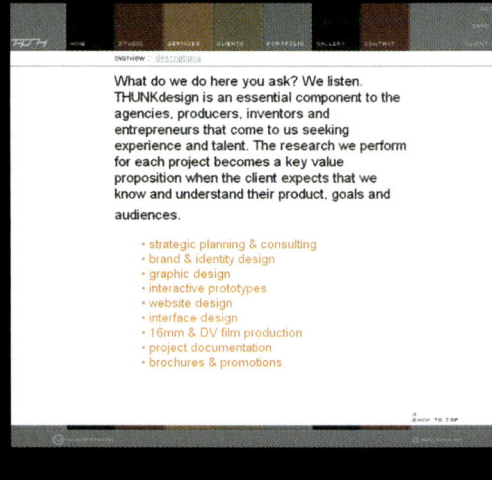

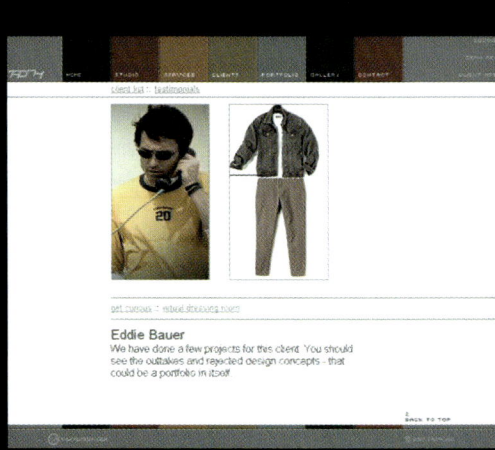

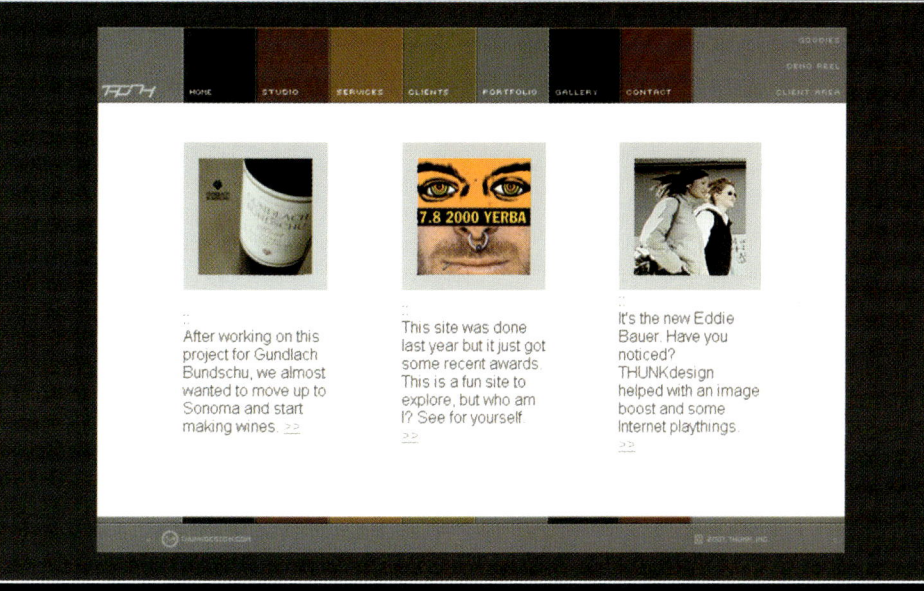

After working on this project for Gundlach Bundschu, we almost wanted to move up to Sonoma and start making wines. >>

This site was done last year but it just got some recent awards. This is a fun site to explore, but who am I? See for yourself. >>

It's the new Eddie Bauer. Have you noticed? THUNKdesign helped with an image boost and some Internet playthings. >>

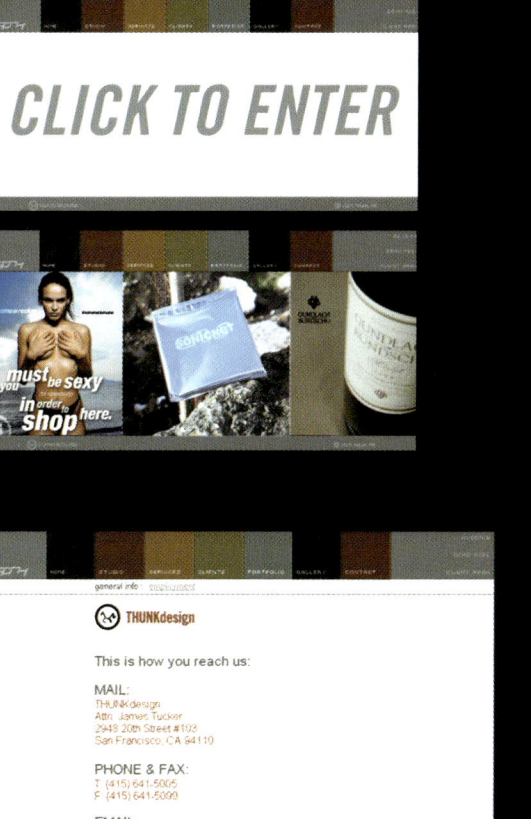

CLICK TO ENTER

must you be sexy in order to shop here.

THUNKdesign

This is how you reach us:

MAIL:
THUNKdesign
Attn: James Tucker
2948 20th Street #103
San Francisco, CA 94110

PHONE & FAX:
T: (415) 641-5005
F: (415) 641-5099

EMAIL:
>>
>>

Howdy! If you are a client of ours then login below. If you want to be a client and have a slick, new, sexy area for the development of your project then contact James Tucker.

Name::
Password::

Login

screen 1

project brief:

Gundlach-Bundschu Winery

Before we started, THUNKdesign recommended writing a project brief that outlined the deployment plan and strategy for the multiple projects that intertwined each other. The 50-page document specified marketing objectives, design goals, advertising strategies, brand essentials, information design, technology, and costs.

BACK TO TOP

> NAME: DILATED STUDIO > SEC-
TOR: MULTIMEDIA DESIGN, PROMO-
TION AND MARKETING > SPECIFICA-
TIONS: FLASH, HTML > RATING:
ORIGINALITY 😐 GRAPHICS 😐
INTERACTIVITY 😊 > DESIGNED BY:
DILATED STUDIO

A SINGLE STRUCTURE UNITES THE
NAVIGATION PROCESS IN THIS SITE.
LINKS TO DIFFERENT SECTIONS ARE
DISTRIBUTED AROUND THE RECTAN-
GULAR CENTRAL DESIGN ELEMENT,
WHICH SERVES AS A WINDOW ON ALL
SUCCEEDING PAGES.

ALL OF THE TEXTUAL INFORMATION
IS PLACED WITHIN THE FRAMEWORK
OF THIS STYLIZED, SOMEWHAT FU-
TURISTIC OBJECT.

THE COLOR IN THIS DESIGN SCHEME
SERVES TO HIGHLIGHT CONTENTS AND
ONLY A SUBTLE VARIATION OF BACK-
GROUND TONES LETS US KNOW THAT
WE HAVE COME UPON A NEW LINK.

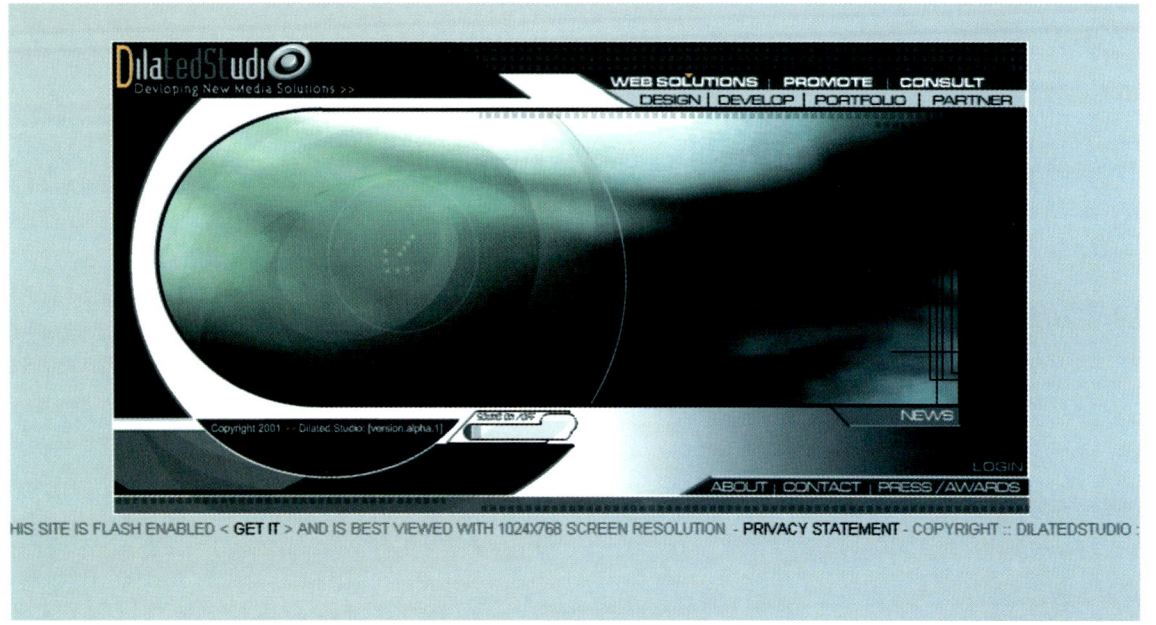

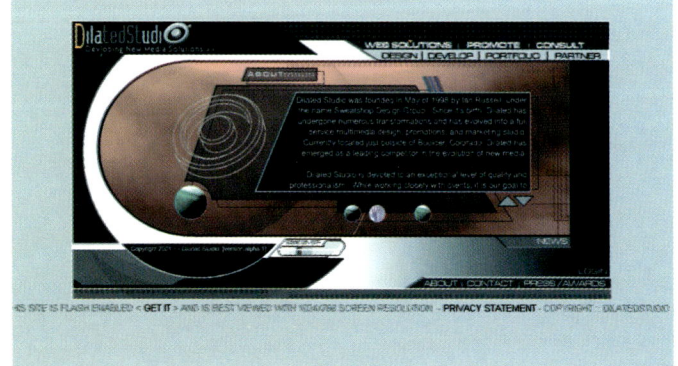

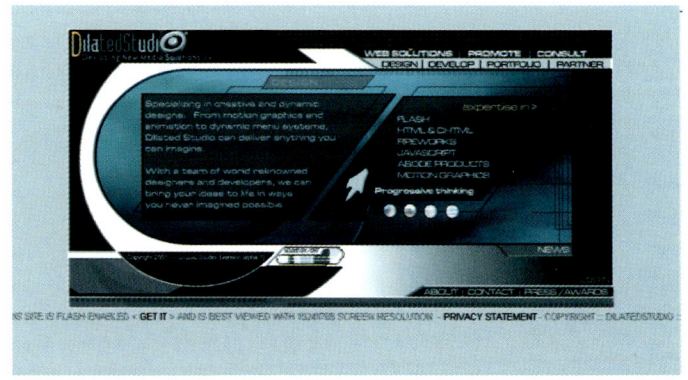

WWW.DILATEDSTUDIO.COM

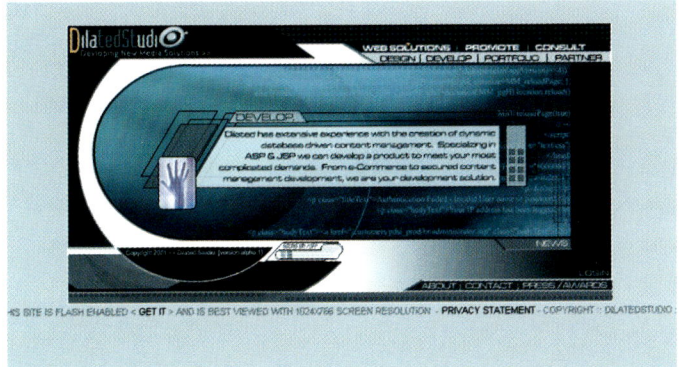

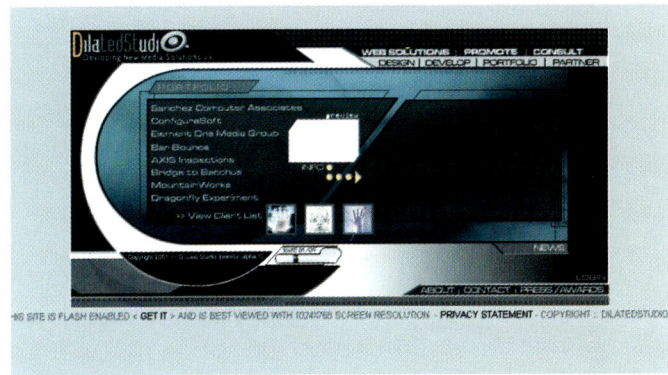

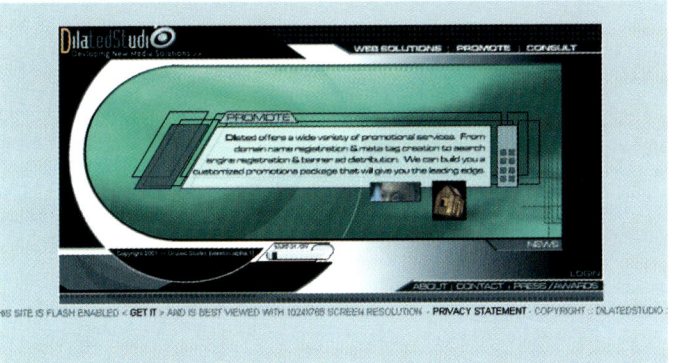

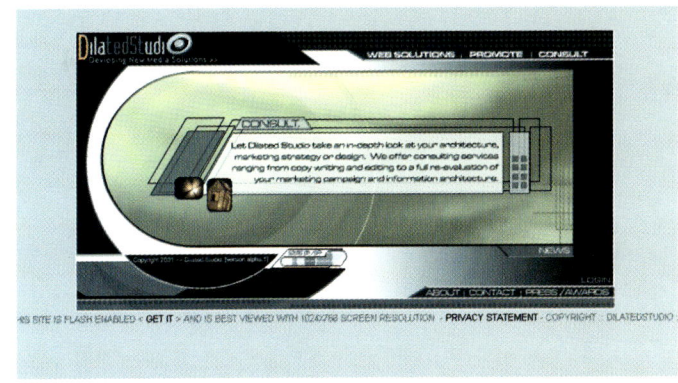

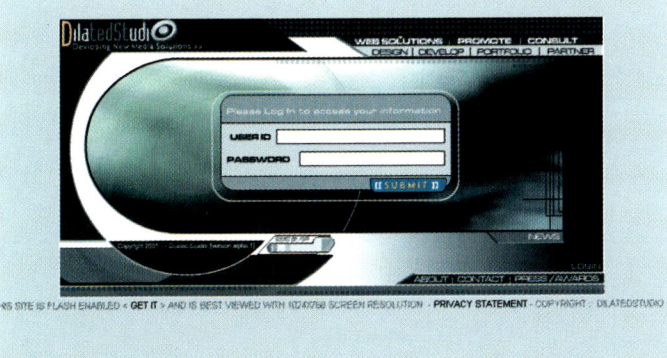

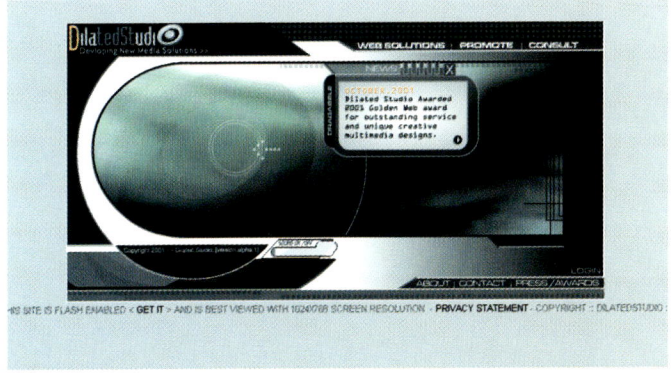

WWW.DAKOTA.DE

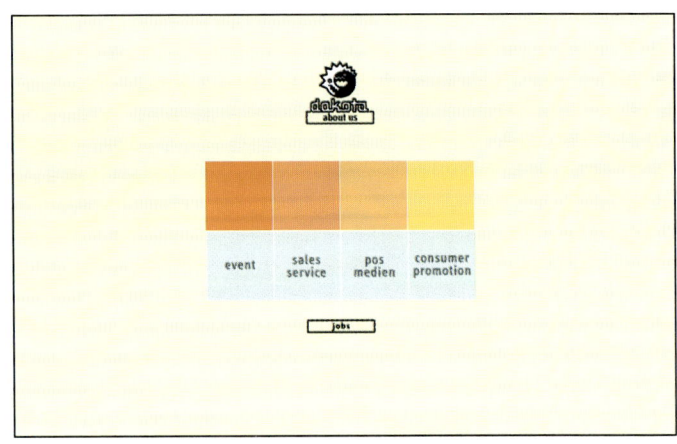

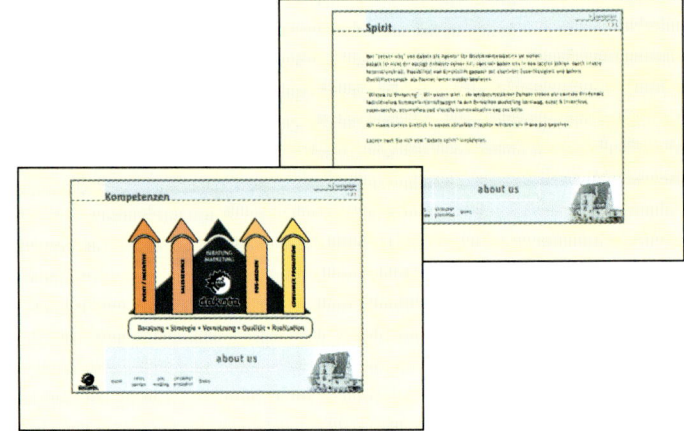

> NAME: DAKOTA > SECTOR: MAR-
KETING > SPECS: FLASH, HTML
> RATING: ORIGINALITY 😐 GRAPH-
ICS 😐 INTERACTIVITY 🙂

THE WARMTH OF YELLOW SERVES AS
THE STRUCTURING PRINCIPLE BE-
HIND A SYMMETRICALLY BALANCED
COMPOSITION, WHICH IS CONTAINED
WELL WITHIN THE LIMITS OF THE DI-
MENSIONS OF THE SCREEN.

HOMOGENEITY IS MAINTAINED
THROUGHOUT THE SITE BY THE SAME
BASIC DESIGN SCHEME. THUS, THE
MESSAGE IS COMMUNICATED QUICKLY,
AND USERS FIND WHAT THEY ARE
LOOKING FOR WITHOUT LOSING TIME
WONDERING WHAT THE SITE IS ABOUT.

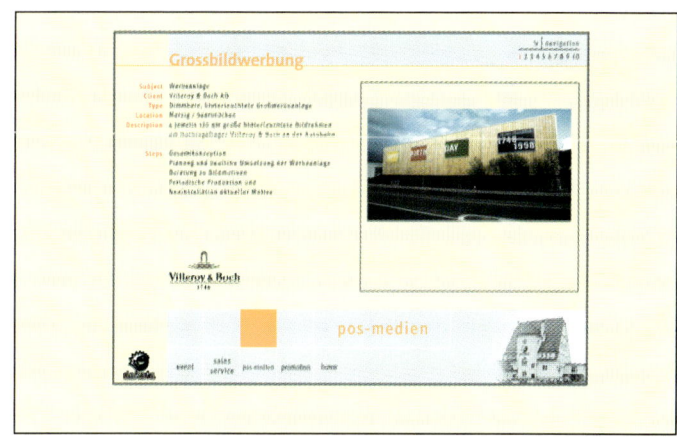

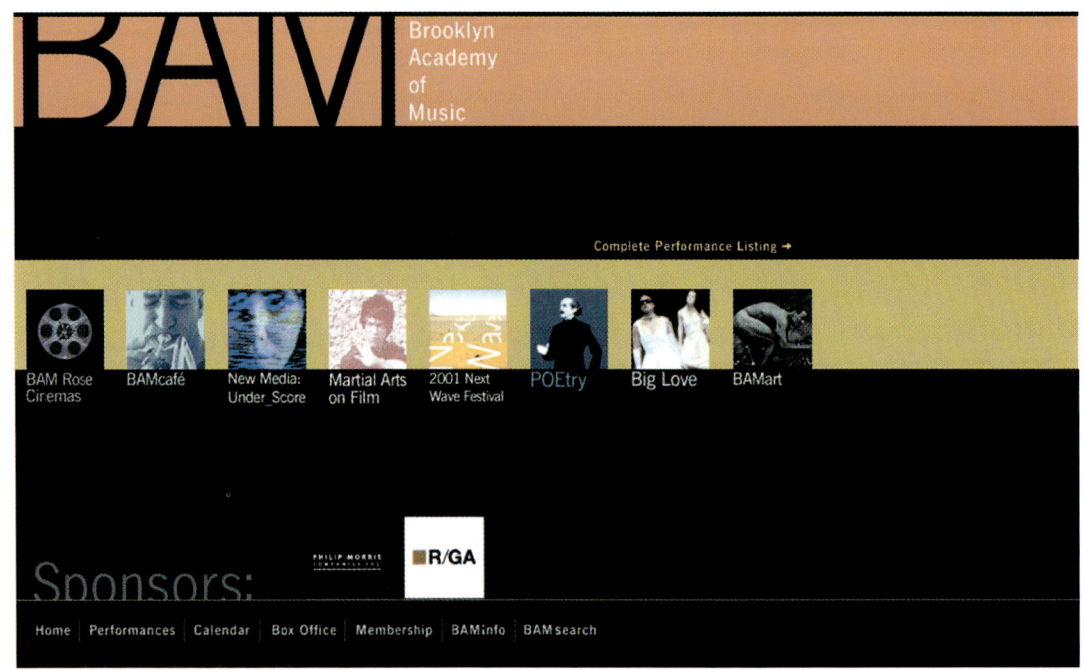

WWW.BAM.ORG

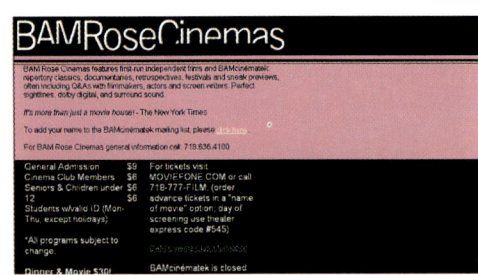

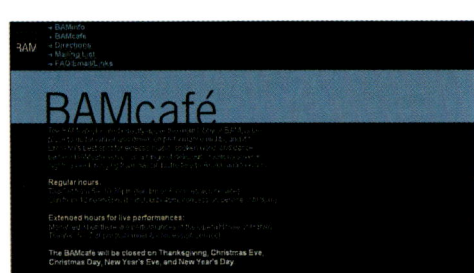

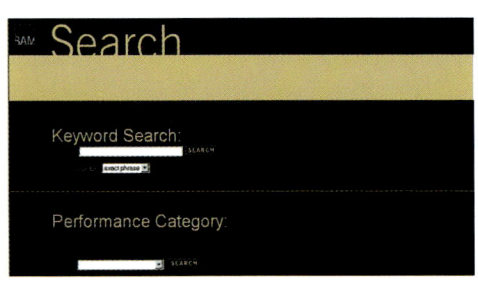

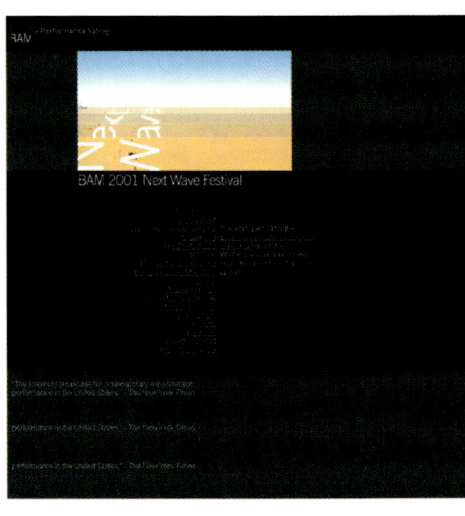

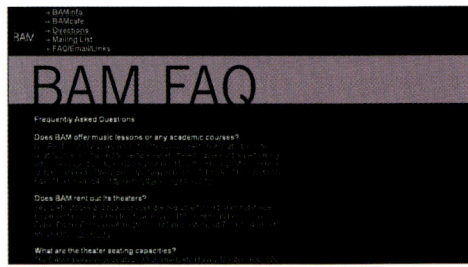

> NAME: BROOKLYN ACADEMY OF MUSIC > SECTOR: MUSIC SCHOOL > SPECS: FLASH, HTML > RATING: ORIGINALITY ☹ GRAPHICS ☹ INTERACTIVITY ☺ > CREDITS: R/GA INTERACTIVE

THE COLOR SCHEME, AS SUCH, CONSISTS ALMOST EXCLUSIVELY OF BLACK, A DRAMATIC BACKGROUND SUPPORT FOR TEXT. HORIZONTAL STRIPES IN DARK TONES BREAK THE MONOTONY AND FOCUS ATTENTION; THE NECESSARY INFORMATION IS PLACED ALONG THESE STRIPES.

THE USER SHOULD FIND NO PROBLEMS GETTING AROUND THE SITE. THE MENU IDENTIFIES EACH SECTION, WHICH IN TURN ARE LAID OUT VERTICALLY, IMPLYING THAT THE WRITTEN INFORMATION HAS BEEN PLACED ABOVE GRAPHIC INGENUITY IN IMPORTANCE.

>FF
00
00

>FF
99
00

>FF
00
00

>00
00
99

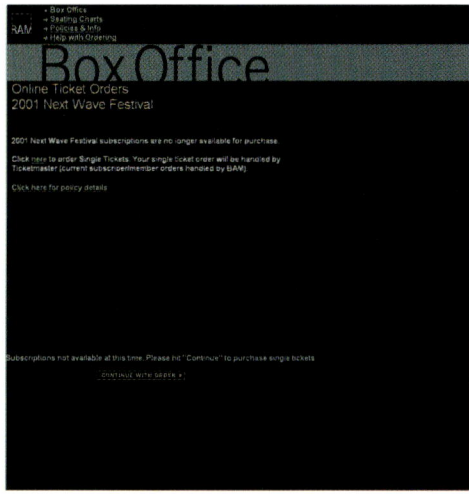

> NAME: ICI > SECTOR: ADVERTISING AGENCY > SPECIFICATIONS: FLASH, HTML > RATING: ORIGINALITY ☺ GRAPHICS ☺ INTERACTIVITY ☺ > DESIGNED BY: ICI

TWO MENUS, ONE AT THE TOP OF THE SCREEN, THE OTHER AT THE BOTTOM, PROVIDE ACCESS TO THE SUBSEQUENT SECTIONS. THE SITE IS UNIFIED BY THE SAME TONE WITH WHICH ALL OF THE PHOTOGRAPHS HAVE BEEN TREATED.

EACH LINK OPENS UP A WINDOW WITH THE RELEVANT TEXTS SUPERIMPOSED ON THE MAIN SCREEN.

WWW.7-ICI.COM

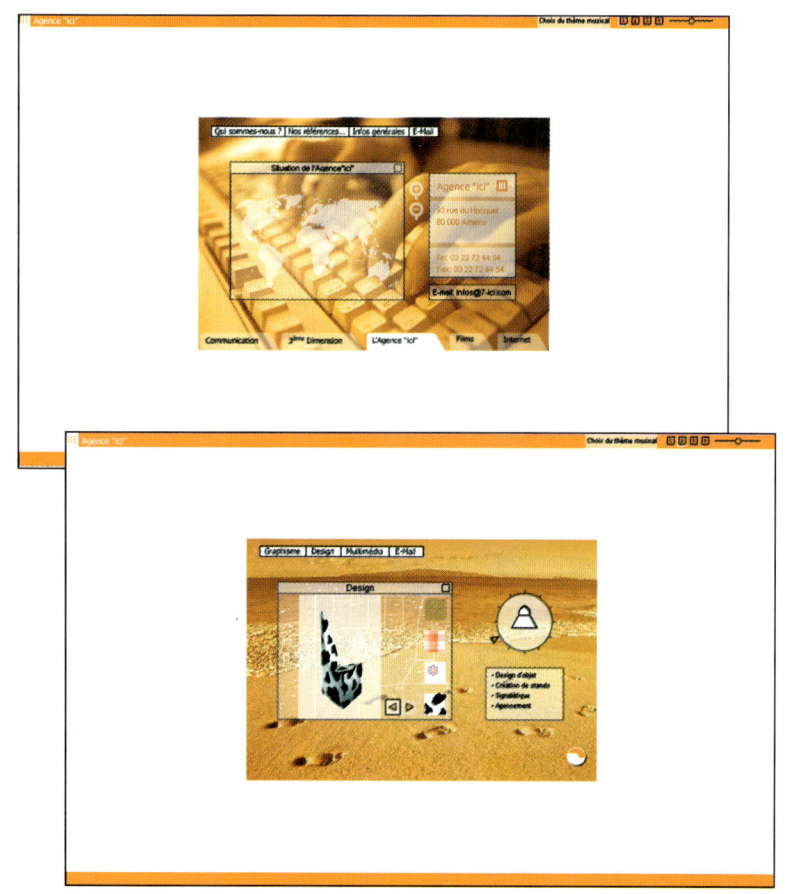

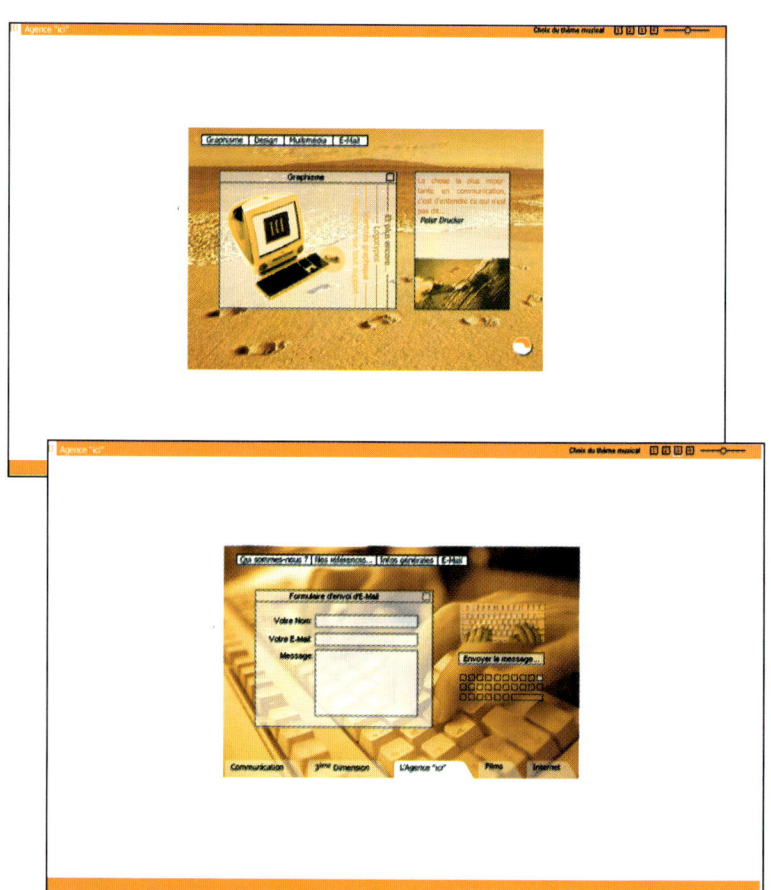

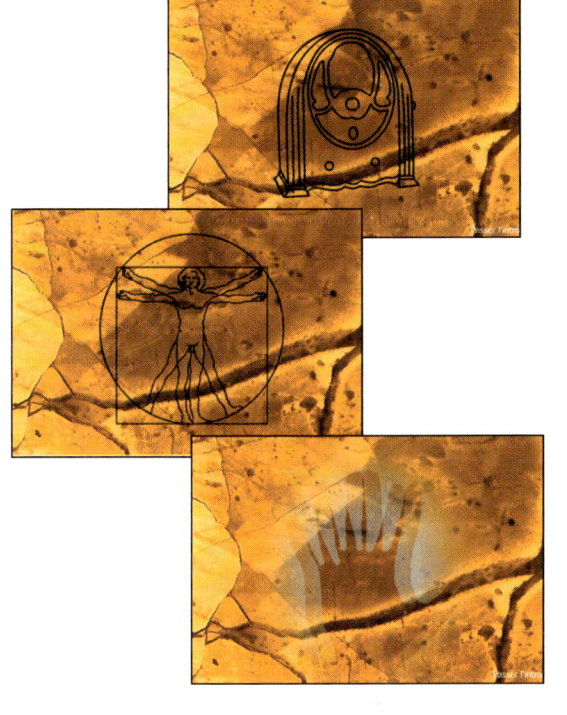

THE USE OF ONLY A PART OF THE SCREEN IS A VALID OPTION WHEN THE INFORMATION TO BE INCLUDED IS BRIEF.

THUS, THE TEDIUM OF SCROLLING UP OR DOWN OR MOVING BACK AND FORTH IS DONE AWAY WITH. THE IDEAS AND CONCEPTS TRANSMITTED ARE SIMPLE AND CAN BE EFFECTIVELY RESOLVED WITHIN A CENTRAL RECTANGLE.

TO THE LEFT, A PAGE DESIGNED FOR USER ENTERTAINMENT.

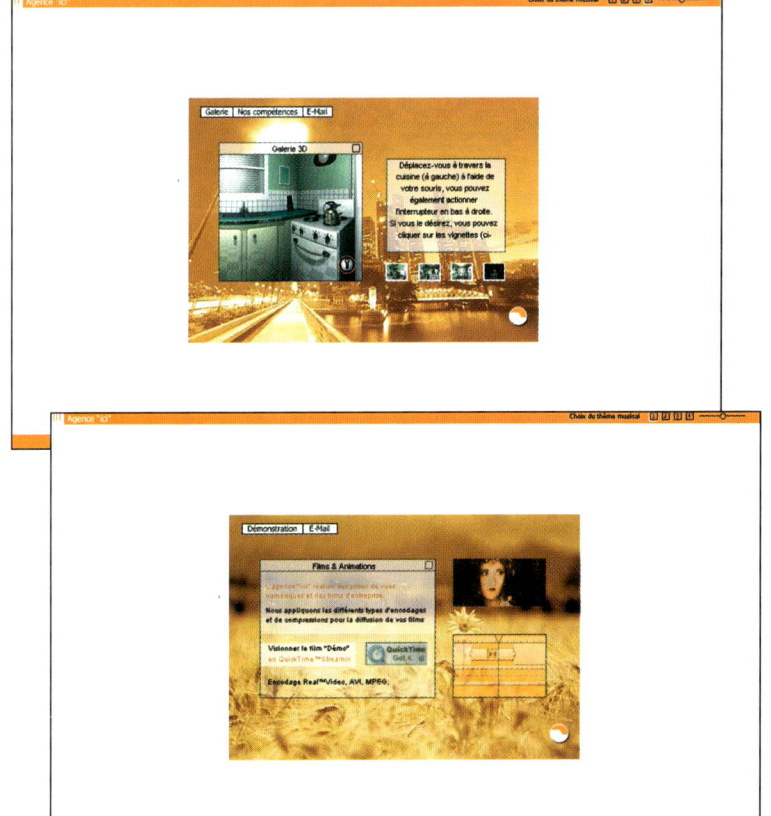

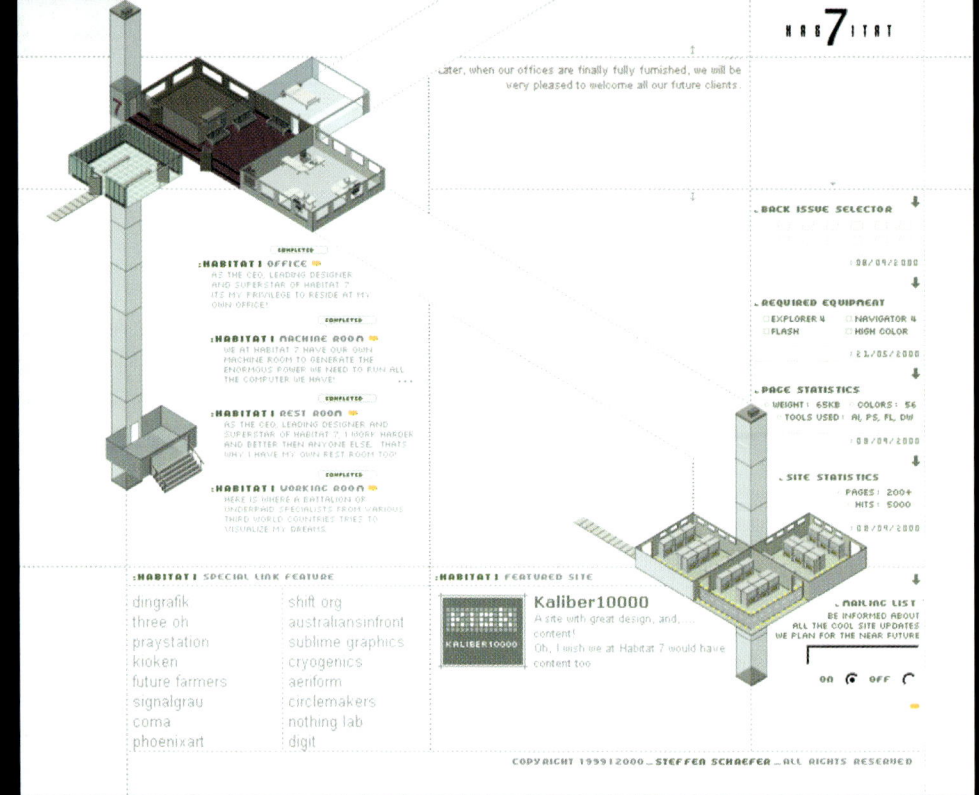

WWW.HABITAT7.DE/DESIGN1

> NAME: HABITAT 7 > SECTOR: WEB-
SITE DESIGN > SPECS: HTML > RAT-
ING: ORIGINALITY ☺ GRAPHICS ☺
INTERACTIVITY ☹ > CREDITS: STEF-
FEN SHAEFER

A VERY TONGUE IN CHEEK LOOK AT
THE DESIGNER'S OWN HOME AND
WORKSPACE - AN OTHERWISE HELP-
FUL METAPHOR FOR FAMILIARIZING
USERS WITH THE SITE.

MOST OF THE CONTENTS ON EACH
PAGE CAN BE SCROLLED UP OR
DOWN, REVEALING THE FULL EXTENT
OF HIDDEN, OVERLAPPING CON-
TENTS, OR WITH ICONS SLIDING UP
TO MEET THE EXPLANATORY TEXT
SLIDING ALONGSIDE THEM.

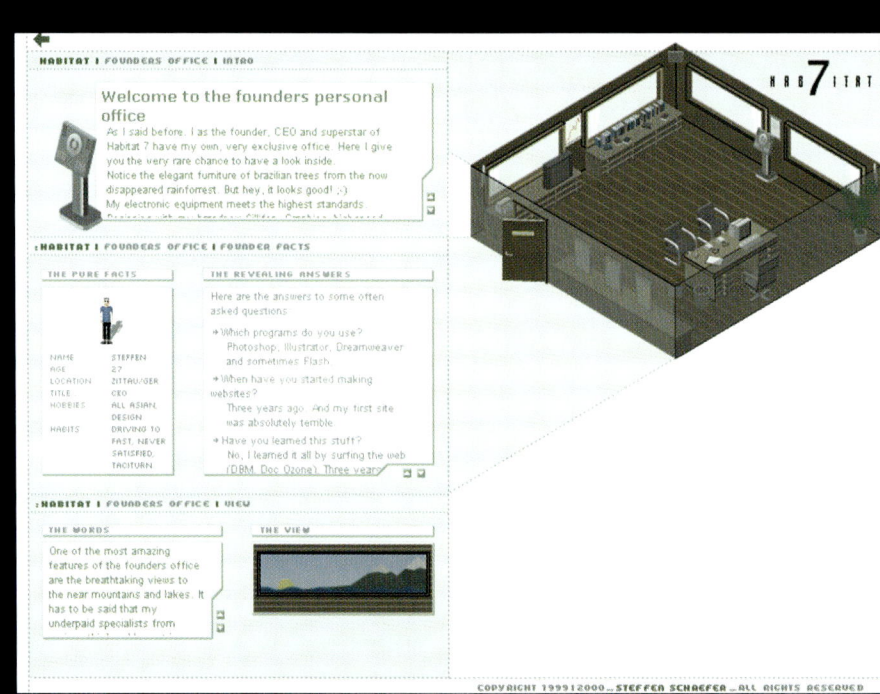

:HABITAT | REST ROOM | INTRO

Welcome to the most exclusive room of the whole Habitat, the rest room of our founder.

We, the specialists from various third world countries, don't know exactly what happens there. OK, some of our female specialists occasionally help our founder in this room, but they never say what they have done exactly. But hear what our founder had to say:

"Ahh, yeah ... my rest room. I need such a privilege because I work so much harder then anyone else. And why I need female specialists to help me? Ahhh ... hmmm ... I need ... OH, shout up and go to work!!! Or I fire you and buy robots."

:HABITAT | REST ROOM | FURNISHING

- TO GIVE YOU A BETTER IDEA OF THE POSSIBILITIES WE GIVE YOU ONE RARE CHANCE TO HAVE A CLOSER LOOK INSIDE

- WE HAVE TO SAY THAT WE, THE SPECIALISTS FROM VARIOUS THIRD WORLD COUNTRIES, DON'T KNOW EXACTLY WHAT OUR FOUNDER MAKES IN HIS REST ROOM. BUT JUDGE FOR YOURSELF.

- OUR FOUNDER IS VERY PROUD TO OWN THIS BOOKS, WHICH LOOK LIKE THE KAMASUTRA BUT EVEN OUR YOUNG SPECIALIST HAVE NEVER SEEN SUCH A LOT OF BOOKS

ITALIAN UNTER-BED
EXPENSIVE   EXCELLENT

KAMASUTRA-BOOKS
RELIABLE   VERY HELPFUL

ORIENTAL PLANT
HERBAL EFFECT   OUTSTANDING

:HABITAT | REST ROOM | FAVS

Heise.de (g)
Der Spiegel (g)
Sueddeutsche (g)
Die Welt (g)
Press-Report (g)
Flatrate.de (g)
BBC-Online (en)
CNET (en/g)
Looks like our founder is a news-junkie!

:HABITAT | REST ROOM | FAVS

Massimos Corner (en)
CGI Resource (en)
SelfHTML (g)
DHV Extensions (en)
Cool Homepages (en)
deformat.de (german)
J-List (en)
BWG Update (en)
Cuisine at (en/g)

:HABITAT | REST ROOM | FAVS

dooyoo.de (g)
Freetextures (en)
Gamecenter (en)
and something different
Karl Fritsch (g)
Haralds Heimseite (g)
Terranet (g)
Dieter Bohlen (g)
Muellseite (g) ... and you feel better!

THIS SITE IS MADE UP OF JUST FOUR MAIN SECTIONS, WITH A LINKS SECTION TAKING USERS TO SIMILAR SITES.

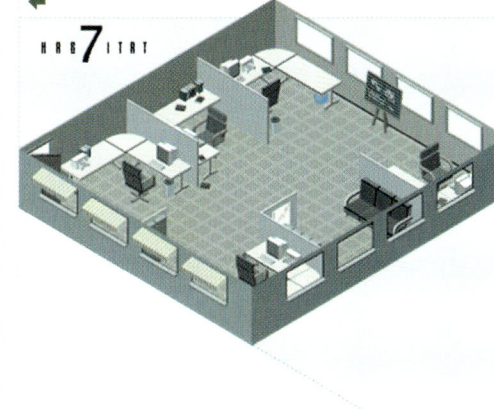

:HABITAT | WORKING ROOM | INTRO

Welcome to the working room of Habitat 7. Here we will give you a exclusive look inside (once again).

One of the most important goals when we furnished this room was to create a focused atmosphere. This task was achieved in association with eHea, a ambitious company from Northern Europe. The workstations (colle...

:HABITAT | WORKING ROOM | SECTIONS

THE DESIGNERS SECTION IS OF COURSE THE MOST IMPORTANT PART OF THE HABITAT 7. DOZENS OF SPECIALISTS FROM VARIOUS (THIRD WORLD) COUNTRIES TRY TO RECREATE THE DREAMS OF OUR FOUNDER.
CLICK TO VIEW THE PERSONALS »»»

THE HABITAT 7 HAS A CODERS SECTION TOO. BECAUSE OUR FOUNDERS DREAMS DON'T INCLUDE ANY CODE THESE SPECIALISTS MUST BE HIGLY INNOVATIVE AND EXTREHELY HIGH SKILLED. THESE PEOPLE HAVE A VERY SHORT LIFE CIRCLE.
CLICK TO VIEW THE PERSONALS »»»

THE THIRD BIG SECTION OF THE HABITAT 7 IS RESPONSIBLE FOR ALL THE MOVIES, SOUNDS AND INTERACTIVE PARTS.
THE FOUNDER IS VERY PROUD THAT SPECIALISTS FROM BOLLYWOOD WORK FOR HIM.
CLICK TO VIEW THE PERSONALS »»»

TONY CHUNG   DESIGNER
21 YEARS   13 MONTH

BRINA FUNOKA   DESIGNER
37 YEARS   2 MONTH

L.X. MUELLER   DESIGNER
32 YEARS   12 MONTH

HRJ MATTALA   DESIGNER
27 YEARS   17 MONTH

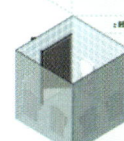

:HABITAT | WORKING ROOM | CONSULTANTS CORNER

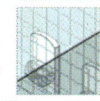

Every company needs consultants. At least that's what the consultants say. So the Habitat has them too. But because our founder does not like them we had to find a place for them where our founder...

> NAME: YOUNG DESIGNERS
> SECTOR: DESIGN COMPETITION
> SPECS: FLASH > RATING: ORIGI-
NALITY ☺ GRAPHICS ☺ INTER-
ACTIVITY ☺ > CREDITS: DEEPEND

THE SITE OPENS WITH ANIMATED CHARACTERS GIVING AN OVERVIEW OF WHAT TO EXPECT, FOLLOWED BY A GENERAL MENU. THE DESIGN IS DIVIDED INTO SIX WELL-IDENTIFIED, CLEARLY PRESENTED —ALBEIT MONOTONOUS— SECTIONS.

THE MAIN LOGO IS THE CENTRAL DESIGN ELEMENT; ALL OTHER GRAPHICS HAVE BEEN KEPT TO A BARE MINIMUM. THE CLICKABLE ICONS FOR MOVING FORWARD OR BACKWARD DISPLAY A SIMPLE, STRAIGHTFORWARD DESIGN.

THE WARMTH AND VIBRANCY OF AN ORANGE BACKGROUND CONTRASTS NICELY WITH SOOTHING BLUE.

WWW.YOUNG-DESIGNERS.COM

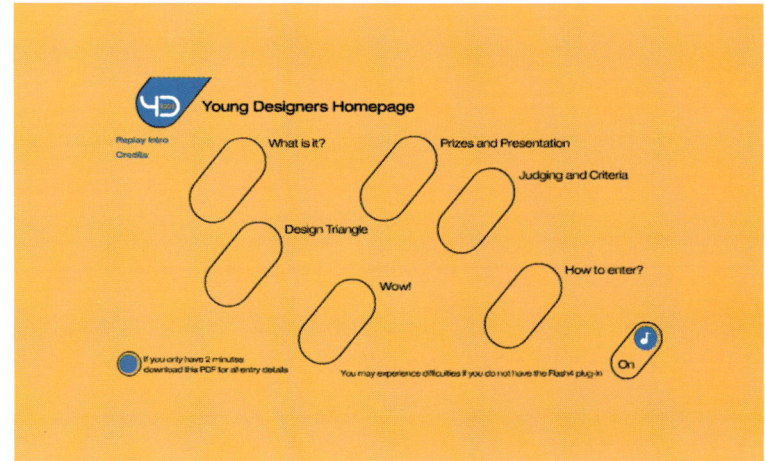

Design Triangle

The Design Triangle is a simple tool to help spark some ideas and develop an interesting design brief.
The Design Triangle is made up of three questions:

- **Who's the user/client?**
- **What's the problem being solved?**
- **What design discipline are you working in?**

Once all three questions have been answered, a design solution should be found. We recommend that when thinking of the user that students find a real life client. It may be a parent or it could be a local company. Of the submissions in 2000, some of the best ideas were by students who had a real client. Send us anything that your students have worked on. We want to see the process behind the entry and how the Design Triangle applies to the work.

Launch Design Triangle   Launch Examples

Interactive Design Triangle

Use the Design Triangle to make up your own brief

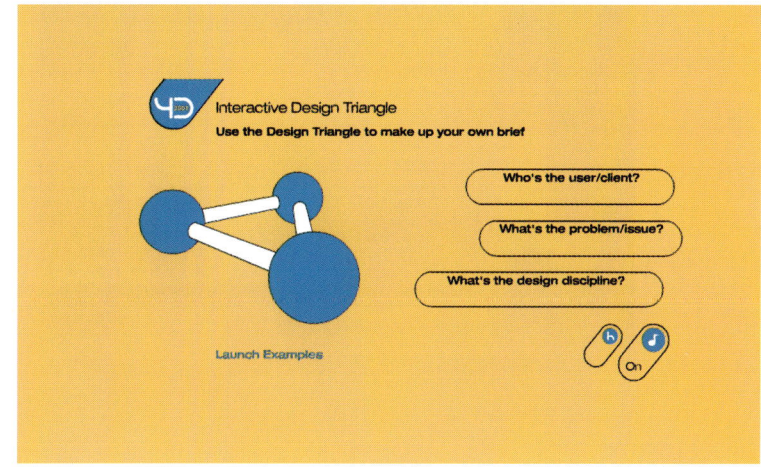

Who's the user/client?

What's the problem/issue?

What's the design discipline?

Launch Examples

Prizes and presentations

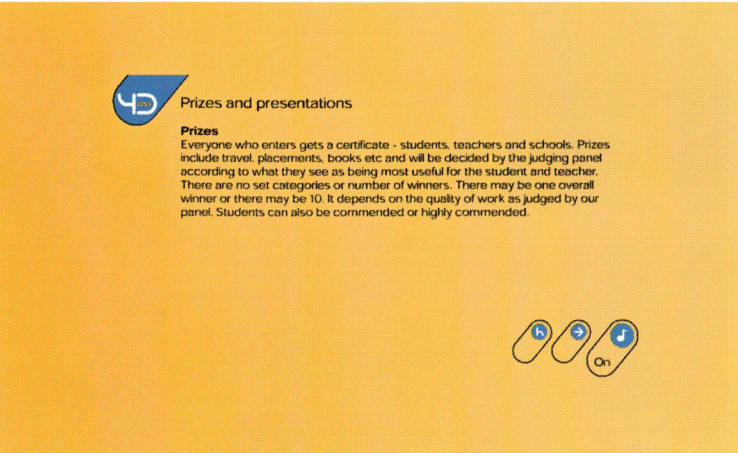

Prizes
Everyone who enters gets a certificate - students, teachers and schools. Prizes include travel, placements, books etc and will be decided by the judging panel according to what they see as being most useful for the student and teacher. There are no set categories or number of winners. There may be one overall winner or there may be 10. It depends on the quality of work as judged by our panel. Students can also be commended or highly commended.

How to enter

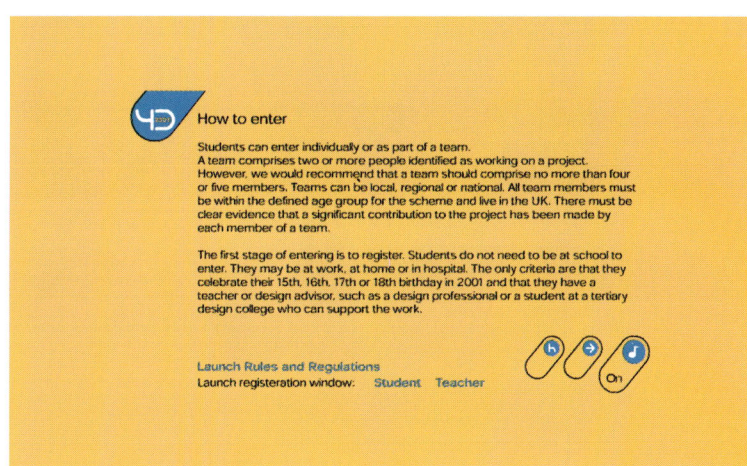

Students can enter individually or as part of a team.
A team comprises two or more people identified as working on a project. However, we would recommend that a team should comprise no more than four or five members. Teams can be local, regional or national. All team members must be within the defined age group for the scheme and live in the UK. There must be clear evidence that a significant contribution to the project has been made by each member of a team.

The first stage of entering is to register. Students do not need to be at school to enter. They may be at work, at home or in hospital. The only criteria are that they celebrate their 15th, 16th, 17th or 18th birthday in 2001 and that they have a teacher or design advisor, such as a design professional or a student at a tertiary design college who can support the work.

Launch Rules and Regulations
Launch registeration window: Student   Teacher

What is it?

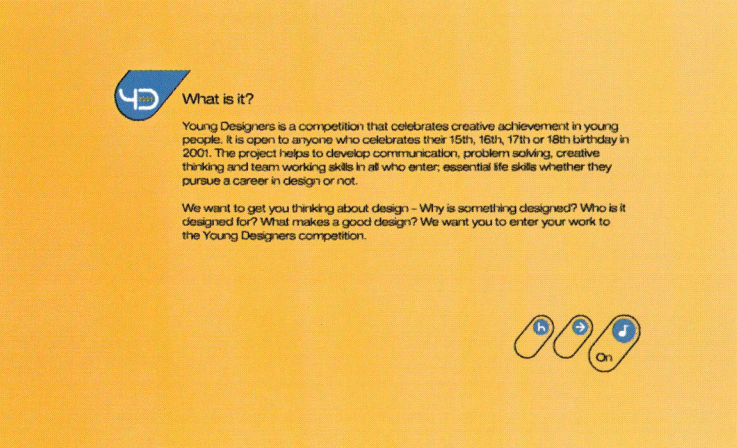

Young Designers is a competition that celebrates creative achievement in young people. It is open to anyone who celebrates their 15th, 16th, 17th or 18th birthday in 2001. The project helps to develop communication, problem solving, creative thinking and team working skills in all who enter; essential life skills whether they pursue a career in design or not.

We want to get you thinking about design - Why is something designed? Who is it designed for? What makes a good design? We want you to enter your work to the Young Designers competition.

Register Now

Teachers register your interest now.

I'm really excited about Young Designers and want to register my interest.

Name:
Position
Date of Birth:
School:
School address:

Telephone:
Fax:
Email:
Submission Type: Individual Entry
How many Design and Technology classes do you teach?
What is the average size of a class?
How many classes are you interested in entering into Young Designers?

Submit

WWW.SIGNLAND.COM

> NAME: SIGNLAND DESIGN & STRATEGY > SECTOR: ADVERTISING AGENCY > SPECS: FLASH, HTML > RATING: ORIGINALITY 😐 GRAPHICS 😐 INTERACTIVITY 😐

THE INTRODUCTORY PAGE PROVIDES THE FORETASTE OF A SOMEWHAT ABSTRACT DESIGN ELEMENT, WHICH, AT FIRST GLANCE, SEEMS SOMEHOW IRRECONCILABLE WITH THE OVERALL SCHEME. THIS RESOURCE, AS IT TURNS OUT, IS THE GUIDING THREAD THROUGHOUT THE SITE.

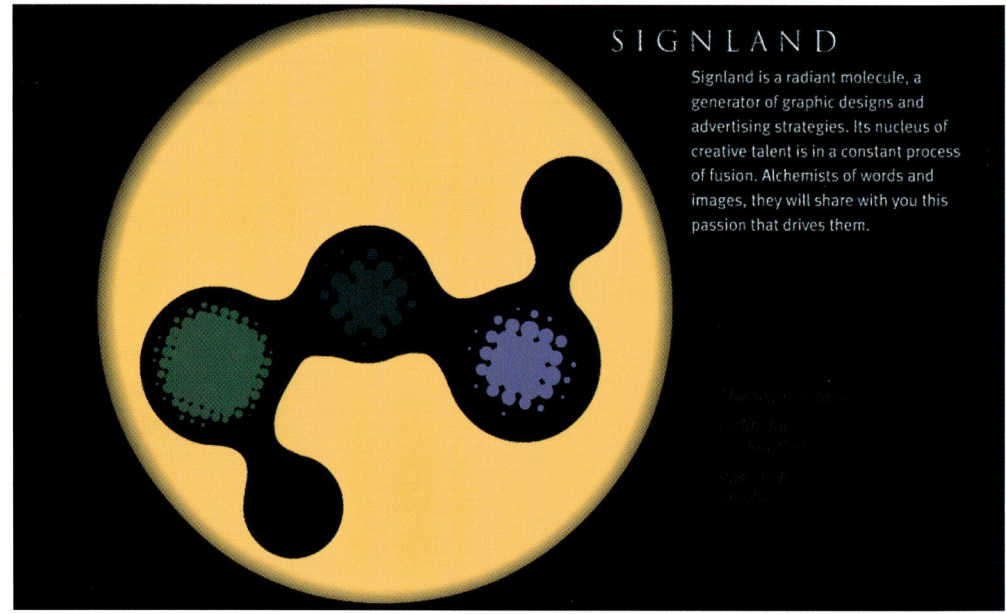

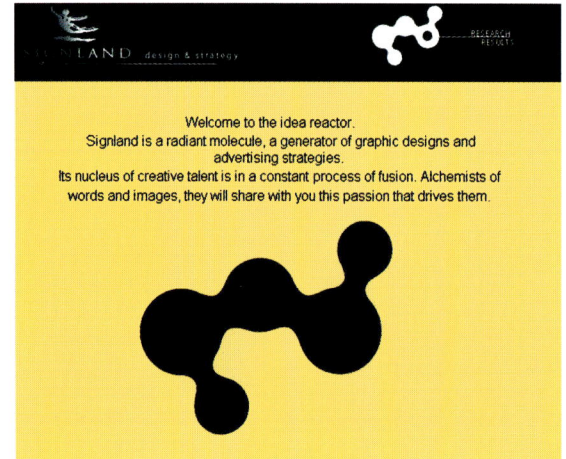

THE SITE'S OTHER UNIFYING ELEMENT, WHICH IS SEEN ON ALL SUBSEQUENT LINKS, IS THE BROAD BLACK BAND AT THE TOP OF THE PAGE.

ONCE EACH SECTION HAS BEEN IDENTIFIED, NAVIGATING IS VERY SIMPLE, ESPECIALLY SINCE THERE ARE FEW LINKS.

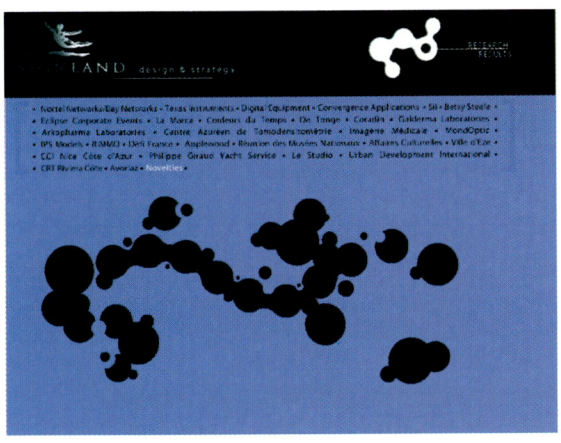
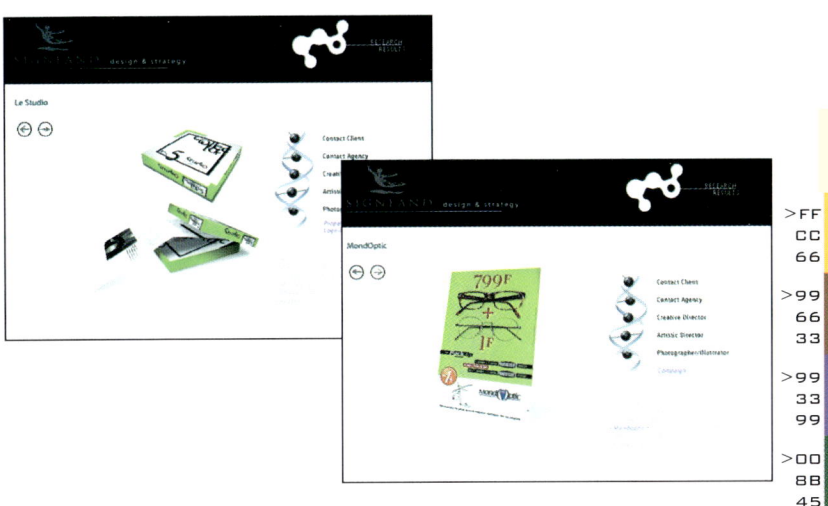

WWW.SOLECUOREAMORE.IT

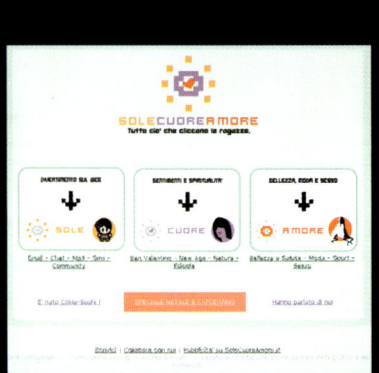

> NAME: SOLE CUORE AMORE > SEC-
TOR: WEBSITE FOR YOUNG WOMEN
> SPECIFICATIONS: HTML > RATING:
ORIGINALITY 😊 GRAPHICS 😊
INTERACTIVITY 😊
> DESIGNED BY: WINKLER & NOAH

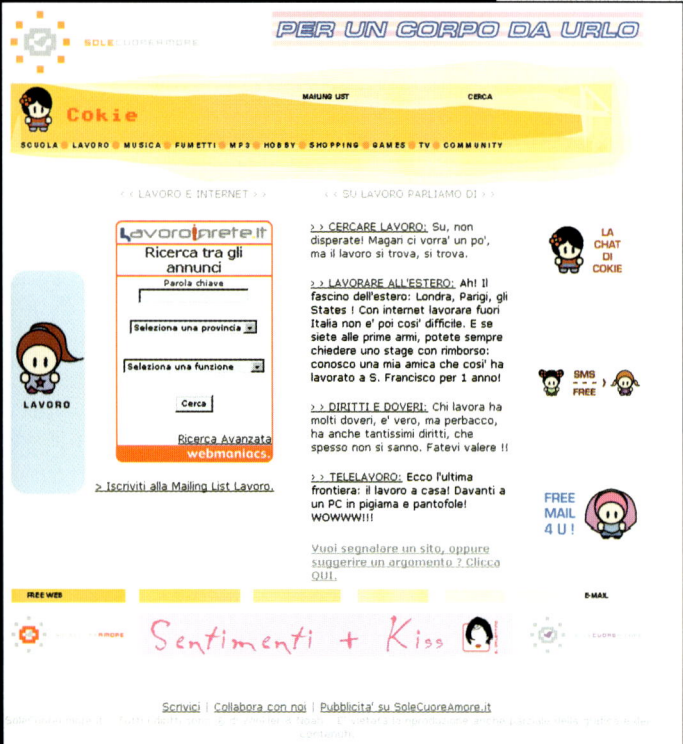

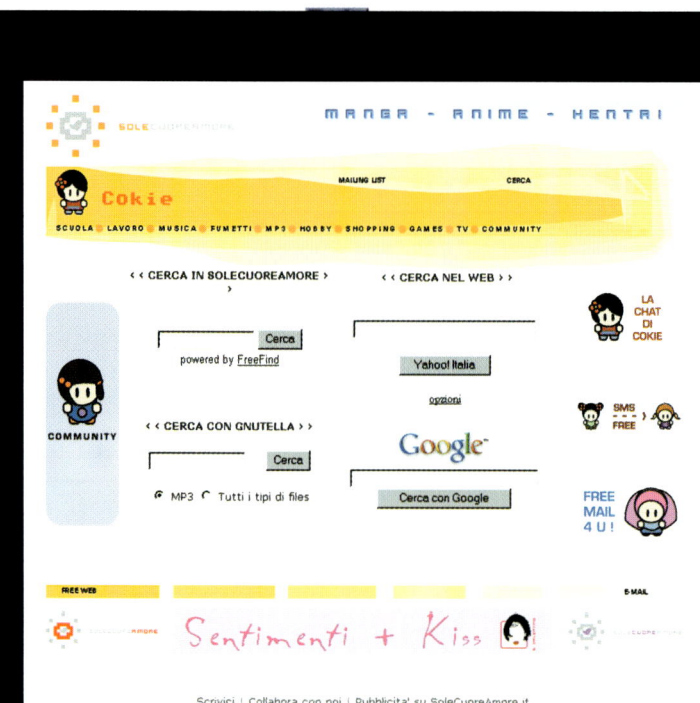

OUT, GRAPHICALLY SPEAKING, THERE ARE THREE CLEARLY DIFFERENTIATED SECTIONS IN THIS SITE. THE ICONS, COLORS AND ILLUSTRATIONS WORK TOGETHER IS SEEN IN THIS FIRST SECTION, WITH BANNERS AT THE TOP OF THE PAGE AND LINKS GROUPED TOGETHER TO THE RIGHT.

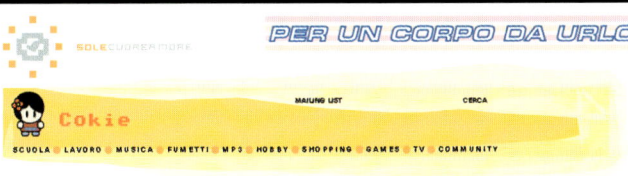

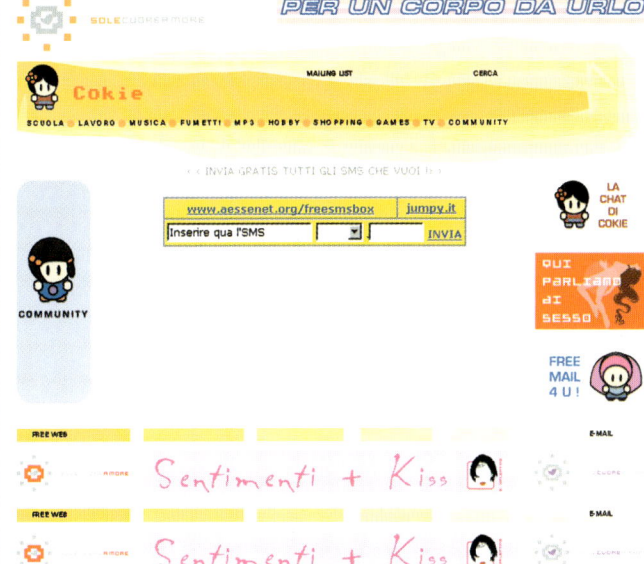

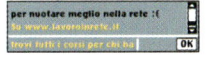

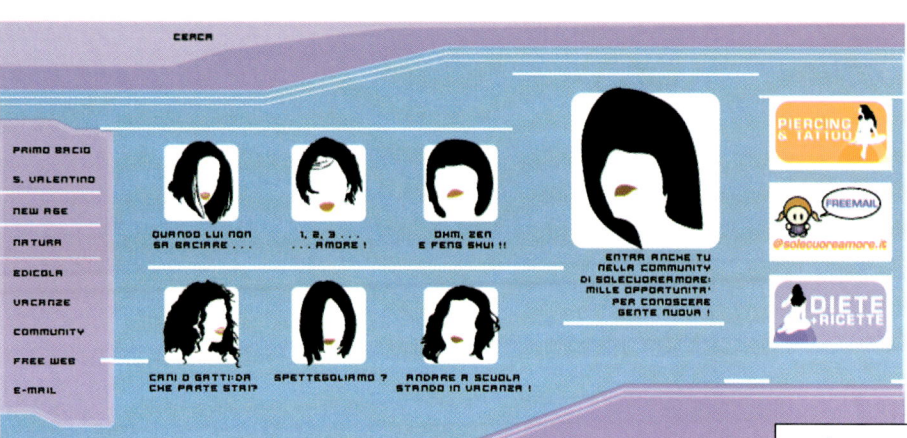

Graphics are highly important in this particular design. Each element carries its own weight and has eye-catching presence on the page.

The color scheme serves to reinforce the graphics, illustrations and backgrounds, especially in the second and third sections.

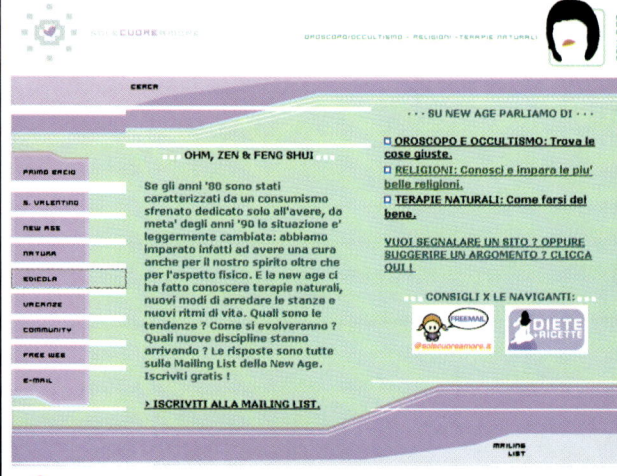

Ease of access, a highly important feature in all hypertextual navigation and present here almost to the point of redundancy, is one of this site's greatest strongpoints.

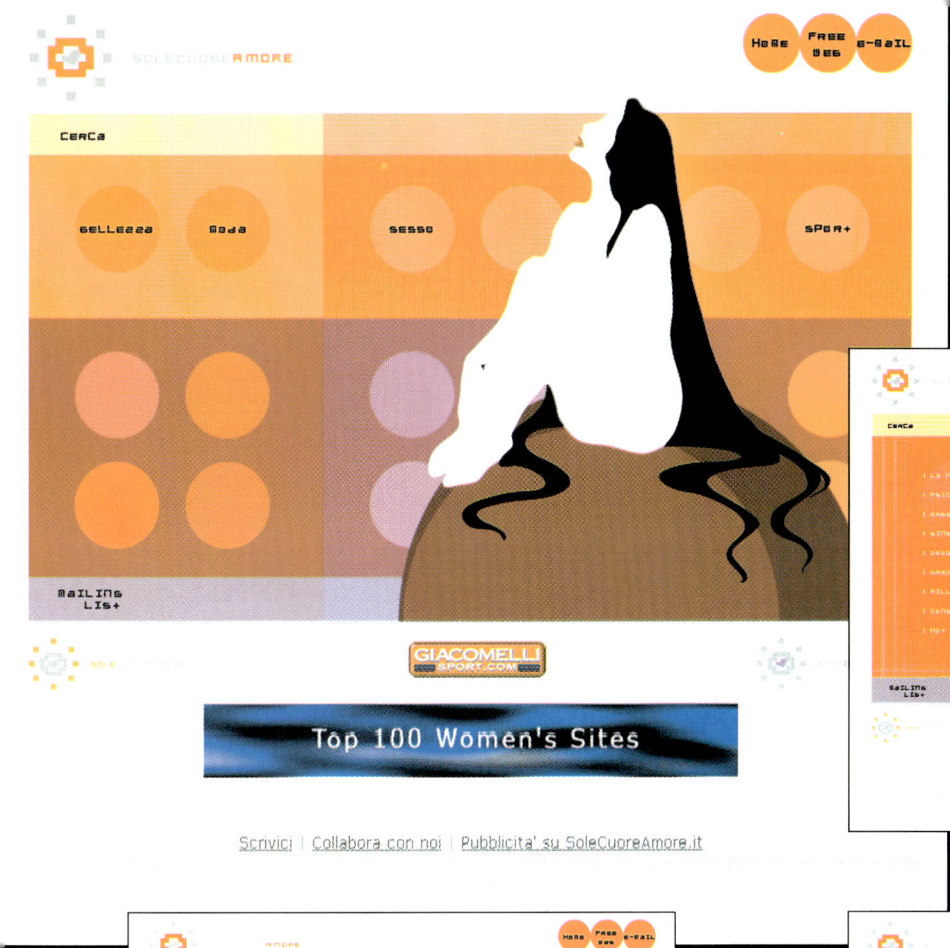

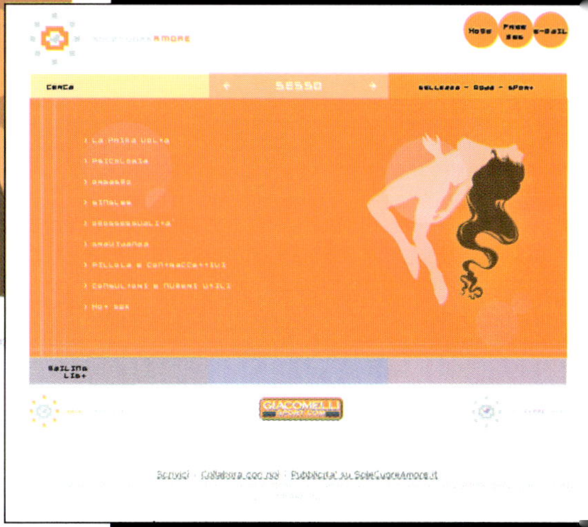

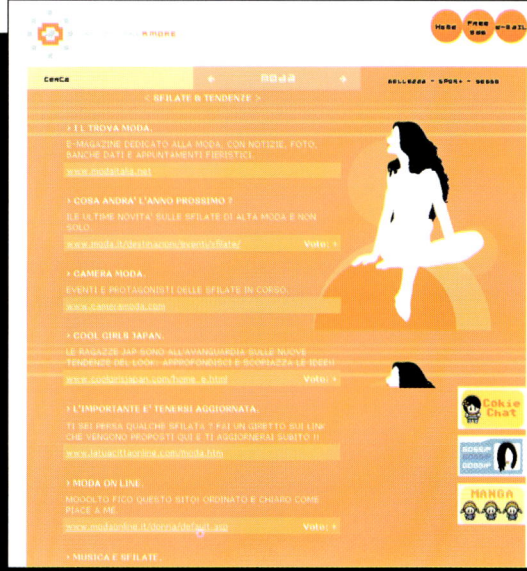

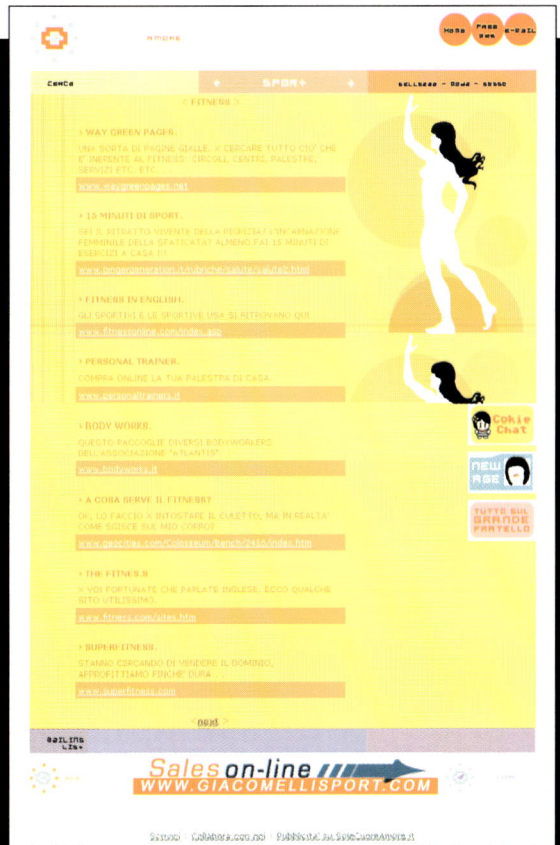

WWW.JOELINNER.NET

> NAME: JOELINNER PROJECT DESIGN
> SECTOR: DESIGN STUDIO > SPECIFICA-
TIONS: FLASH, HTML > RATING: ORIGINAL-
ITY 😊 GRAPHICS 😊 INTERACTIVITY 😐
> DESIGNED BY: PEDRO GARCÍA-QUIJADA,
SATURNINO AND FIDEL ESTEBAN QUIROGA
ARROJO

THERE ARE MANY PAGES TO THIS SITE,
ALTHOUGH THE CLICKABLE PART OF
EACH LINK IS OFTEN DIFFICULT TO
FIND. LIKEWISE, THE USER MIGHT HAVE
PROBLEMS FINDING THE WAY OUT OF
CERTAIN SECTIONS.

A BASICALLY MONOCHROMATIC SCHEME
WITH TOUCHES OF CONTRASTING COL-
ORS IS A BOLD PROPOSAL A STATEMENT
WHICH DISPLAYS CONFIDENCE.

A WIDE RANGE OF ICONS, PICTOGRAMS
AND GRAPHICS, ALL TINGED WITH A
CERTAIN RETRO FLAVOR, KEEP THE EYE
ENTERTAINED.

THIS IS A DYNAMIC AND ORIGINAL
PROJECT. THE GRAPHIC COMPOSI-
TION, IN WHICH THE INTERPLAY BET-
WEEN THE ILLUSTRATIONS AND CO-
LORS TAKES CENTER-STAGE, HAS
BEEN HANDLED ADEPTLY.

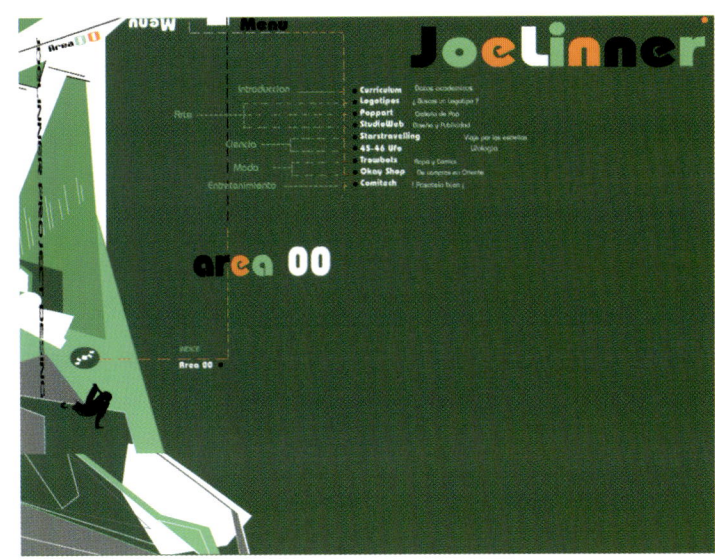

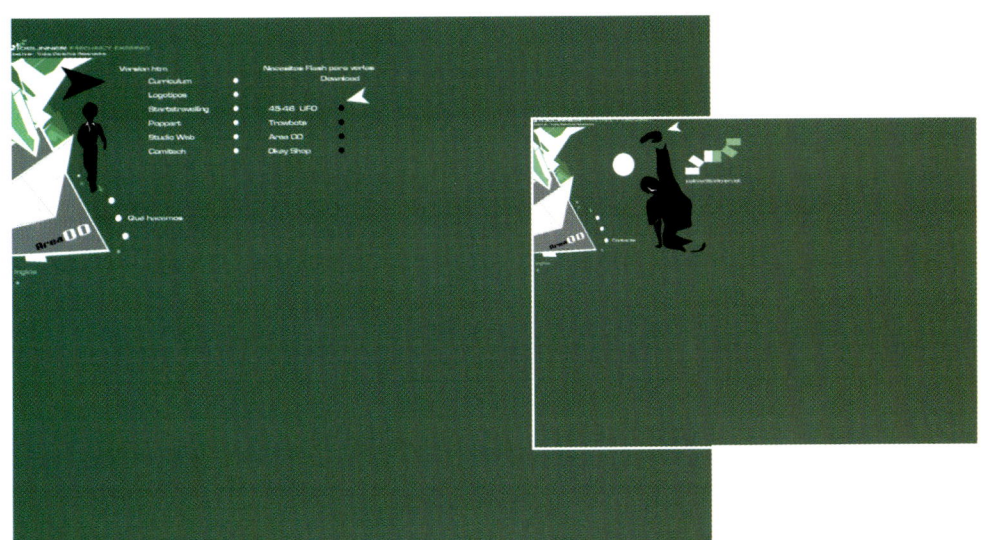

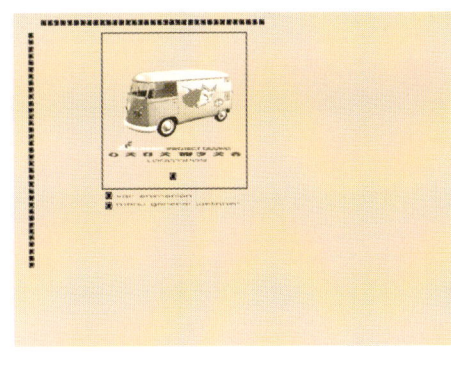

WWW.THEORY7.COM

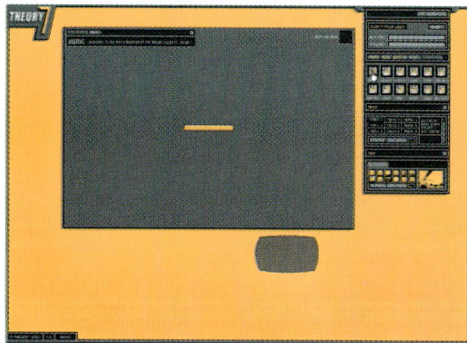

THE COMBINATION OF CONTRASTING TONES HAS LAID THE GROUND WORK FOR A DYNAMIC COMPOSITION.

THIS STRUCTURE, MEANT TO RESEMBLE SOME SORT OF CONTROL PANEL, IS THE PLACE WHERE THE MULTIPLE CONTENTS CAN BE VIEWED, CHOOSING FROM PALETTES LOCATED TO THE RIGHT.

> NAME: THEORY 7
> SECTOR: DESIGN STUDIO
> SPECS: FLASH, XML
> RATING: ORIGINALITY ☺
GRAPHICS ☹ INTERACTIVITY ☺

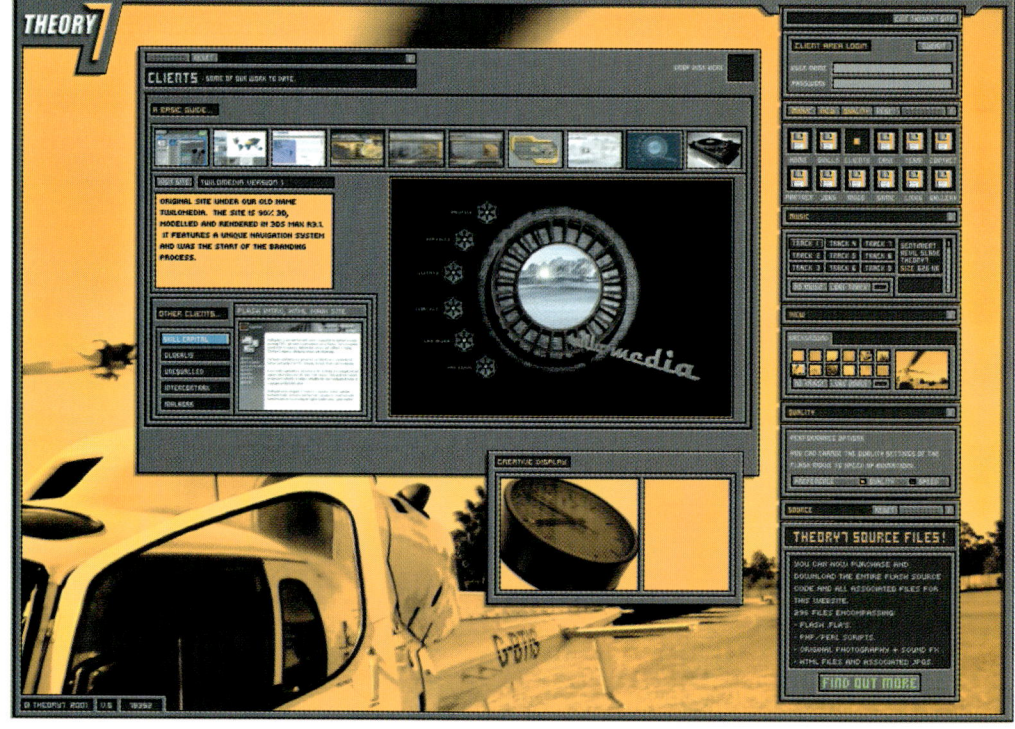

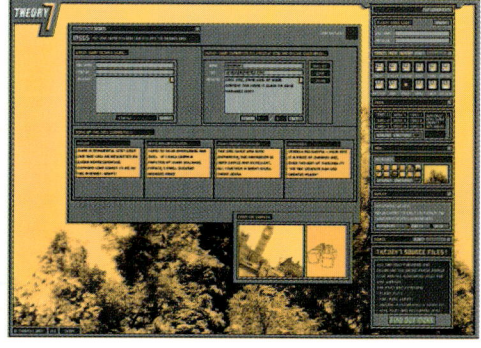

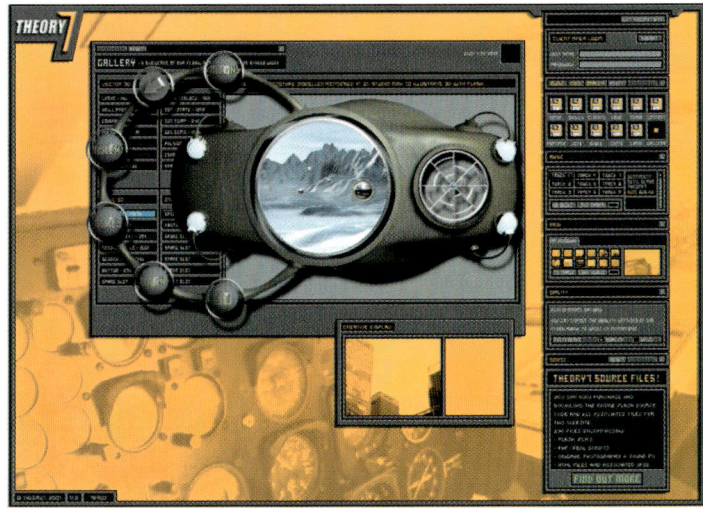

THE PERSONALIZATION AND SELEC-
TION OF BACKGROUNDS AND SOUNDS
IS A PARTICULARITY OF THIS DESIGN,
THE IDEA BEING TO TAILOR THE SITE
TO THE TASTES OF EACH USER. THERE
IS EVEN A GAME INCLUDED FOR THE
SOLE PURPOSE OF ENTERTAINMENT.

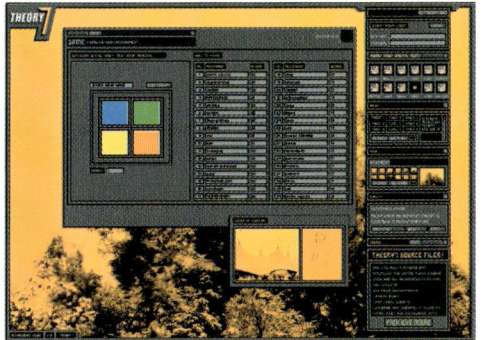

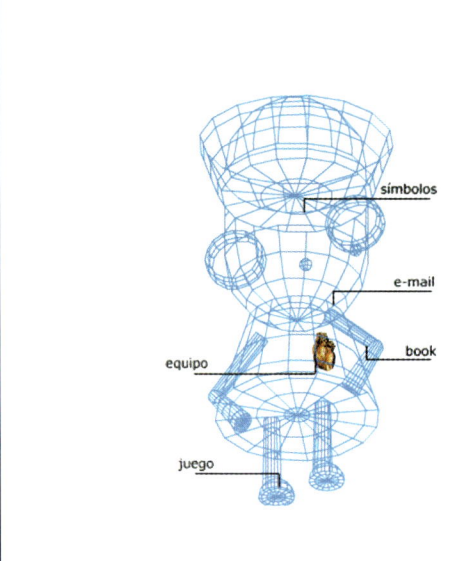

símbolos

e-mail

equipo

book

juego

factoría creativa
Salvador Espriu, 89, local 2
08005 Barcelona
tel.93 225 51 17
fax 93 225 48 95
www.frontiera.net
frontiera@frontiera.net

frontieradiligent

WWW.FRONTIERA.NET

> NAME: FRONTIERA DILIGENT
> SECTOR: COMMUNICATION AND DESIGN > SPECS: FLASH, HTML
> RATING: ORIGINALITY ☺ GRAPHICS ☺ INTERACTIVITY ☺ > CREDITS: FRONTIERA DILIGENT

An expanse of white dominates the screen. Blue, which brings stability and tranquility, has been entrusted with giving shape to the company's message. Nothing more than a subtle change of tone and the contrast between black and white were used to tie the contents together. Likewise, in order to make the process more dynamic, small windows announcing new sections open and close on the home page.

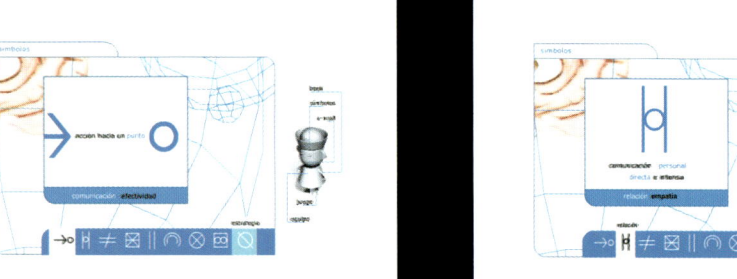

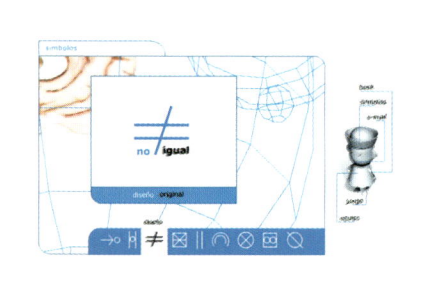

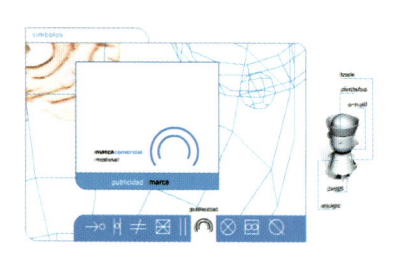

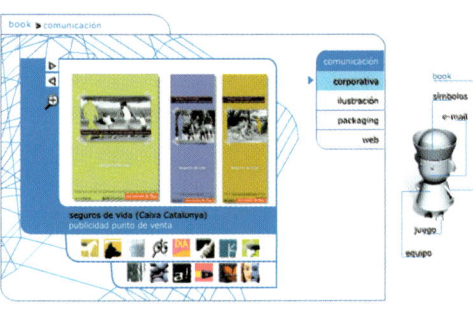

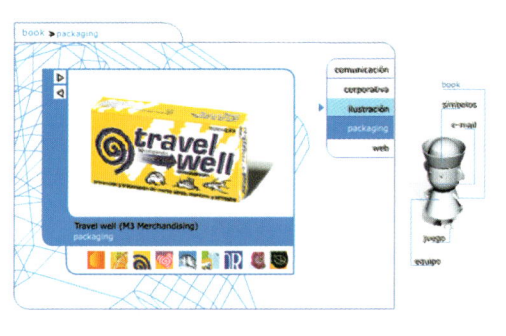

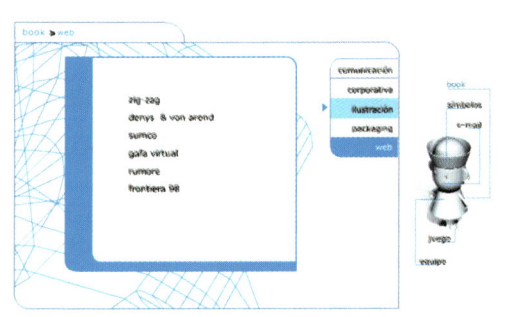

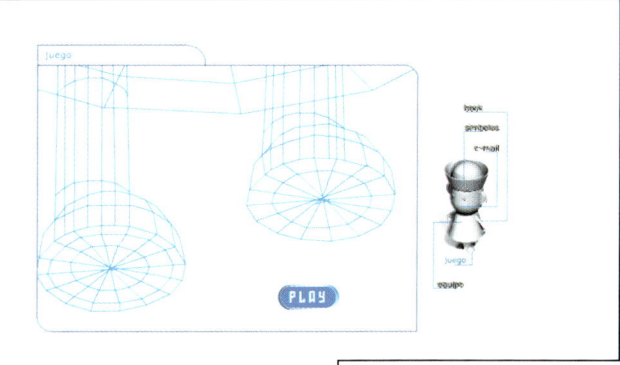

Simplicity is rarely at odds with good taste and effectiveness in transmitting information. This project is proof positive of that: a polished animation with simple graphics are used as resources throughout the various links. The clickable sections are in continuous movement, beckoning the user to come for a visit.

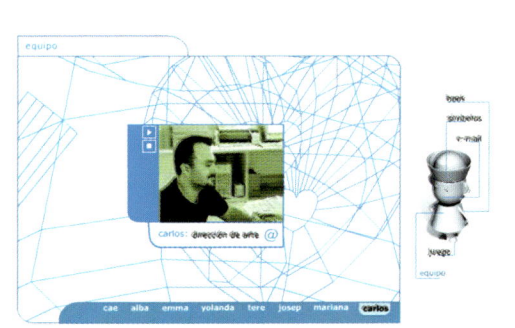

WWW.THEKRUNK.COM

> NAME: THE KRUNK > SECTOR: ON/OFF-LINE DESIGN > SPECIFICATIONS: FLASH, HTML > RATING: ORIGINALITY ☺ GRAPHICS ☹ INTERACTIVITY ☺ > DESIGNED BY: THE KRUNK

THIS IS NAVIGATION MADE EASY, WITH NO SUPERFLOUS GIMMICKS GETTING IN THE WAY WHILE BROWSING.

A MASS OF BLACK PROVIDES A MARKED CONTRAST TO THE VIVACITY OF THE YELLOWS, BLUES AND REDS OF THE REST OF THE PAGES. A SENSE OF BALANCE AND STABILITY IS PROPORTIONED BY PLACING THE BLACK AT THE BOTTOM OF THE COMPOSITION TO FORM A SOLID BASE. AS THERE ARE RELATIVELY FEW BUTTONS AND ICONS, THE WRITTEN TEXT PREDOMINATES IN IMPORTANCE.

THE SAME COMPOSITION, CONSISTING OF SUPERIMPOSED HORIZONTAL BLOCKS, IS CONSERVED ON EACH OF THE SITE'S PAGES.

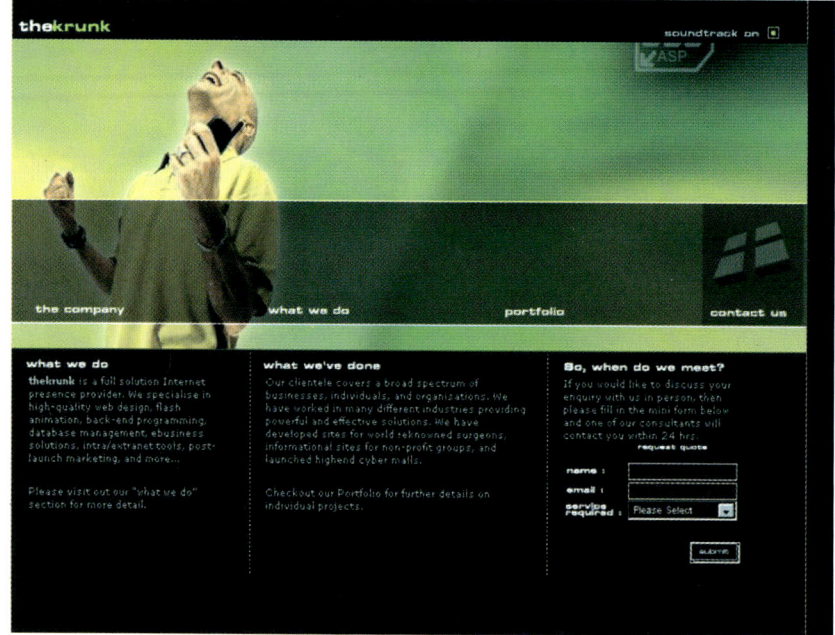

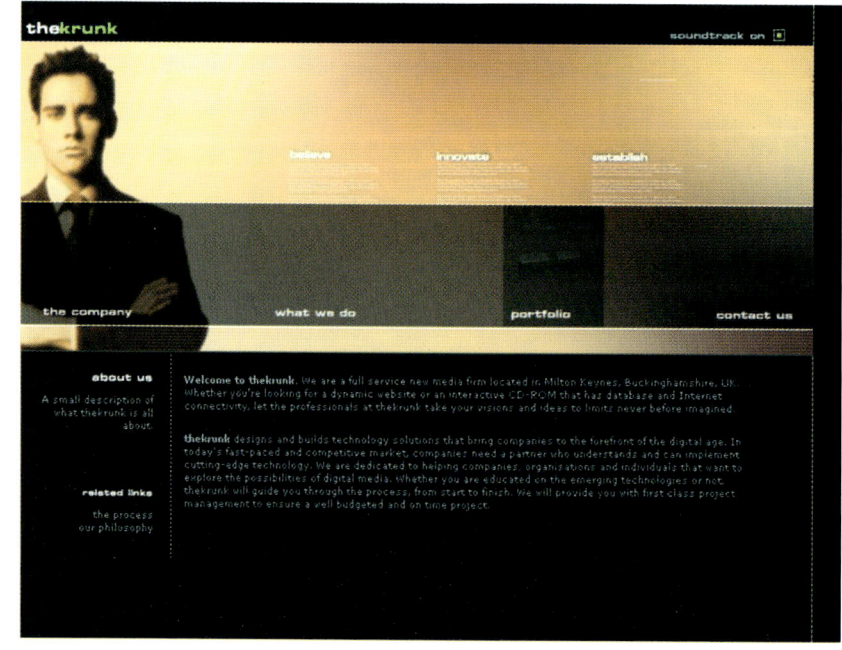

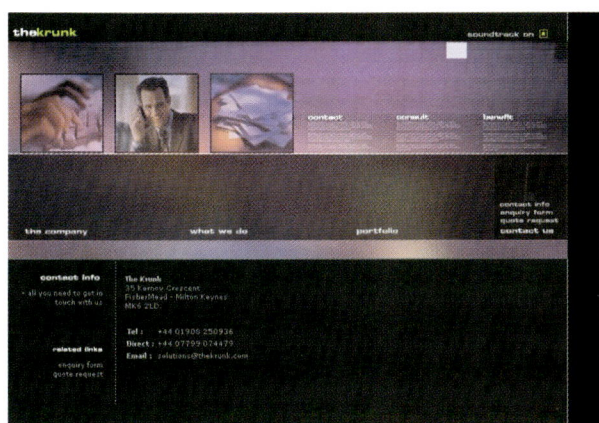

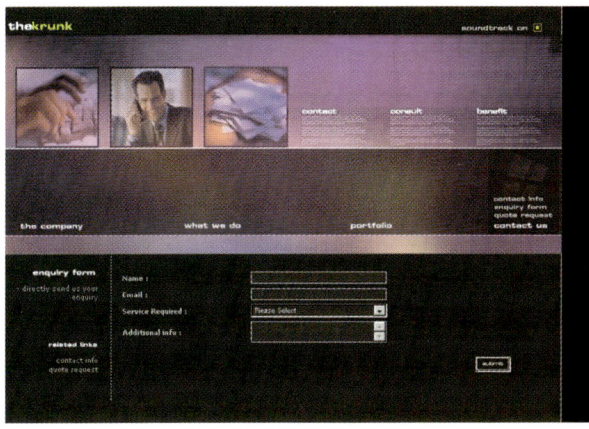

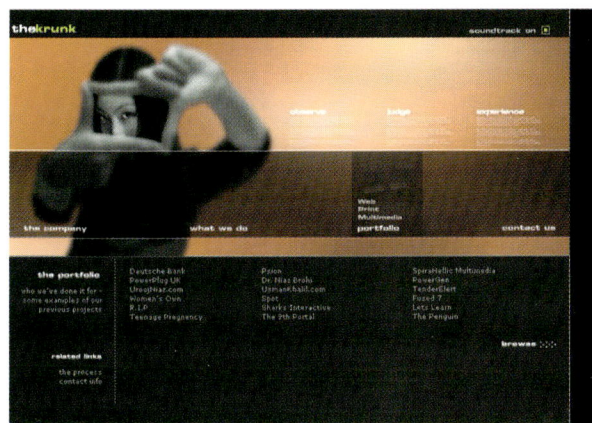

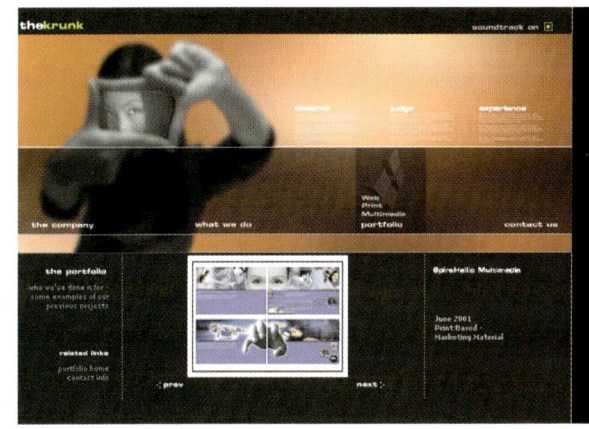

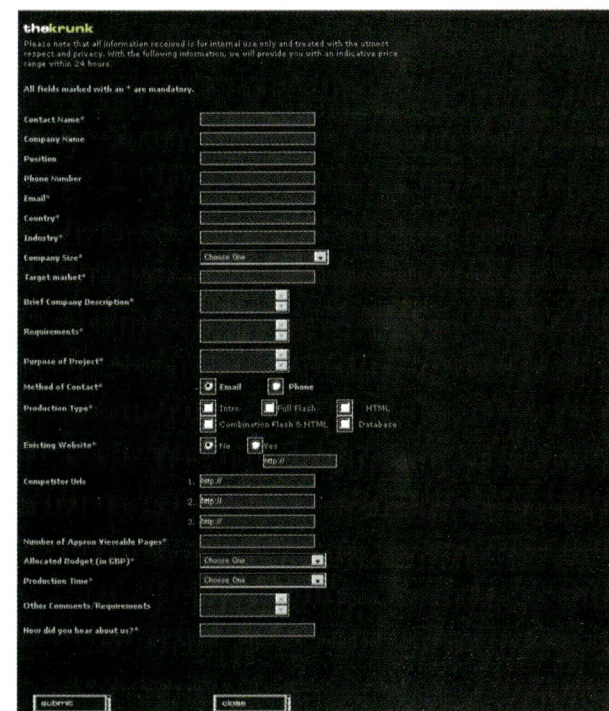

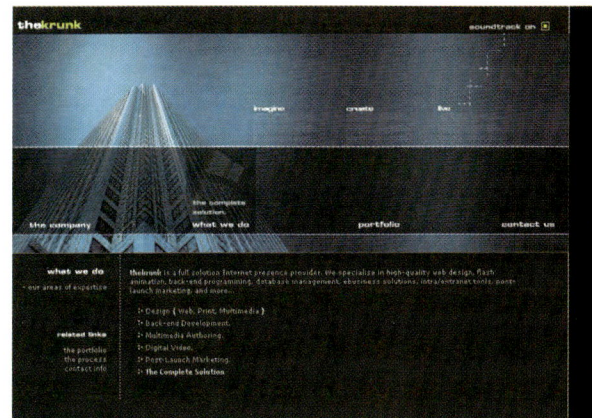

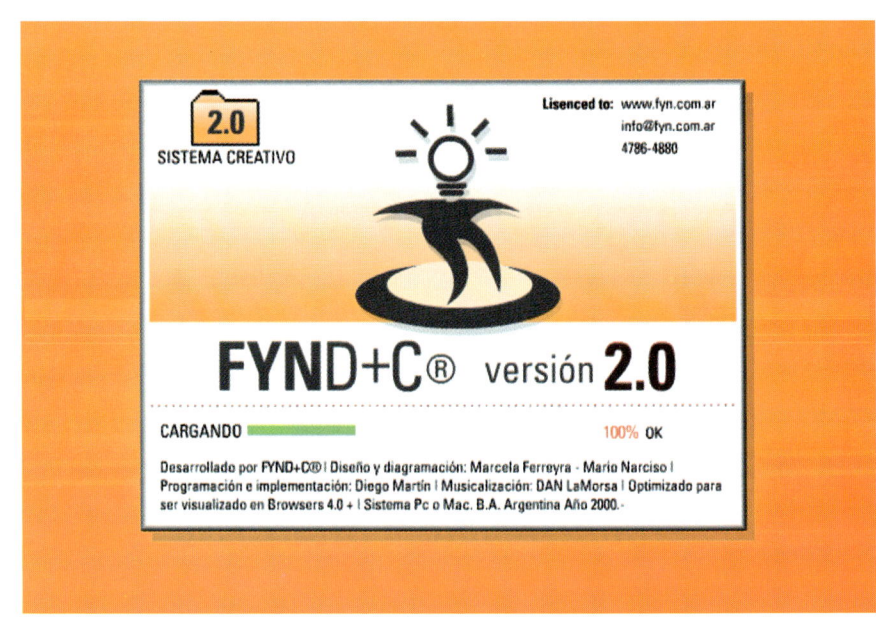

WWW.FYN.COM.AR

> NAME: FYN D+C > SECTOR: DESIGN STUDIO > SPECIFICATIONS: FLASH, HTML > RATING: ORIGINALITY ☺ GRAPHICS ☺ INTERACTIVITY ☺ > DESIGNED BY: FYN D+C

THE INGENUITY OF THIS PARTICULAR DESIGN LIES IN THE WAY THAT IT EMULATES THE IDEA OF THE DESKTOP, THEREBY CREATING AN IMMEDIATELY RECOGNIZABLE REFERENCE, SEEN AND USED ON A NEAR-DAILY BASIS. ALREADY FAMILIARIZED WITH THIS FORMAT, BROWSING BECOMES AN INTUITIVE PROCESS FOR THE USER.

ON THIS PAGE, SOME OF THE SEQUENCES FROM THE START-UP PAGES.

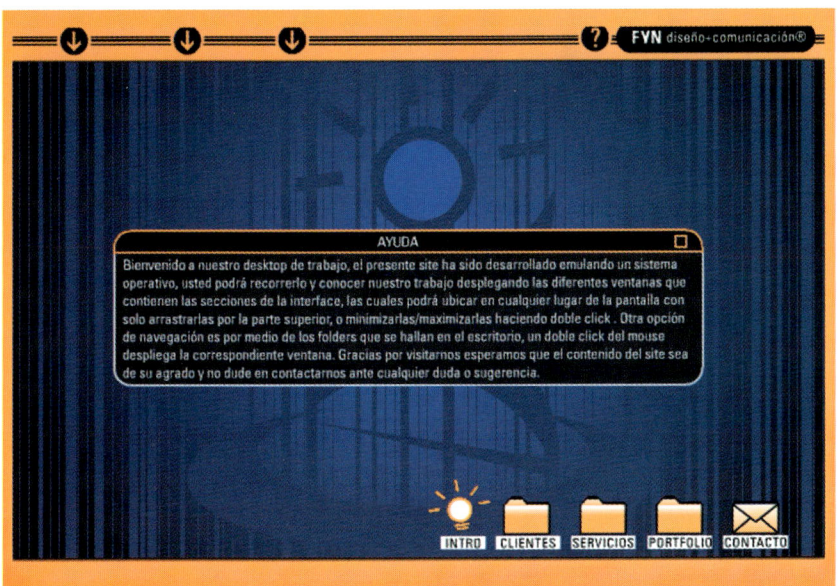

The user can browse the contents using either the bar at the top of the page or selecting the file folders at the bottom. Either way, the same contents are pulled up.

The color scheme has been designed so as to call special attention to the background icons. As with the traditional desktop, users can also personalize the main screen to fit their preferences.

>FF
00
00

>00
00
99

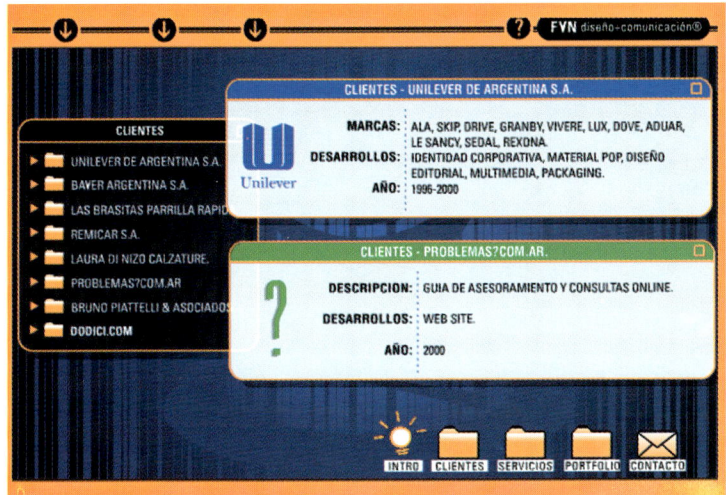

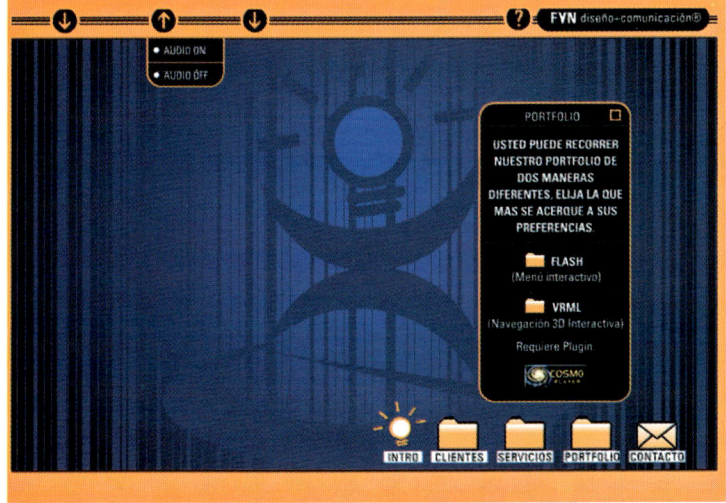

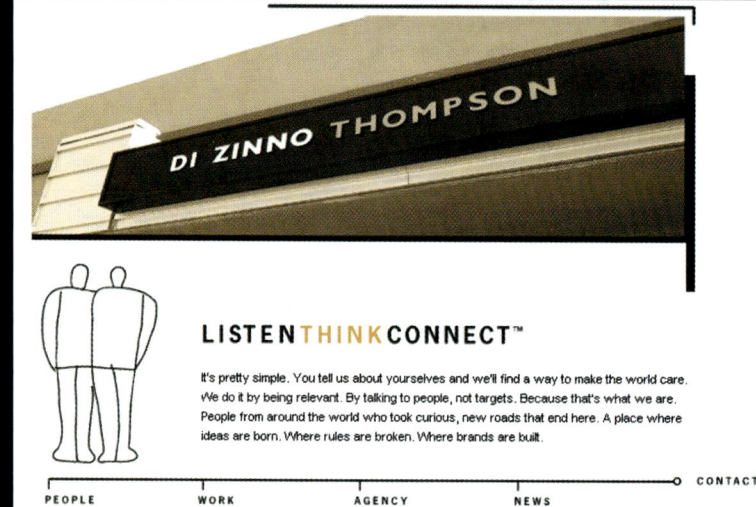

DZT.COM

THIS IS AN EXAMPLE OF AN AUSTER

DESIGN WHICH RETAINS ALL OF IT

EFFECTIVENESS. THE TWO-TON

TREATMENT OF THE PHOTOGRAPH

GIVES THE SITE ITS OWN UNIQU

CHARACTER. AN EFFECTIVE AN

SOBER MESSAGE IS CONVEYED WIT

THE SIMPLE USE OF JUST TWO COL

ORS, ORANGE AND BLACK.

A PALETTE AT THE BOTTOM OF TH

PAGE DISPLAYS THE FIVE LINK

COMPRISING THIS WEB. EACH SEC

TION HAS BEEN DEVELOPED WIT

COHERENCY, MAKING NAVIGATIN

CLEAR AND SIMPLE.

THE OVERALL PROJECT MANAGE

TO AVOID GRAPHIC OVERLOAD

OPTING FOR A DIRECT APPROAC

TO THE CONTENTS.

THE DESIGN IS STREAMLINED AN

AUSTERE, WITH A BALANCED USE O

TEXTUAL AND GRAPHIC INFORMA

TION. THE FOCAL POINT OF THE DE

SIGN IS THE TOP PORTION OF TH

> NAME: DI ZINNO THOMPSON

> SECTOR: ADVERTISING AGENCY

> SPECIFICATIONS: FLASH, HTML

> RATING: ORIGINALITY ☹

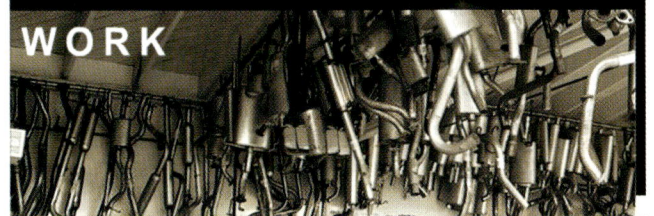

WORK

We don't believe people really want to hear advertising messages. They're already bombarded with 10,000 "marketing impressions" every day. So we create messages that mean something to them. Relevant messages they'll pay attention to, understand and embrace.

DI ZINNO THOMPSON

AGENCY

SERVICES

CATEGORY EXPERIENCE

PROCESS

HISTORY

LOCATION

We're made up of people from around the world who took curious new roads that end here. Our collective experience covers just about every category out there. Take a look.

Strategic Planning

Interactive

Creative Solutions

Public Relations

Media Planning/Buying

Event Marketing

Project Management

Promotions

Broadcast Lab

Direct Marketing

DI ZINNO THOMPSON

DZT IN THE NEWS

PRESS RELEASES

CLIENTS IN THE NEWS

DI ZINNO THOMPSON

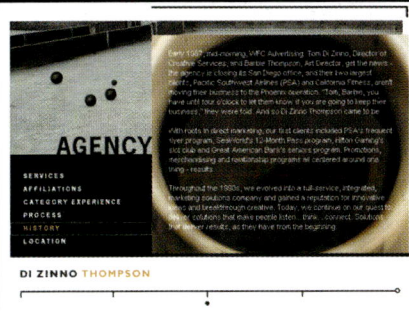

AGENCY

SERVICES

AFFILIATIONS

CATEGORY EXPERIENCE

PROCESS

HISTORY

LOCATION

DI ZINNO THOMPSON

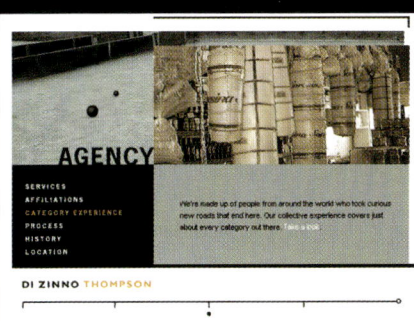

AGENCY

SERVICES

AFFILIATIONS

CATEGORY EXPERIENCE

PROCESS

HISTORY

LOCATION

We're made up of people from around the world who took curious new roads that end here. Our collective experience covers just about every category out there. Take a look.

DI ZINNO THOMPSON

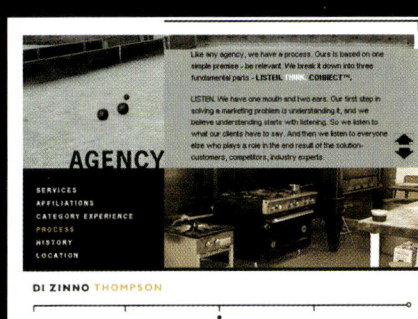

AGENCY

Like any agency, we have a process. Ours is based on one simple premise - be relevant. We break it down into three fundamental parts - **LISTEN. THINK. CONNECT.™**

LISTEN. We have one mouth and two ears. Our first step in solving a marketing problem is understanding it, and we believe understanding starts with listening. So we listen to what our clients have to say. And then we listen to everyone else who plays a role in the end result of the solution - customers, competitors, industry experts.

SERVICES

AFFILIATIONS

CATEGORY EXPERIENCE

PROCESS

HISTORY

LOCATION

DI ZINNO THOMPSON

AGENCY

SERVICES

AFFILIATIONS

CATEGORY EXPERIENCE

PROCESS

HISTORY

LOCATION

We work in a gutted-out, revamped warehouse with big windows and no doors. While not much for privacy, it encourages the collaborative spirit we need to do what we do. And done interesting whiffle Ball games. You'll find us in San Diego's Little Italy district bordered by the ocean, downtown and the airport. Come by sometime. We'd love to show you around.

By the way, did you know San Diego has the second best climate in the world? (We'll tell you what's first next time we talk.)

DI ZINNO THOMPSON

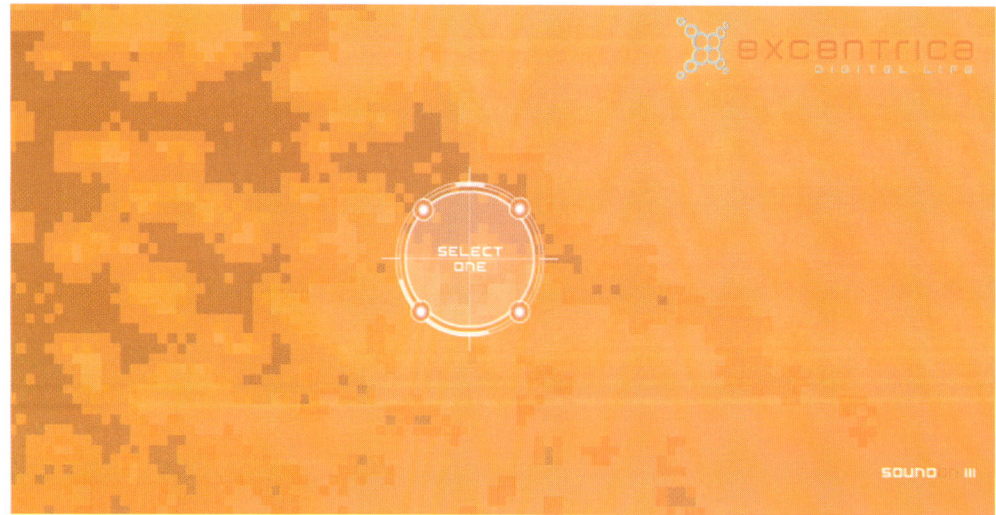

> NAME: EXCENTRICA > SECTOR: DESIGN STUDIO > SPECS: FLASH, HTML > RATING: ORIGINALITY ☺ GRAPHICS ☺ INTERACTIVITY ☺

A SMALL CIRCULAR MENU IS THE GUIDING PRINCIPLE FOR UNDER-STANDING THE SUBSECTIONS, EACH OF WHICH HAS BEEN TREATED WITH ITS OWN COLOR SCHEME, PIXELAT-ING AND ADDING TEXTURE TO THE GRAPHICS. INDEPENDENT LINKS, CAPABLE OF STANDING ON THEIR OWN WITH DISSIMILAR DESIGN CRI-TERIA, ARE THEREBY CREATED.

WWW.EXCENTRICA.COM

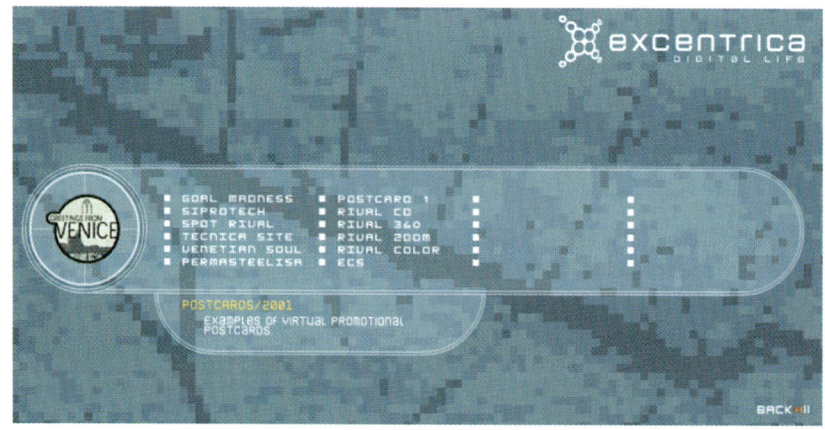

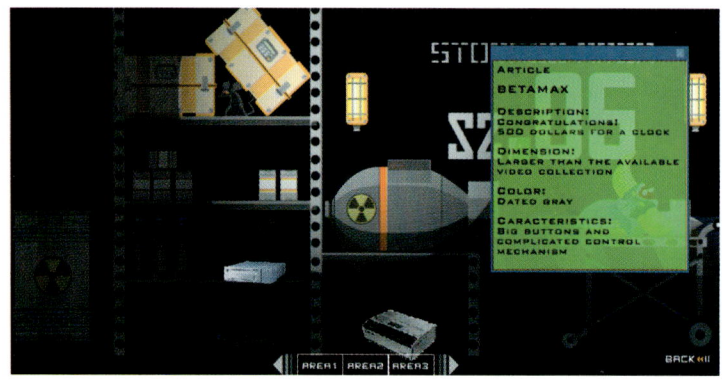

ORGANISM:
ALFA TURKEY 85

DESCRIPTION:
ANAEROBIC
HERBIVORE

DIMENSION:
543 MILLIPEDES
AROUND THE HIPS

COLOR:
TOOTHPASTE WHITE

CHARACTERISTICS:
SOFT SPOT FOR
BIKINI SWIM SUIT
CALENDARS

ANALIZE
LIFE
405205
.COM

excentrica
DIGITAL LIFE

NIK - MULTIMEDIATOR

AGE:
4 DOG YEARS

ORIGIN:
HARMONIOUS EVOLUTION

BIO-STRUCTURE:
INERT

ROLE:
SUPERVISOR OF HUMAN
EXPERIMENTS

AREA OF COMPETENCE:
ADVANCED REAR-END DIGITAL
PROTOTIPES

ATTENTION SPAN:
EXCELLENT WHEN CORNERED

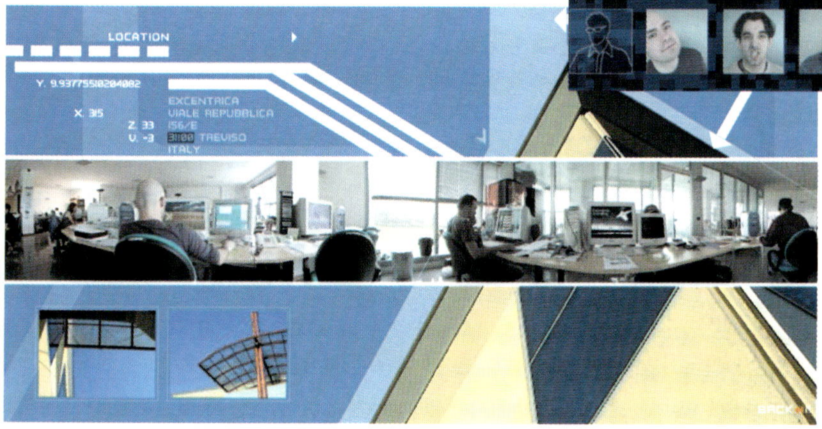

SOUND ON

LOCATION

Y. 9.9377550204002
X. 315   EXCENTRICA
Z. 33   VIALE REPUBBLICA
U. -9   156/E
         31100 TREVISO
         ITALY

BACK

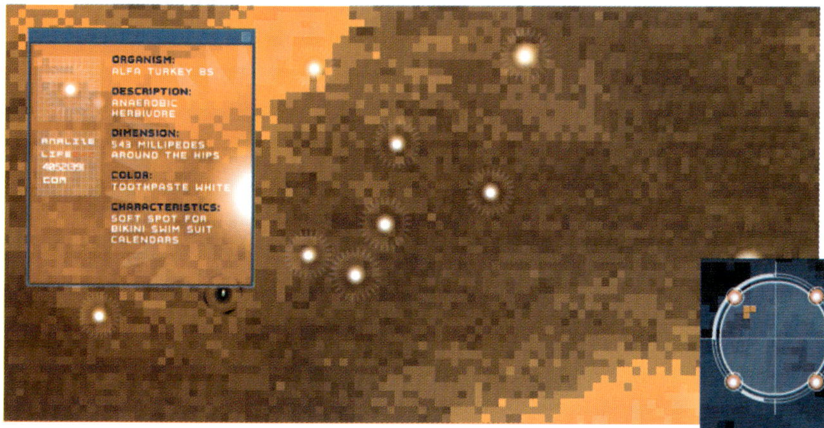

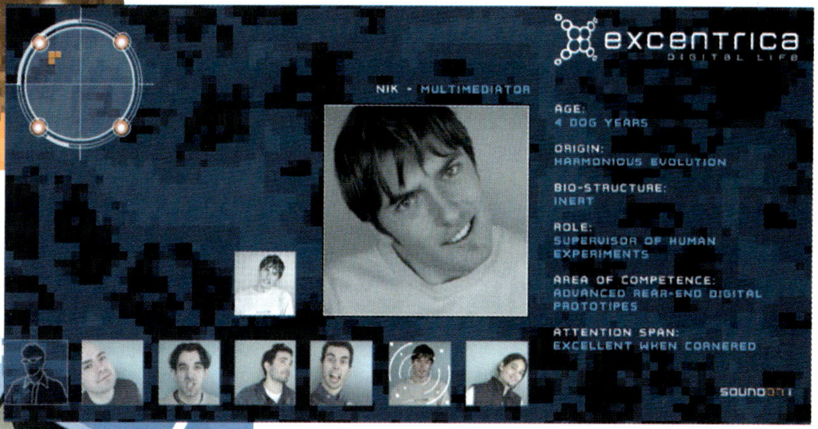

BELOW, A SEQUENCE FROM AN EX-
PERIMENTAL SECTION - NOTICE THE
VERTICAL LAYOUT - AND A GAME.

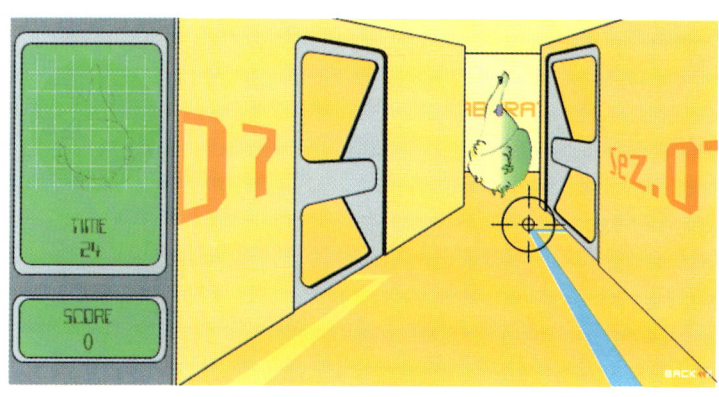

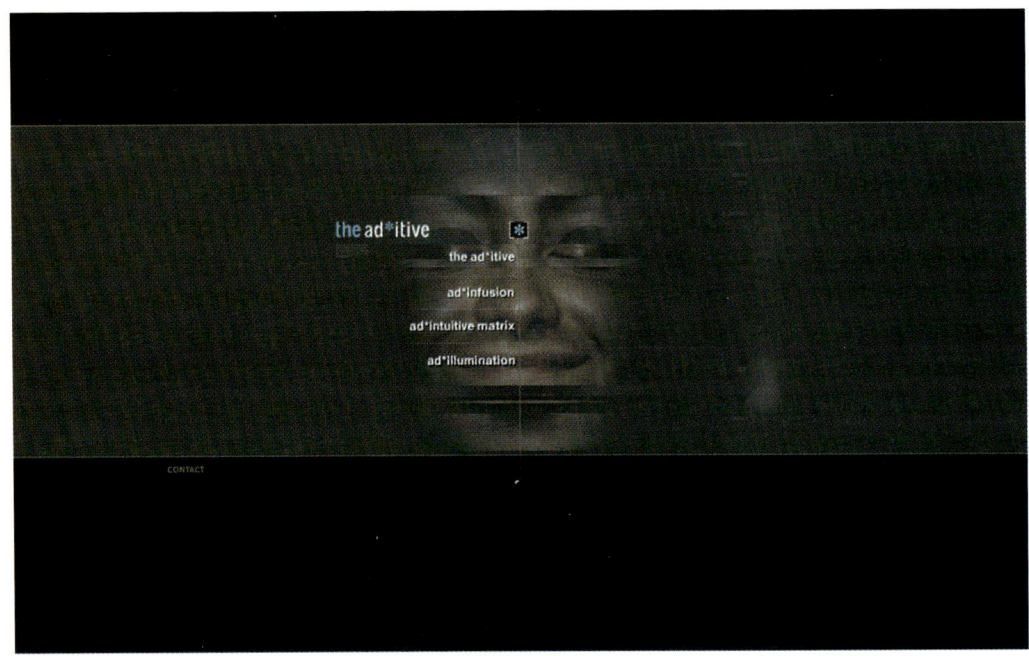

WWW.AD-ITIVE.COM

> NAME: THE AD*ITIVE > SECTOR: ADVERTISING AGENCY > SPECIFICATIONS: FLASH, HTML > RATING: ORIGINALITY ☺ GRAPHICS ☺ INTERACTIVITY ☺

A BLACK BACKGROUND BRINGS STRENGTH AND CHARACTER TO THIS PROJECT AS WELL AS HIGH-LIGHTS THE INFORMATION. LIKE-WISE, THE BLUE TONE, ALTHOUGH DARK, CREATES AN INTERESTING INTERPLAY WITH THE BLACK AND WHITE, CREATING AN ATMOSPHERE IN CONSONANCE WITH THE CONTENTS: ABSTRACT, YET DISCREET, AGILE, WITHOUT CLAMORING FOR ATTENTION.

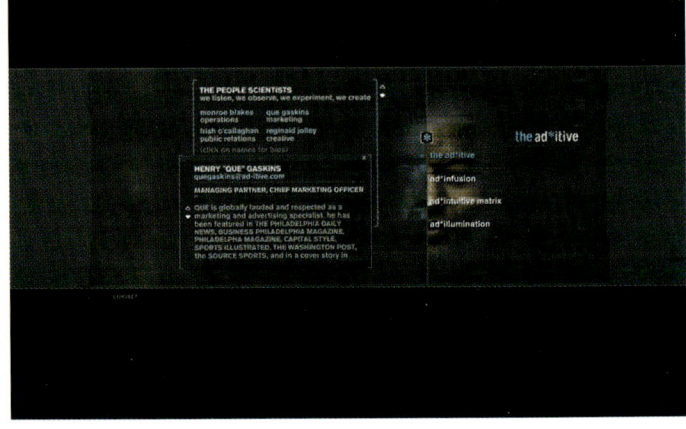

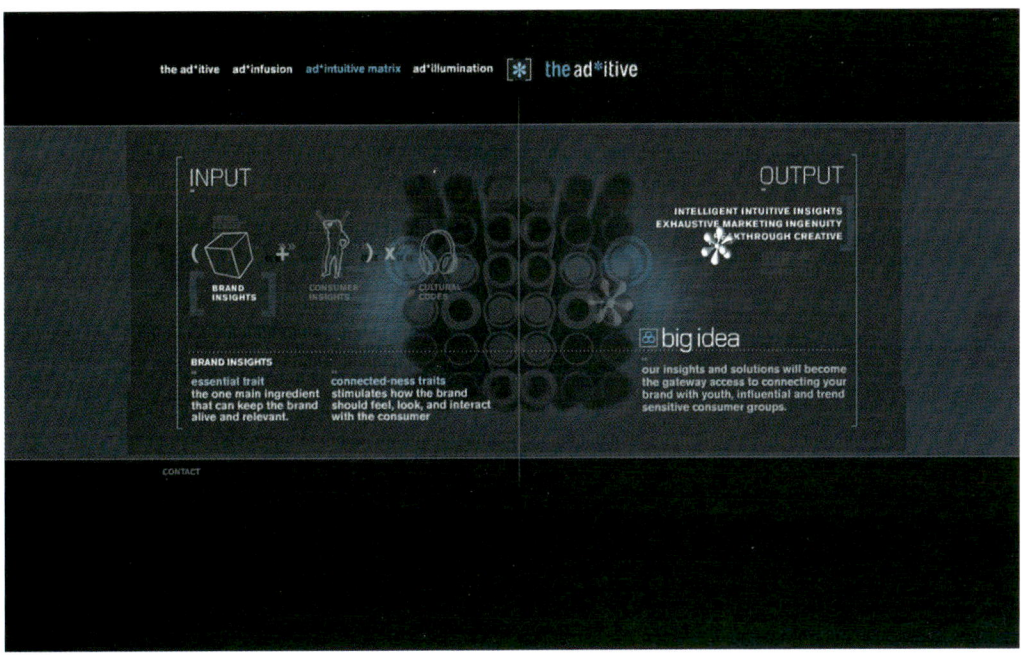

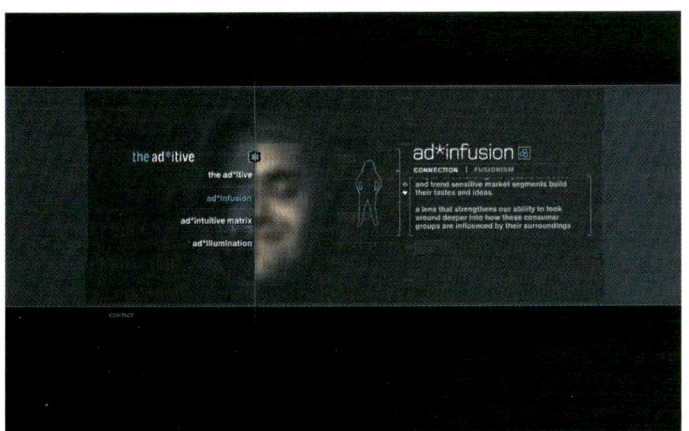

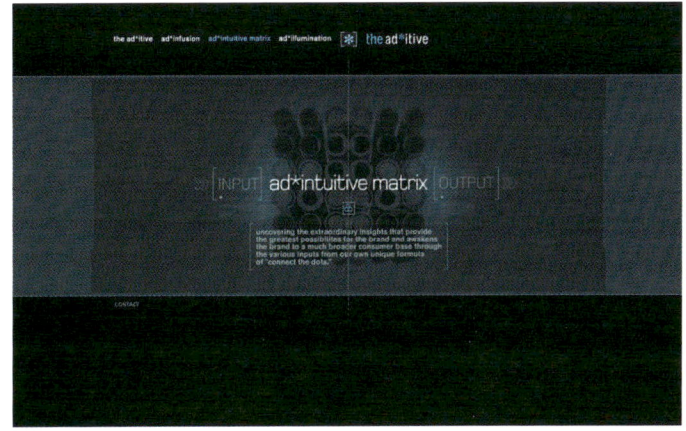

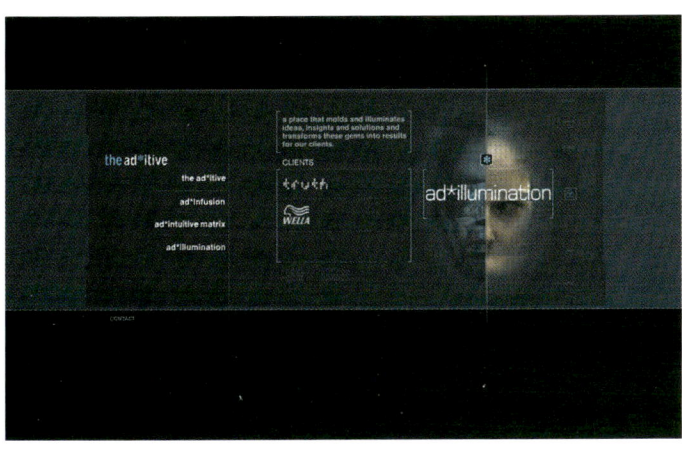

The graphics, animation and texts all hold equal sway in the overall design and manage to capture the user's attention, making a browse through this site anything but monotonous and linear.

Movable graphics also confer a sense of visual versatility to this innovative design.

AN ICON FLOATING ON THE INTENSE
RED OF THE START-UP PAGE TAKES
USERS TO THE MAIN MENU. EACH
SECTION USES A PLAYFUL INTERAC-
TION OF COMPLEMENTARY COLORS;
ONLY IN THE LAST SECTION DO ALL
OF THE TONES CONVERGE.

THE METAPHORE OF THE PERIODIC
TABLE OF THE CHEMICAL ELEMENTS
SERVES AS A MODEL FOR PROMOT-
ING THE WORK OF THIS DESIGN
TEAM. EACH SECTION DISPLAYS A
CLEAR ORDER AND THE GRAPHICS
ARE EASILY RECOGNIZED.

EACH LINK MAINTAINS THE OVERALL
DESIGN'S COHERENCY, WHICH IS RE-
PEATED IN EACH SECTION, WHILE
COLOR CLASSIFIES THE CONTENTS.

> NAME: HOLLIS DESIGN > SEC-
TOR: ON/OFFLINE DESIGN > SPEC-
IFICATIONS: FLASH > RATING:
ORIGINALITY ☺ GRAPHICS ☺ IN-
TERACTIVITY ☺ > CREDITS: HOL-
LIS DESIGN

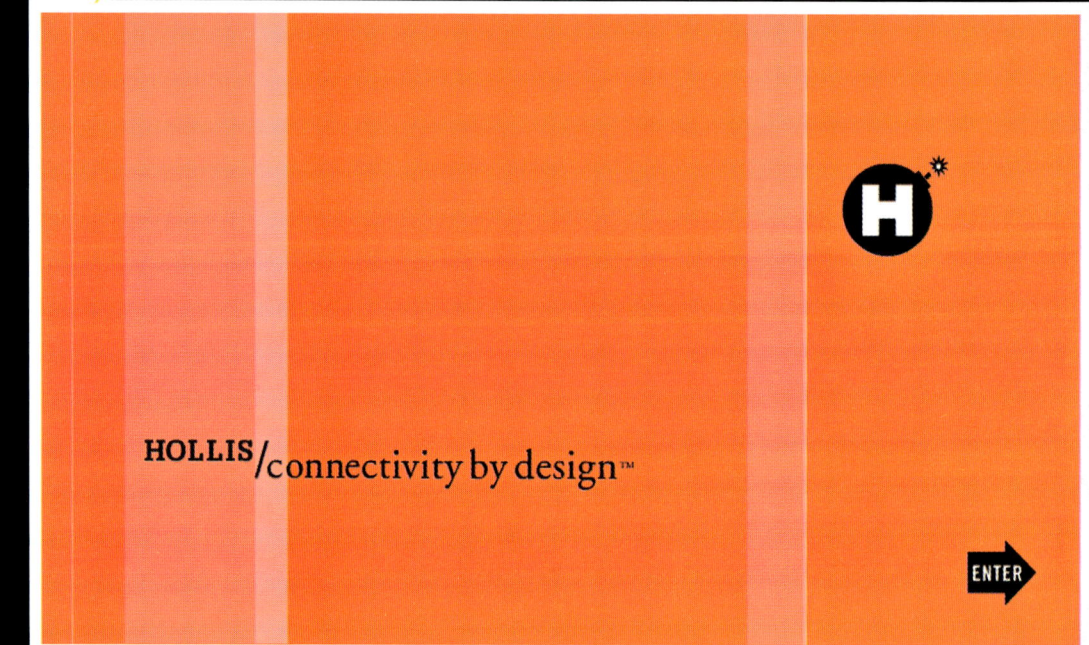

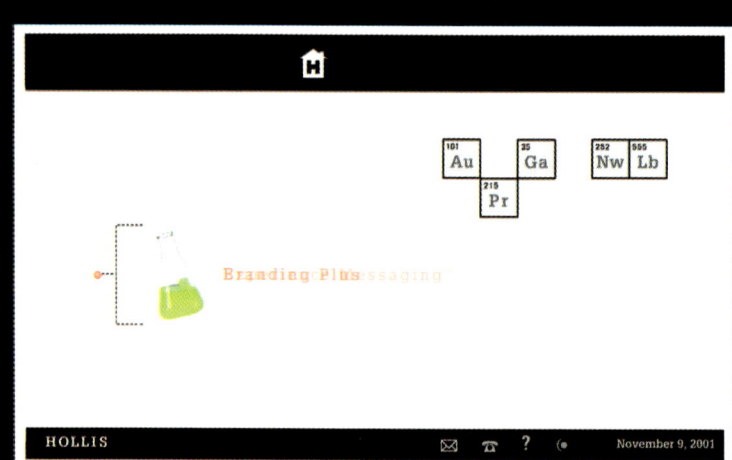

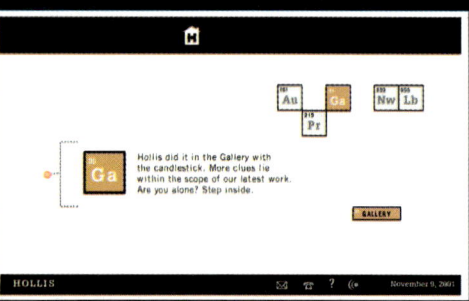

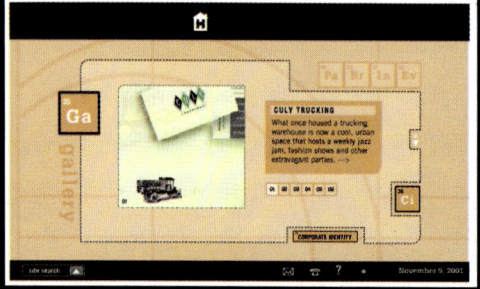

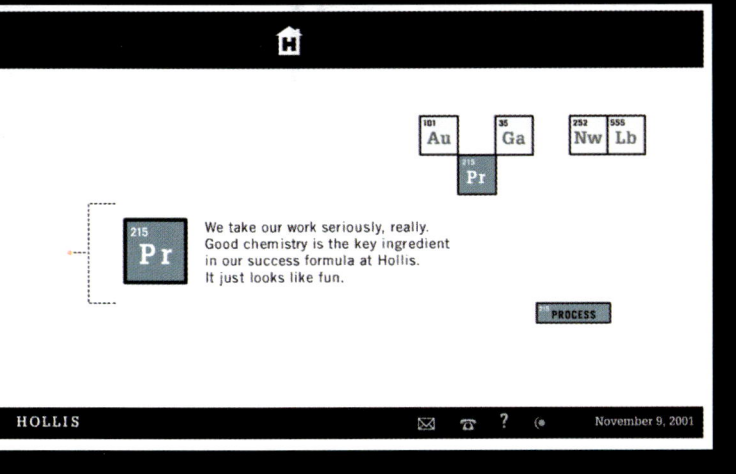
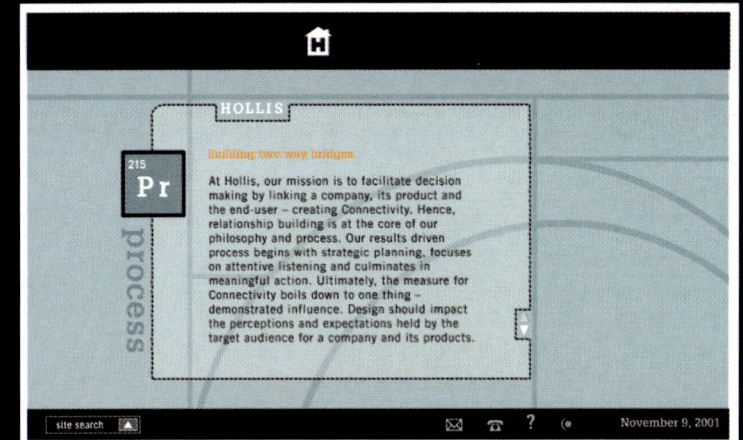
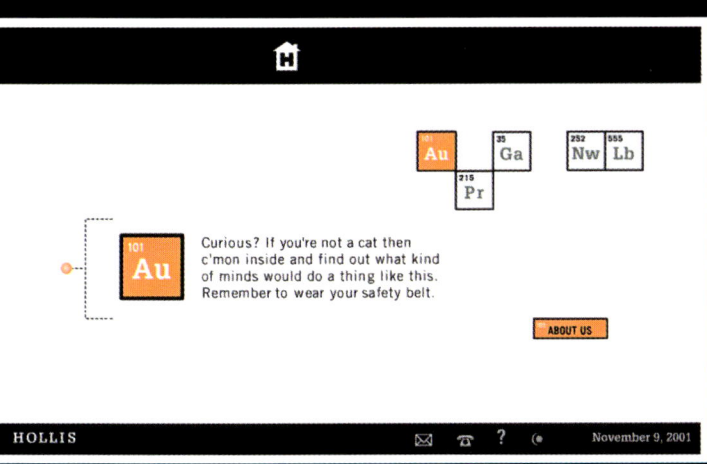
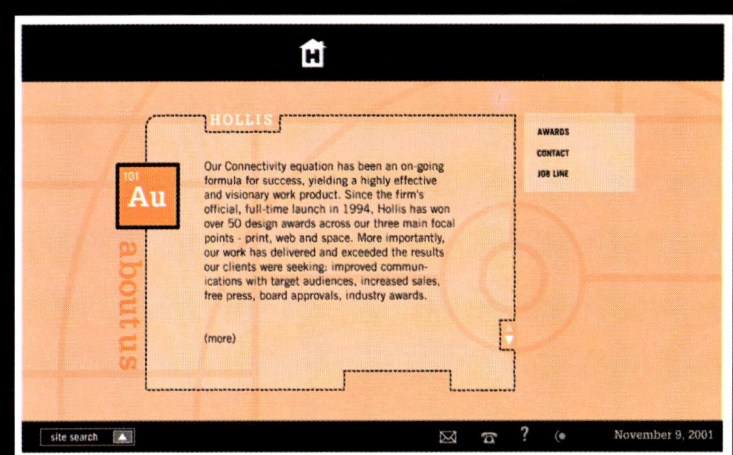
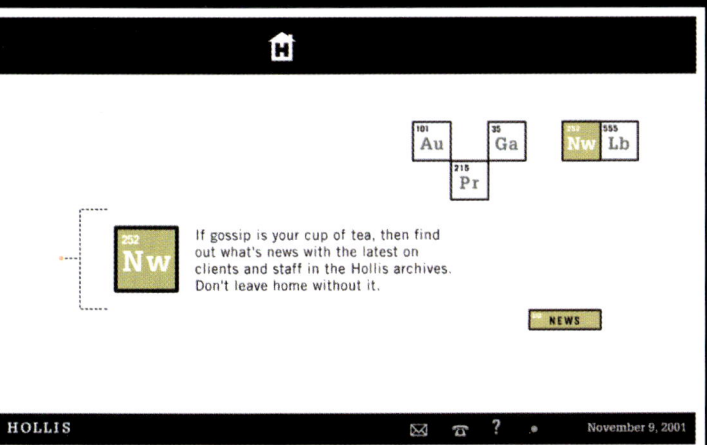
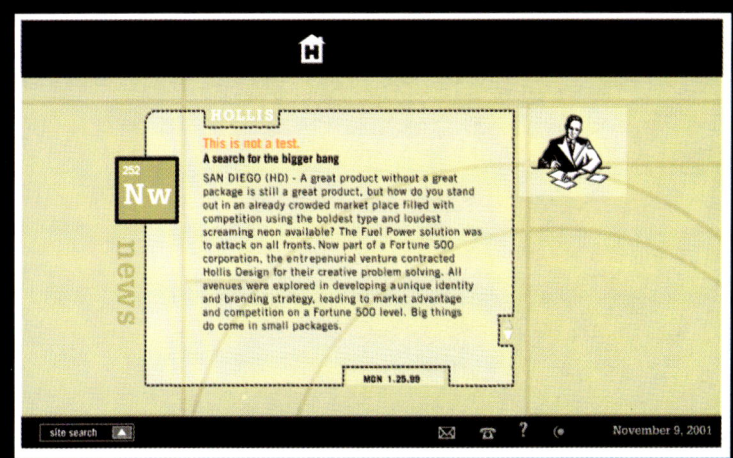
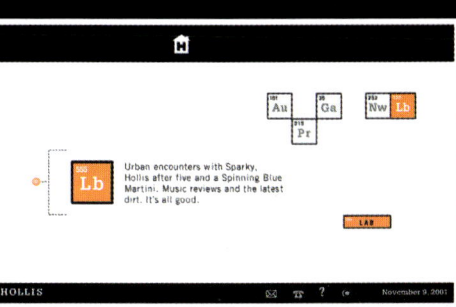

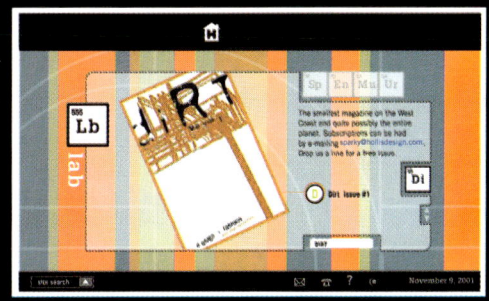

> NAME: TRY GROUP > SECTOR: ONLINE CHILDREN'S EDUCATION > SPECS: SHOCK-WAVE, HTML > RATING: ORIGINALITY ☺ GRAPHICS ☺ INTERACTIVITY ☺ > CREDITS: TRY GROUP

WHAT MAKES THIS SITE ESPECIALLY APPEALING IS THE COMPLETE INTERACTIVITY THAT IT REQUIRES OF THE USER. THE VARIOUS OPTIONS ALLOW AN IMAGINATIVE UNFOLDING OF CONTENTS DEPENDING ON SUCH BASIC ELEMENTS AS A CIRCLE AND STRAIGHT AND CURVED LINES.

THE BLACK BACKGROUND HIGHLIGHTS THE SHAPES THAT APPEAR, A SITUATION WHICH WOULD NOT HAVE MATERIALIZED HAD WHITE, WHICH GIVES MUCH MORE LIGHT TO THE SCREEN, BEEN CHOSEN INSTEAD.

WWW.WILLING-TO-TRY.COM

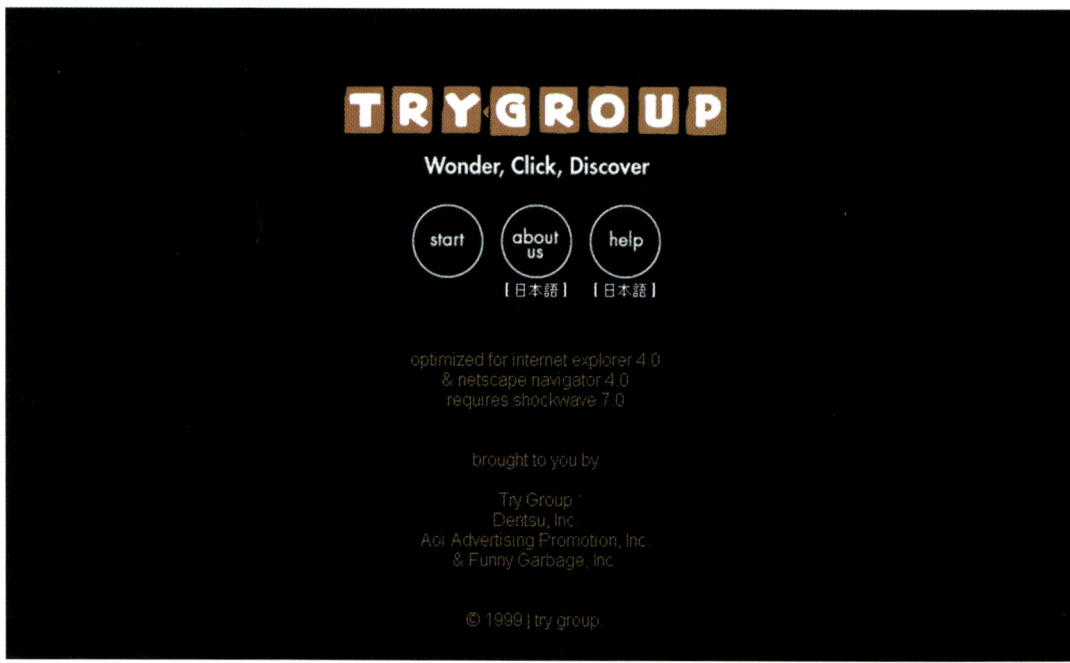

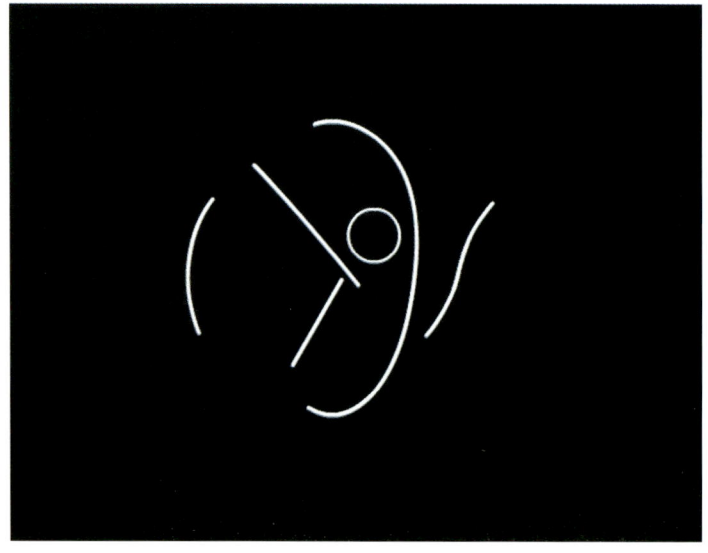

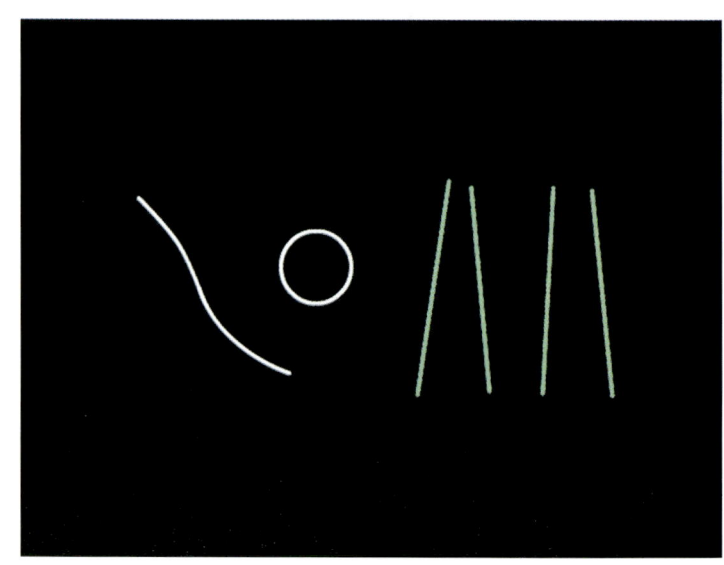

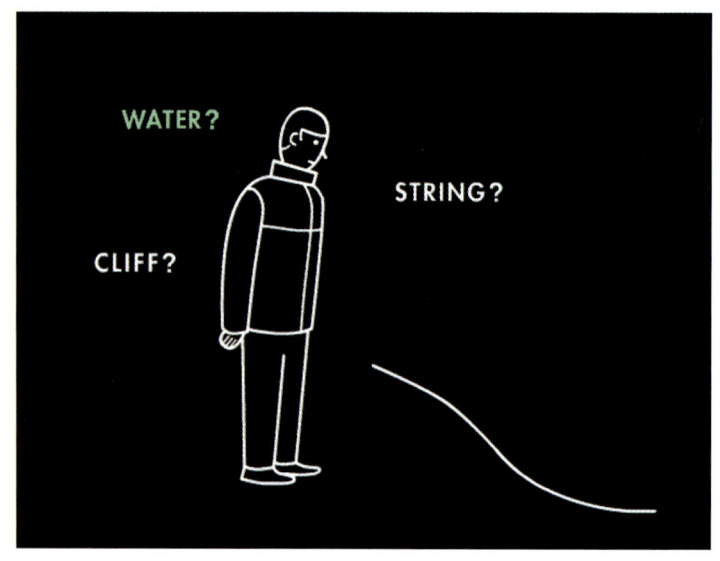

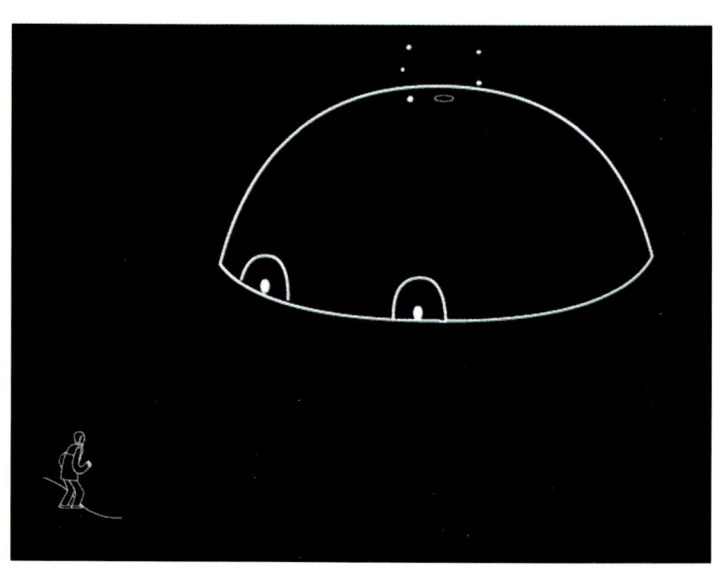

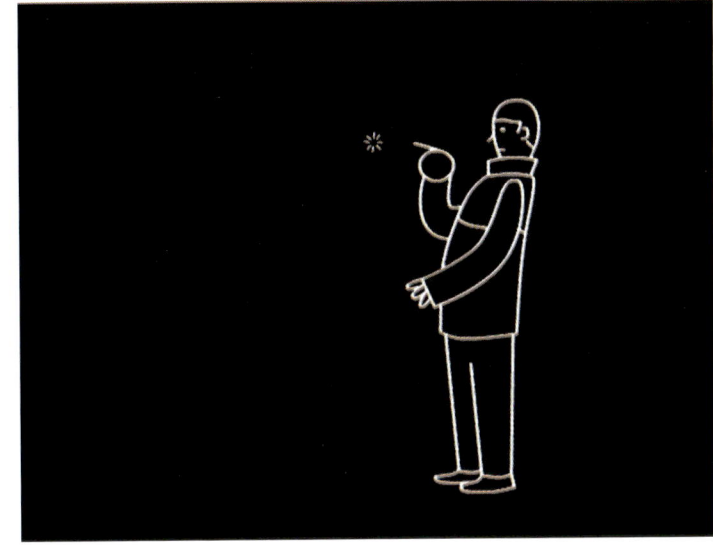

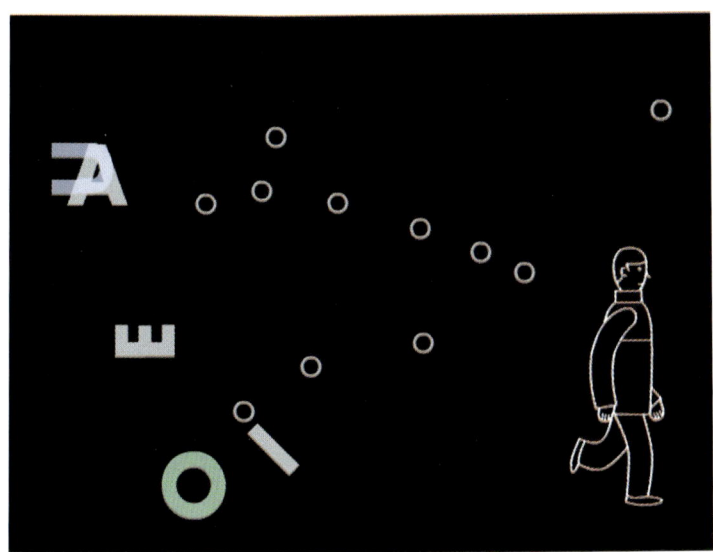

THIS SITE IS AN EXAMPLE OF CRE-ATIVITY SUCCESSFULLY APPLIED TO ONLINE LEARNING FOR CHILDREN. IN ORDER TO ACHIEVE EFFECTIVE COM-MUNICATION WITH THIS KIND OF PUB-LIC, A SIMPLE VISUAL LANGUAGE AND ELEMENTARY SHAPES AND CON-CEPTS ARE USED. THE DYNAMIC QUALITY OF THIS SITE INDICATES A TOTAL MASTERY OF THE MEDIUM AND THE RESOURCES INVOLVED.

CONCERNING COLOR, THE INTERPLAY OF A BLACK BACKGROUND WITH WHITE SKETCHED LINES IS ENOUGH TO CRE-ATE A RICH AND INGENIOUS DESIGN.

About the Author

Héctor Navarro Güere has dedicated his professional career to the study of User Interface Design, Web Design, Graphic Design, Journalism and all aspects of Internet development, channeling his training toward effective communication in the user/interface relationship.

He has spent his education and professional life between Europe and South America, and currently resides in Barcelona, where he is Editor and Head Designer at Links International Publishing House, as well as visiting Professor of Visual Interface Design at UPC University, and of Typography and Hypermedia at the LAI design school.

Mr. Navarro Güere holds a degree in Journalism and a doctorate in Fine Arts. He has worked as both Journalist and Graphic Designer for numerous magazines and newspapers and has received awards for his research. His first book, published in 1995, was "Perception in Kinetic Art: 3 Venezuelan Artists".